Colored Travelers

THE JOHN HOPE FRANKLIN SERIES IN
AFRICAN AMERICAN HISTORY AND CULTURE
Waldo E. Martin Jr. and Patricia Sullivan, editors

Colored Travelers

Mobility and the Fight for Citizenship before the Civil War

Elizabeth Stordeur Pryor

The University of North Carolina Press CHAPEL HILL

This book was published with the assistance of the Authors Fund of the University of North Carolina Press and a Smith College faculty grant.

Set in Espinosa Nova by Westchester Publishing Services
Manufactured in the United States of America
The University of North Carolina Press has been a member of the Green Press Initiative since 2003.

Library of Congress Cataloging-in-Publication Data
Names: Pryor, Elizabeth Stordeur, author.
Title: Colored travelers : mobility and the fight for citizenship before the Civil War / Elizabeth Stordeur Pryor.
Other titles: John Hope Franklin series in African American history and culture.
Description: Chapel Hill : University of North Carolina Press, [2016] | Series: The John Hope Franklin series in African American history and culture | Includes bibliographical references and index.
Identifiers: LCCN 2016019962| ISBN 9781469628578 (cloth : alk. paper) | ISBN 9781469628585 (ebook)
Subjects: LCSH: African Americans—Travel—United States. | African Americans—Civil rights—History—19th century. | Freedom of movement—United States—History—19th century. | Travel restrictions—United States—History—19th century. | United States—Social conditions—19th century.
Classification: LCC E185.18 .P75 2016 | DDC 323.1196/07309034—dc23
LC record available at https://lccn.loc.gov/2016019962

Jacket illustration: J. Dupreys (Duprys), *The Stranger*, ca. 1840–1850. Oil on canvas, 18¼ × 25 in. (46.4 × 63.5 cm). The Menil Collection, Houston.

Chapter 1 was previously published in a different form in *Journal of the Early Republic* and is used here with permission.

For Jerry, Lilli, and Henry,
the loves of my life

Contents

Figures

Acknowledgments

I was in a graduate seminar at the University of California Santa Barbara (UCSB) when the ideas for this book began to coalesce. I offer Jane DeHart unending gratitude for wooing me into the class and, really, the UCSB history department, and then following through as a perfect first mentor. After I presented a paper on Frederick Douglass's 1845 voyage to England, Jane put me in touch with her colleague Patricia Cline Cohen, insisting that we would bond over our mutual interest in travel. And bond we did. Pat became my advisor, and her nuts-and-bolts sensibility inspired me to think of travel itself as a point of departure. Pat, I have since learned, is an "intellectual mother" to a host of students and junior colleagues, and I am more than a little bit lucky to be one of them. From the time I became her student until now, Pat has read in record time everything I've ever sent her and has offered astute and probing comments. A mere "thank you" seems inadequate, and although Pat is not a fan of gushing, sometimes it needs to be done. It is safe to say that without her deep commitment to me and to this project, I would not now be writing the acknowledgments to my first book.

I am grateful to so many intellectual brothers and sisters and aunts and uncles who have remained steadfast cheerleaders throughout this process. I shower light, love, and thanks over them all. They include Leila Rupp and Eileen Boris, who pushed me to think of gender and citizenship in more sophisticated ways. Jane DeHart remains a mentor. She not only introduced the project to the folks at UNC Press but also, after a four-hour post-Berks dinner for two, became mishpucha. April Haynes, a scholar who can connect the dots like no other, cracked open my thinking on racial passing but has also passed glorious hours with me gossiping about folks such as Douglass and William Wells Brown as if we had partied with them the night before. Our paths have crossed many times, and I'm always the better for it. During my Cornell days, Leslie Alexander took me under her wing the first day of graduate school and cultivated my passion for history by showing how it was fun, funny, and also devastating. Our many conversations and her important book inspire my thinking here. Others who in graduate school guided and/or pushed me onward include the late Michael Kammen, Mary Beth Norton, Lois Brown, John Majewski, Nelson Lichtenstein, Erica Rappaport, Michelle Scott, Jessica Chapman, Vanessa Crispin Peralta, and Kathryn Wollan.

Three colleagues have read nearly every page of this manuscript and managed to reinvigorate me along the way. I am so grateful to Barbara Krauthamer, Ted Melillo, and Dawn Peterson—each more well read than the next. Together we spent hours at my dining-room table talking race and U.S. history, laughing out loud, and, sometimes, even tearing up a little bit when the historical insights got that deep. Dawn is likely the only person who has read every single word of multiple drafts, and her brilliance never fails to awe. By sharing with me her generous intellect, she has also become one of my very closest friends. I am privileged to have connected with so many people whose beautiful readings of history continue to stun me. They include Ed Baptist, Emily Bernard, Scot Brown, the late Stephanie Camp, Corey Capers, Brian Connolly, Jim Downs, Douglas Egerton, Sharla Fett, Bridget Fielder, Aisha Finch, Tanisha Ford, Leigh Fought, Jen Fronc, Thavolia Glymph, Leslie Harris, Graham Hodges, Vanessa Holden, Jessica Johnson, Martha Jones, Robin D. G. Kelley, Andrea King, Jen Manion, Joanne Pope Melish, Jessica Millward, Jennifer Morgan, Sowandé Mustakeem, Richard Newman, Chantal Norrgard, Tamika Nunley, Deirdre Cooper Owens, Alyssa Mt. Pleasant, Khary Polk, Vijay Prashad, Stacey Robertson, Seth Rockman (and his invitation to share my work at Brown University's 19th Century US History Workshop), David Roediger, Patricia Schechter, Manisha Sinha, Stephanie Smallwood, Ula Taylor, and Heather Andrea Williams. At different moments, their work and their friendship have kept foremost in my mind not only the fact that black lives matter but that they always have.

Teaching at Smith College has likewise introduced me to a world of rich intellectual bounty. From students to colleagues, I find myself immersed in a community of intellectual rigor, curiosity, humility, playfulness, and commitment. First, to my students, I must say that when I met you I was terrified, and I should have been. I could write a book about the things you've taught me in the last seven years. You have helped me create a pedagogical approach for bringing racist language (in its historical context) into the classroom. Our wild and profound discussions have taught me that the word "nigger" not only represents a national and historic trauma but for nearly all of us, no matter our race, a personal one. Our conversations planted the seeds for the ideas in the first chapter of this book. It's no surprise that the rare genius of Smith students is mirrored in their teachers, many of whom, as friends and mentors, have read drafts of this project and/or fostered my teaching. I offer my warmest gratitude to Jeff Ahlman, Marnie Anderson, Lisa Armstrong, Payal Banerjee, Ernest Benz, Joshua Birk, Darcy Buerkle, Ginetta Candelario, Floyd Cheung, Dawn Fulton, Paula Giddings, Sergey Glebov, Helen and Dan Horowitz, Daphne Lamothe, Richard Lim, Neal Salisbury, Nadya Sbaiti, Kevin Quashie, Danielle Ramdath, Shani Roper, Louis Wilson, and Ann Zulawski. A special shout out goes to Jennifer Guglielmo, who has not only read chapters but also spent countless hours debriefing with me about the processes of teaching, writing, professional development, and life. Jennifer is one of those unusual people who is unafraid to acknowledge that at the heart of teaching and research lies the heart.

Of course, none of this would be possible without generous institutional support. Smith College provided research grants and time off from teaching to write. I'm also indebted to Lyn Minnich in the history office, librarian Pam Skinner for her research assistance, and copy editor, Kristy Johnson, whose services were made possible with Smith funds. I am very grateful to my two research assistants, Mallory Strider and Cade Johnson for help on this project. A year-long postdoctoral fellowship from the University of California's President's Postdoctoral program allowed me time for the project to, as Pat Cohen says, soak. As a fellow, I was able to shift gears and conduct new research at the UCLA School of Law, working with Cheryl I. Harris as mentor and with Devon Carbado. I was also fortunate to be granted a Kate B. and Hall J. Peterson Fellowship from the American Antiquarian Society (AAS). If you've never been to the AAS, you should go. The archivists, curators, and fellows trade information and images with a divine nerdiness and camaraderie that I've only seen echoed while watching my son play *Magic: The Gathering.* Thank you to the AAS and Paul Erickson, Elizabeth Pope, Tracey Kry, April Haynes, Ezra Greenspan, and Lloyd Pratt for sharing your findings with me. Lloyd kindly brought to my attention the painting that became the cover of this book. I also give thanks to Nicole Joniec from the print department at The Library Company of Philadelphia who located several important images, and Jennifer Fauxsmith, archivist at the Massachusetts Archives, who guided me toward the antisegregation petitions from the late 1830s and 1840s. Chuck Grench, my editor at UNC Press, was always patient and encouraging. The two UNC anonymous readers each floored me with their feedback. I hope they know how influential their comments were. I also want to thank the anonymous readers from *Journal of the Early Republic* (*JER*) for their comments on my first chapter, and Cathy Kelly at *JER* for her enthusiasm for the piece.

Any person who is a parent and has undergone the process of writing a book knows that it can be hard on families. My husband, Jerry, my kids, Lilli and Henry, and I were carried from beginning to end by so many people, including my spiritual sisterhood and also family that are friends and friends that are family. To my spiritual guides who picked me up, dusted me off, and gave me hope, none of this would be happening without your fellowship. I thank Sue H., Bonnie, Cynthia, Carrie, Vanessa, Allison, Thea, Roxane, Teresa, Diana, Gabe, Linnea, Lisa, Sara, Carol, Nathalie, and so many more for reminding me to put first things first. My family and friends are shining lights. My mother, Maxine Pryor, was a devoted grandmother, and it's unfair that she didn't get to watch the kids grow up or to see this book finished. I credit my father, Richard Pryor, with my interest in black history and, especially the word "nigger." His undeniable genius landed squarely in my kids, and I know he would be tickled by them. Thank you to my in-laws Jerry and the late Lillian Stordeur, Christopher Stordeur, and Pam Estrada. To my siblings Rain, Richard Jr., Steven, Franklin (aka Mason), Kelsey, and Renee, and to Jules Merson and Richie Rothenberg, Nina and Bud, Sara Berrisford, Andrea Meyer and Harlan Bosmajian, Aidan Boo Bosmajian, Katya Meyer, Miriam and Michael Meyer, Lizzy Cohen, Lisa Tittemore, Nina Smith, Sheryl Kalis, Lili Taylor, the Wilsons—Lucas, Martha, Nehemiah, and Olivia—Uncle Maury and Aunty Sylvia Silverman, and the cousins, Jill Silverman and Bill Gross, Michael and Nancy Silverman, Robyn Silverman and Dave Pratt, and Leah, Tom, Tommy, Kyle, Maggie, Danny, Haley, Jackie, and Sean. I also thank Christy and Andre Warren, Alisa Garrett Davis, Kristine Belson, Amy Russell and Miles Coolidge, Rey and Vivian Rodriguez, and the mamas from Oakwood School in L.A., as well as Charlie Spencer, Josie, Barb, and everyone from the Greenfield Center School. Thank you to Joani, Marty, and Max Walder for supporting and caring for our daughter. Thanks to the folks at the Pioneer Valley Ballet for introducing our boy to his favorite thing.

I am not exactly sure how to properly express my gratitude to my family, who waited so patiently for me to finish this book. I am blessed with two kids of whom I am ridiculously proud. Lilli and Henry, thank you. I don't know why, but you have never failed to love me and treat me with the admiration and respect usually reserved for a mama who bakes cookies and makes homemade Halloween costumes. Although I am not that lady, each time we crack up at the breakfast table, *go off* on an egregious Facebook post, or just settle in for some ear flicks, I am fortified for another day. I have no doubt that both of you are so well adjusted because of your dad. He's the angry chef, but he does everything for us. Jerry, I fell head-over-heels the first moment you smiled at me in front of the First Presbyterian Church in Ithaca. But even then, I could never have imagined the tremendous sacrifices you would make for your kids and for me. You are up at the crack of dawn to turn up the heat and are the very last one to go to bed. I hope I make you feel as safe and as loved as you make me feel every day. If this project is my third baby, there is no doubt you are the baby daddy. Congratulations, it's a book!

Colored Travelers

Introduction

"I am unable to travel in any part of this country without calling forth illustrations of the dark spirit of slavery at every step."[1] The words of black abolitionist Frederick Douglass, written in 1852, were literal. He meant not only that slavery infiltrated every aspect of American life but also that traveling was hard. From at least the 1810s and until the Civil War, free African Americans in the antebellum North confronted obstacles to their mobility, including racial segregation in public space. It was difficult for a person of color to walk across town without being harassed, but the vehicles of public transportation—stagecoaches, steamships, and railroads—emerged as one of the most notorious spaces for antiblack aggression. Even so, when Douglass voiced his complaint, segregation was not yet the law of the land. It was not until the 1860s that southern states passed segregation laws, and it was not until 1896 that the federal government institutionalized "separate but equal" legislation in the United States.[2] Instead, free people of color in the antebellum North were facing an antecedent to government-sanctioned segregation. Through a combination of social customs, racial codes, and popular culture, U.S. whites worked vigorously to construct a system that surveilled, curtailed, and discouraged black mobility. White racism in public space was arbitrary and inconsistent, but it nevertheless rendered a jaunt across town and a voyage to England equally fraught endeavors. It was a practice, as Douglass noted, that was born out of slavery, but it was also one decidedly separate from it. It was also so insidious that Douglass could justifiably lament, "such is the hard fate of the colored traveler."[3]

This book tells the story of free people of color in the antebellum North who had the financial resources and social networks to be able to travel. When they traveled, they faced mounting white opposition, a circumstance that prominent black activists vehemently resisted. As a result, these men and women birthed, shaped, and cultivated the equal rights movement in the United States. I call the subjects of this study "colored travelers," a term that activists such as Douglass used to describe himself and others.[4] "Colored" is a fitting descriptor because black activists in the nineteenth century consciously chose it to signal racial unity.[5] The term appeared at least as early as 1829, when black Bostonian David Walker, one of the most influential activists of the period, harnessed it in the title of his antislavery manifesto *Appeal: To the Coloured Citizens of the World* . . . .[6] In 1830, black leaders in New York also used it when they named the Colored Convention movement in order to assert black consensus in the quest for U.S. citizenship.[7] Of course, the term "colored" was not uncomplicated, because it also announced class standing.[8] In 1837, an African American minister from Connecticut described as "colored travellers" the people who dodged white racists as they walked through the streets of Hartford.[9] In so naming, he conveyed that they were not only people who made their way through the city. They were also respectable men and women, and they were activists.

By necessity, the pillars of black communities throughout the North were colored travelers. They were people who traveled to nourish the American and transatlantic abolitionist movements, to foster other national organizations, to preach, to attend church, to conduct business, and to visit friends and relatives. They moved through major cities such as Boston, Philadelphia, and New York, but also through smaller ones such as Augusta, Maine; Salem and New Bedford, Massachusetts; Albany, New York; and Cincinnati, Ohio, to name but a few. The most elite of these activists became transatlantic abolitionists and crossed the ocean to visit cities such as Liverpool, London, Bristol, Dublin, Edinburgh, Paris, and Berlin. The question of how colored travelers were able to take these trips is profoundly important. A close look at the ways in which free people of color negotiated white hostility in public space and how they constructed strategies to resist segregation highlights the stakes of black activism before the Civil War. It also demonstrates that, for African Americans, acquiring equal access to public space was paramount to citizenship.

Indeed, colored travelers recognized that being able to travel freely was a crucial component of U.S. citizenship. The breadth of their travels made it plain that they not only understood travel as a cog to geographic mobility but also imagined it as a type of currency. Access to travel opened up economic, political, and social possibilities. As such, segregation and exclusion from the vehicles called "public conveyances" was particularly pernicious. By protesting against segregation, colored travelers identified the cars, compartments, and cabins of public conveyances as critical sites for equal rights protest. They wrote letters to sympathetic editors to expose the outrageous behavior of white racists, and they eventually stood up to transportation proprietors, putting their own bodies in harm's way in the fight. Moreover, in their lectures and memoirs, they insisted that, outside of slavery, there was no better way to understand the oppressive nature of white supremacy in the so-called free states of the United States than to take a good hard look at travel.[10] In their quest for inclusion and citizenship, colored travelers redefined segregation as a crime, reframed ideas about what constituted respectable behavior, took on the federal government, shaped definitions of freedom, and, probably most importantly, no matter what the risks, they traveled anyway.

From the vantage point of the twenty-first century, it might seem commonplace that protests erupted on the vehicles of public transportation. Yet, the colored travelers of this study were pioneers. People such as Douglass, Paul Cuffe, Robert Purvis, Susan Paul, Samuel Cornish, David Ruggles, Charles Remond, William Wells Brown, Elizabeth Jennings, and J. W. C. Pennington were among the first activists to make equal access to public conveyances a central feature of black protest. Their activist work identified segregation in travel as the most significant symbol of U.S. racism. For starters, the term "Jim Crow," often used as a nickname for the style of segregation practiced in the American South after the Civil War and throughout the twentieth century, was invented on the Massachusetts railroads in the 1830s. That was when conductors and railroad officials forced colored travelers to ride in the separate "Jim Crow car," a practice that black activists passionately resisted. Moreover, it was in response to organized black protest against separate car laws on the Louisiana railroads that in 1896 the U.S. Supreme Court decided *Plessy v. Ferguson*, a case that legalized "separate but equal" accommodations for black people. Access to the vehicles of public transportation figured into what is arguably one of the most iconic moments of U.S. civil rights history. In 1955, Rosa Parks, an activist from Alabama, broke segregationist law when she refused to move to the back of a commuter bus in Montgomery, a move that launched the Montgomery Bus Boycotts.

Every historic contest over travel and freedom of mobility in public space can trace its roots to white oppression and black resistance in the antebellum North. In recent years, scholars have increasingly recognized the significance of these fights to the black protest tradition in the United States. These studies acknowledge that before the twentieth century, black activists fought to integrate public conveyances, especially railroads and streetcars.[11] Yet, looking at freedom of mobility more broadly demonstrates how contests over travel had a significant political and social context, and that black activists developed their protest strategies over space and time. Robin D. G. Kelley, when examining black responses to twentieth-century segregation, has argued that "the success of organized, collective movements" was contingent on "the everyday posing, discursive conflicts, and physical battles" endemic to individual racial interactions in public space.[12] Looking at *travel itself* as a critical site of racial and spatial contestation—from leaving home, to arriving away, to using public conveyances in between—amplifies how a collection of individual skirmishes worked together to create a movement.

The point of this exploration is not to suggest that black activists always won these battles, because they often did not. Instead, free people of color in the early nineteenth century established two important ideals of black protest that still resonate. First, they contended that access to transportation, the processes of travel, and indeed mobility itself were core features of American citizenship. Next, they insisted that black people had a right to independent movement and, if such movement was denied, they were willing to fight for it. As free people focused their battle for citizenship in the very spaces where they most often encountered white brutality, they not only contested segregation but also elevated public conveyances to the front lines of the battle over equal rights in the United States.

THE REMAINDER OF THIS BOOK is divided into five chapters and an epilogue, which are organized to replicate the processes of travel. It takes colored travelers from home and examines their journeys until their arrival abroad. Thus, it begins in chapter 1 with a discussion of the complexities of the racial climate at home in the United States and then, in chapters 2 and 3, looks at spatial and temporal factors shaping race and resistance on public vehicles. It then shows, in chapter 4, how the federal government was invested in delimiting the free mobility of colored travelers by refusing to grant them official U.S. passports. Next, in chapter 5, it looks at the transatlantic crossing and the ship itself as a liminal site between American racism and what colored travelers perceived to be the egalitarianism of Great Britain and Europe. Finally, the epilogue reflects once more on the meanings of home for colored travelers by analyzing their insistence that, on foreign shores, they had, for the very first time, experienced freedom.

Chapter 1 is an etymology of the word nigger. An examination of that single word might seem a strange place to begin a story of black travel and activism. Yet, there is no better way to understand the racial violence of public space in the antebellum North than by acknowledging the ubiquity of the epithet nigger. Colored travelers described the word and the ideology it represented as a constantly looming threat. White children chased free people of color down the street shouting the word. White satirists and performers repeated it in literary and theatrical blackface productions that often depicted black caricatures as being dangerous precisely because they freely traversed the nation. In the nominally free states, nigger threatened brutal reprisals and thus shaped the black experience of mobility. Importantly, this chapter argues that the source of the word's virulence resided in the fact that African Americans in antebellum America had long used the word nigger to describe themselves and others. Black laborers adopted the word into their own vocabularies to subvert white authority. Whites therefore very much understood the word as part of the black lexicon. In turn, they ventriloquized nigger to mock black speech, black mobility, and, ultimately, black freedom. Considering nigger not solely as a white antiblack epithet but also as a word rooted in African American cultural and protest traditions goes a long way toward solving the perennial American racial conundrum of why black people can say nigger and white people should not.

A note on the term nigger: The word is *not* bracketed with quotation marks here. It was a point with which I grappled considerably. In part, this is because, as I argue, the violence of the word is directly connected to the fact that when northern whites spoke it, they largely imagined they were quoting black people. Likewise, when black activists later uttered the word themselves, they imagined they were quoting white racists. Therefore, quotation marks would have indicated what was true, that many who spoke the word in the nineteenth century did so reflectively, to emulate the vocabulary of someone else. Yet, in the twenty-first century those same quotation marks are used to set the word nigger apart from other words, to flag it as one that is offensive, a word that no respectable person would dare to speak. Flanking the word in "scare quotes" creates a barrier meant to protect the reader or to signal the squeamishness of the writer who would have chosen any other word if only she or he could.[13] Most significantly, the quotation marks also indicate a presumption. Using them suggests that we all know exactly what this word means. It is my contention, however, that we should not be so sure. For the same reason, although I will never personally speak the word in a public forum, opting instead for the colloquial (and admittedly problematic) phrase, "the n-word," I choose here not to replace the actual word with the popular surrogate because it too supposes an agreed-upon history and understanding, one that I hope this chapter challenges.

Chapter 2 traces the dawn of the age of segregation in the United States. Between the 1780s and the 1850s, two separate and interconnected historical developments led to segregation as a method of social control. The first was black emancipation in the North, the result of a prolonged and uneven process that lasted decades. In light of African American freedom, white northerners began to imagine black people as immutably slavish and backward and thus as people, although nominally free, in need of regulation. As a result, whites scrutinized the travel of free people of color with a level of suspicion previously reserved for slaves. Thus, a process best thought of as *the criminalization of black mobility* emerged that deputized all whites to surveil any black person in motion. This was highly deleterious to African Americans because it fostered antiblack vigilantism in public space. At the same time, advances in technology brought on a "transportation revolution."[14] It was a moment that signaled American progress and, as such, U.S. whites imagined the interiors of public conveyances as white-only space. As an elite cohort of newly freed African Americans sought equal access to public vehicles, transportation proprietors and white passengers in the North viciously guarded the thresholds of stagecoaches, steamships, and railroads. By deploying vigilantism, whites segregated or refused service to free people of color, using a range of methods from verbal abuse to violent expulsion. Colored travelers fought back against exclusion in a variety of ways that highlight the importance of travel in their conceptions of citizenship. The protest strategies of these earliest activists planted the seeds of the nineteenth-century equal rights movement.

Chapter 3 identifies the moment when colored travelers launched a movement in earnest. They argued that free and equal access to public conveyances was a legal right. The movement took off in the late 1830s and early 1840s, when segregation on the Massachusetts railroad turned brutal. In part, this was because steam-powered passenger railroads were new. It was also because the president of one of the foremost Boston railroad lines created a novel invention, a separate car to carry black people and the poor. It was a system quickly adopted by several other railroad companies. The railroads used dirty cargo cars for this purpose, and railroad workers in Massachusetts dubbed the space the "Jim Crow car." It was a method of racial control that institutionalized segregation as no method of transportation had before. In keeping with the criminalization of black mobility, the railroad directors not only insisted that people of color ride in the dirty, cramped spaces, but officials also employed conductors who served as enforcers and routinely beat, kicked, and ousted colored travelers who attempted to ride in the first-class car. Activists fought hard against the Jim Crow car and, in so doing, revised their ideas of what constituted respectable activism. To them, standing up and risking white violence in the name of equality became a mark of black masculinity. Activists spoke of segregation not only as injurious but also as a crime. And, in a strategy that continues to buttress civil rights protest today, colored travelers held the state accountable by turning to the courts for redress. Finally, the fight over racial segregation allowed activists to formally articulate equal access as a central quality of citizenship.

Chapter 4 tells the story of how, between 1834 and the 1860s, the U.S. Department of State refused to grant free people of color official passports for international travel. During a period when passport policy was still nascent, by rejecting black applicants, the federal government illustrated how travel and citizenship were inextricably linked in the United States. At the same time that African Americans could not get passports, state laws and customs required some people of color to carry a series of identification papers best thought of as *racialized surveillance documents*, including slave passes, black sailors' passports, and free papers. Demonstrating how fundamentally raced the idea of carrying papers was to white Americans, when white people traveled abroad, they consistently grumbled about having to show their papers. They argued that when European officials demanded to see the U.S. passport, they did so at the expense of individual liberty. For colored travelers, however, the passport was an object of desire because it denoted U.S. citizenship. Colored travelers battled passport rejections with much the same vigor as they fought segregation on public conveyances. In the late 1840s and early 1850s, by pushing the federal government to address racial restrictions for acquiring the U.S. passport, colored travelers rendered the question of black citizenship a matter of national import almost a decade before the 1857 *Dred Scott* decision did the same.

Chapter 5 looks at the Atlantic crossing from the United States to Great Britain, where colored travelers shifted their protest strategies at sea. Black abolitionists made this journey between the 1830s and the 1860s, and they found that even British-owned steamship companies practiced segregation. Interestingly, however, black activists did not take on Atlantic captains and ship proprietors with the same ferocity that they had conductors back home. In part, this was because the ocean voyage, which lasted between nine and fourteen days, was too confining and dangerous to defy white vigilantes. Yet, more importantly, colored travelers also knew that desegregating Atlantic steamships was hardly the endgame. Rather, colored travelers relaxed their protest strategies while on board and remained focused on the significance of the trip itself. They wanted to reach foreign shores, connect with British abolitionists, and most of all see if the promises were true that abroad African Americans could experience true freedom of mobility, a right that eluded them at home. This is not to suggest that activists did not protest segregation on British steamships. They did, but without the physical assertiveness they adopted in the fight against the Jim Crow car. The story of Frederick Douglass's harrowing transatlantic voyage in 1845 shows this. An analysis of early nineteenth-century shipboard culture and the British-owned Cunard steamship line illustrates how, for colored travelers, the transatlantic voyage emerged as a liminal phase between American racism and their perceptions of British and European egalitarianism.

Finally, the epilogue returns to the theme of home, but this time as imagined by colored travelers who went to the British Isles and Europe. When they stood on foreign shores, black men and women said that they felt free for the very first time in their lives. It is important to note that during the same period, more people of color traveled and even emigrated to places such as Liberia, Haiti, and the Middle East than they did to Europe and Great Britain.[15] Yet, it was only in Europe and Great Britain that they made the profound discovery that the U.S. style of racism and white supremacy was not natural or innate to white people. By walking around without hearing nigger shouted at them and being refused access to public space, colored travelers came to understand freedom of mobility as a visceral, sensory phenomenon. They found that freedom could be heard, seen, inhaled, and touched when they found themselves abroad. Although the sense of liberation they experienced while in the British Isles was stunning, most colored travelers still returned home. They went abroad not to expatriate but to invest in the future of a nation that, despite its cruelty, they saw as their own. Seeing their own mobility as a vital part of this nation-building project, colored travelers used the trip abroad to inform and imagine the battle for freedom at home.

THE FOLLOWING STORIES ILLUMINATE the historic struggle for the right to travel. In the early twenty-first century, they have a striking ring of familiarity. Entities ranging from police departments, to neighborhood watches, to good Samaritans continue to criminalize black mobility in the United States. State and local governments, along with popular culture, have deputized certain Americans to keep watch over black people on the move. In the last several years and with the help of social media, the vulnerability of young black and brown women and men has become increasingly visible. Young people have become household names not because of their accomplishments but because they were killed by cops or vigilantes while "walking while black."[16] In response, there is a movement underfoot. It is taking place on social media, on college campuses, in city streets, and under the auspices of an organization known popularly as #BlackLivesMatter. It is a movement in which people of color refuse to accept the notion that respectability means tolerating antiblack aggression in public space. It is also a movement that can chart its birth to the men and women who fought for freedom and citizenship in the antebellum North.

CHAPTER ONE

Nigger and Home
An Etymology

In 1837, Hosea Easton, a black minister from Hartford, Connecticut, was one of the earliest black intellectuals to write about the word nigger. In several pages, he documented how it was an omnipresent refrain in the streets of the antebellum North, where it was used by whites to terrorize colored travelers. Reflecting on the ways in which the word nigger impacted African Americans, Easton painted a picture of an urban landscape in which "little urchins of Christian villagers" pestered black men and women as they passed. He said white parents and teachers used the word to instruct children that blacks were deficient but also to show how their own racial status was precarious. These adults disciplined white children with stories of nigger bogeymen and promised them that they would "have no more credit than a *nigger*" if they misbehaved. Children absorbed their racial lessons and reacted with open hostility when they saw real black people. White children taunted, "see nigger's thick lips—see his flat nose—nigger eye shine—that slick looking nigger—nigger, where you get so much coat?—that's a nigger priest." As he moved throughout the North, Easton experienced a cacophony of children's voices that "continually infest[ed] the feelings of colored travellers, like the pestiferous breath of young devils." White adults were "heard to join in the concert."[1] Also in 1837, a white abolitionist concurred and highlighted how whites deployed the word nigger to hamper black mobility, noting that "if a negro walked the street, he was often hailed by men and boys with '*Cuffee—nigger!*' or the like."[2]

In the antebellum United States, colored travelers were acutely aware that travel at home—not the houses in which they lived but the streets, towns, and cities they traversed—was fundamentally inhospitable. Going out in public meant confronting the verbal assault nigger. This single word captured the magnitude of antiblack feeling and was unleashed on free people as they moved through urban space, rode public vehicles, and even ventured abroad. For free African Americans, independent travel within their hometowns and beyond was stressful, dangerous, and sometimes even deadly, and the ubiquity of the word nigger illuminated the limits of their freedom. Despite the fact that, by 1800, Vermont, New Hampshire, and Massachusetts were ostensibly free states, and that between 1780 and 1804, New York, Connecticut, Rhode Island, Pennsylvania, and New Jersey had passed a series of gradual abolition laws to end enslavement, the institution still left an indelible mark on the region.[3] Without the racial control that slavery ensured, antiblack violence increased in the 1820s North.[4]

Before the 1770s, the labels "nigger" and "slave" were interchangeable, each describing an actual social category of involuntary black laborers. As African Americans became free in the North, however, nigger latched on like a shackle. White Americans of all classes and ages hissed out the word, branding free black people as foul smelling, unproductive, licentious, and unfit for self-rule. By the 1820s, blackness, not slavery, marked people of color as occupying a fixed social class. Most significantly, the word nigger became a slur in conversation with black social aspiration. In the early nineteenth century, a small but influential black middle class—a group characterized by education and activism, not necessarily prosperity—began to defy their prescribed roles as laborers.[5] They asserted their right to have equal access to the goods and services designed for public consumption, including entrée into vehicles of transportation, theaters, taverns, and inns. To prevent such freedom of mobility, nigger emerged as a weapon of racial containment, a barometer against which to measure the increasingly rigid boundaries of whiteness as well as a mechanism used to police and cleanse public space.

Colored travelers such as Hosea Easton, David Walker, Frederick Douglass, J. W. C. Pennington, William Wells Brown, and Harriet Jacobs used the word nigger in their lectures and literary productions to expose and protest the complex relationship they had with the place they called home. An etymology of the word from descriptor to epithet shows how and why black activists designated it a verbal symbol of U.S. racial repression, even as African American laborers continued to use it.[6] Indeed, the word became virulent precisely because black laborers integrated it into their own vocabularies, a practice that is an understudied and overlooked aspect of African American history. In other words, the label carried so much discursive weight because black laborers spoke it; self-identified with it as such; and thus, subverted notions of race and class identity in the United States. In turn, whites disavowed the word's traceable European origins and by the 1820s were using it largely to mock black speech. In so doing, they placed the onus of black subordination on black people themselves, using African American vernacular to make inequality appear both logical and natural. By the 1830s, the transatlantic abolitionist movement was under way, and black activists unmasked the venomous dialectics of nigger. They elevated the word to an epithet, uttering it publicly with reluctance and only to demonstrate the oppressive inequality and political hypocrisy endemic to the country of their birth.

Making Sense of Nigger

By the 1830s, the term nigger reverberated with white belonging and black exile. To presume that it was always a white-only epithet, however, misses the point of its virulence. Instead, it was a word with multiple vantage points, a word whose meanings were complicated by the race and class of the person who spoke it. This is a fact exemplified by a close look at how David Walker used it in his famous 1829 manifesto *Appeal: To the Coloured Citizens of the World.* . . . Walker, a free man of color who penned his abolitionist pamphlet when he lived in Boston, used his writing as a forum to indict U.S. whites for slavery and their demeaning treatment of free people of color in the North. In *Appeal*, he invoked the word nigger four times, twice in the body of the work and twice in separate footnotes. Walker's most familiar description confirms what modern readers already know. The word, he said, had Latin roots and had once designated "inanimate beings . . . such as soot, pot, wood, house, &c," as well as animals. But Walker argued that by 1829 it had become the purview of U.S. whites, who spat it out at "Africans, by way of reproach for our colour, to aggravate and heighten our miseries, because they have their feet on our throats."[7] With this description, Walker signaled that nigger had become a powerful antiblack epithet, that whites used it with intention, and that its essence could only be illuminated through the use of a violent metaphor.

Even as Walker's definition of nigger held whites solely accountable, when the word surfaced three more times in the pamphlet, each instance inadvertently revealed that black people used the word too. In one instance, the black abolitionist blurted it after a several-page diatribe. In his typical radical style, he debunked the prevailing white notion that in truth black men who sought equality wanted nothing more than to marry white women. Walker found such a proposition preposterous and, to prove his point, raged that any black man who wanted to marry a white woman "just because she was *white*, ought to be treated by her as he surely will be, VIZ: as a NIGER [*sic*]!!!!"[8] At first glance, it seems that Walker was simply repeating the language of antiblack whites. If you fetishize whiteness, he declared, you deserve to be treated as badly as whites are sure to treat you. But whether ironically or not, Walker also unabashedly conjured an image of subservience to rebuke black men who sought intimacy with white women. In so doing, he himself actively called other black men niggers.

It might sound jarring to modern ears to hear a nineteenth-century black intellectual use nigger both unapologetically and against black people, but two more illustrations from the pamphlet illustrate that Walker was not the only person of color to do so. Walker devoted a large section of the provocative manifesto to analyzing the effects of slavery's trauma on people of African descent.[9] He argued that one of the most debilitating aspects of this trauma was that some African American men and women openly resisted a militant strategy for change. These were black folks who Walker dubbed the "ignorant ones," meaning people he believed were satisfied not with slavery necessarily, but with its legacy, calling themselves "free and happy" in the face of their "wretchedness."[10] In the South, those he called the ignorant ones were slaves; in the North, Walker thought they were people who worked in service to whites without complaint, shining shoes, barbering, and laundering. To illustrate this subservience, Walker said he met an enslaved man in North Carolina who reasoned "a Nigar [*sic*], ought not to have any more sense than enough to work for his master."[11] Walker saw this particular self-naming and self-description as demeaning and obsequious. In an attempt to rectify such ignorance, Walker urged his proselytes to educate these black laborers, particularly in the North. He also warned that their conversion would not be an easy one. It seemed that the laboring poor did not think of themselves as ignorant and instead defied and dismissed other people of color who insisted they were. Walker cautioned, "when you speak to them for their own good, and try to enlighten their minds, [they] laugh at you, and perhaps tell you plump to your face, that they want no instruction from you or any other Niger [*sic*]."[12] Here is another example of African Americans conjuring the word nigger, but this time it was poor men who deployed it as a social leveler. It was as if to say, "you are not better than us." In her study of pre–Civil War New York City, historian Leslie Harris has identified similar instances where African Americans refused to privilege "middle-class, educated blacks and their tactics for racial improvement above more grass-roots political efforts that involved working-class blacks."[13] Like the subjects of Harris's study, black laborers in Walker's Boston similarly refused to assume that there was only one viable strategy for liberation, and they called out Walker and his followers for insisting there was. Still, of all the names they might have called Walker, why did they choose nigger? Moreover, if nigger had been white-only English, why would Walker portray African Americans who spoke it? And if the word was only an antiblack epithet, why might a free person of color rely on language meant to subjugate him?

These questions remain unanswered because even though David Walker's *Appeal* offers just one of many instances in which African Americans used the word nigger in the nineteenth century, scholars have yet to fully analyze this practice. The idea that nigger was a seminal antiblack term that gained virulence as a slur in the 1820s and 1830s is a fact on which scholars agree. Cultural theorists such as Randall Kennedy and Jabari Asim and, for the early nineteenth century, historians David Roediger and Patrick Rael have done marvelous work demonstrating that white northerners became invested in wielding the word precisely at the moment when gradual abolition and emancipation began to free people of color in the North, a development that deeply impacted African American understandings of public space and mobility in the United States. Moreover, in an important observation, Rael even argues that, by the end of the antebellum period, middle-class whites and some southern gentlemen refused to use the word, not because they were antiracists but because they recognized nigger as the vocabulary of the lower classes.[14] If Rael is correct that white people of a certain class felt too superior to utter (or at least admit to uttering) the word, it seems more likely that their aversion stemmed from African American usage rather than that of vulgar whites. Nevertheless, because scholars have shied away from the discussion, questions remain about the process by which nigger was transformed from a harsh descriptor to a violent epithet. Perhaps scholars fear that doing so might detract from social histories that foreground black agency and resistance.[15] Ultimately, this avoidance diminishes understandings of the profound impact such language had on people of color in public space.

Notwithstanding scholarly reticence on the subject, there is ample evidence to suggest that from at least the early part of the eighteenth century, if not before, nigger was a multifaceted and complex part of black English that some people of color, most notably black laborers, used to refer to themselves and other African Americans. That black people spoke the word is substantiated in the sources by the observations of white Europeans who visited the United States in the early nineteenth century. This is a fact that has posed an intellectual problem for scholars because these travelers interpreted such black usage as yet another example of servility, obsequiousness, and backwardness. These observers claim to have "frequently" overheard people of color calling out to each other, "you niggar," on southern plantations and in northern cities alike. Each time, the white listener believed she or he had heard an instance of "unbounded insolence and tyranny" or that black people who spoke it were striving to "imitate their superiors."[16] These foreign witnesses asserted that nigger was the vocabulary of white supremacy and that African Americans who used it attempted, however failingly, to cross into a social space reserved for whites.

Most scholars in turn have tended to interpret the black use of nigger much as the nineteenth-century foreign observers had: African American speakers were simply adopting the language of the oppressor and thus mimicking Anglo-American racial conventions in the process. In turn, scholars have glossed over, justified, or condemned this behavior—calling the historical black usage a sign of affection at its best or of class arrogance or counterrevolutionary ignorance at its worst.[17] Of the few scholars who examine the black use of nigger in the nineteenth century, only Sterling Stuckey acknowledged the historical nuance of the word, that it could have different meanings at different moments.[18] And while Jabari Asim's important book on who can and cannot say the "n-word" is insightful in many ways, he wrongly asserts that antebellum African Americans who used the word were playing "into the hands of those who opposed their cause."[19] As the writings of Walker attest, the black use of nigger was more complicated than one simple explanation can neatly convey. Instead of thinking of nigger purely as a word that African Americans borrowed and mimicked from white English, it is more accurate to conceptualize it as a word and a social identity that black laborers ultimately shaped for themselves as they made sense of their lives in a hostile environment.

I Rather Be a Nigger Dan a Po' White Man

Nigger did not start out as part of African American vocabulary. From at least 1619, when British settlers described the first twenty involuntary black laborers in Jamestown as "Negars," the term emerged as a common colonial descriptor.[20] In British North America, it flattened all workers of African descent into one racialized identity. A nigger was the property of whites, she was black, her bondage was hereditary, and it lasted in perpetuity. A nigger was a slave, a real social category that described an actual class of laborers. When whites used the word nigger, it was neither a compliment nor an epithet. It identified a recognizable, albeit degraded, group of workers.

As black freedom began to unfold in the postrevolutionary North, however, the descriptor nigger remained steadfast. It announced that black people's condition as laborers would not change, no matter their legal status. This was in large part because involuntary labor persisted throughout the process of gradual abolition under the guise of indentured servitude. Yes, the legislatures of Massachusetts, Vermont, and New Hampshire ended slavery before 1800, but five other northern states—Rhode Island, Connecticut, Pennsylvania, New York, and New Jersey—passed a series of convoluted gradual abolition laws that honored the rights of northern slaveholders and did not actually free enslaved people.[21] Instead, these lawmakers freed the children of slaves, but only after the child served out a protracted labor contract. This is a liminal status that historian Joanne Melish aptly calls "statutory slavery."[22] These contracts usually lasted from birth until the person was in his or her mid-twenties, after the best working years of a person's life had been used up.[23]

The categories "slave" and "indentured servant" were so tightly entangled that some indentured servants found little difference between their own status and that of enslavement. James Mars, an indentured servant from Connecticut who was born to enslaved parents in 1790 and thus technically free, nevertheless titled his 1868 narrative *Life of James Mars: A Slave Born and Sold in Connecticut*. He detailed a life that mirrored enslavement, including harsh punishments, separation from family, and the threat of sale.[24] According to common parlance, someone like Mars would have been referred to as a nigger because, as a black involuntary laborer, he was one. Using the word in this way was not understood as an epithet as demonstrated by the fact that black intellectuals did not take issue with this casual usage. For example, Walker's angry name-calling suggested that he too recognized nigger as a degraded social class, although he was emphatic that he did not belong to it. In 1837, Hosea Easton, the black minister from Connecticut, also acknowledged that nigger described an actual social category, explaining that "the term in itself, would be perfectly harmless, were it used only to distinguish one class of society from another."[25] The problem, he argued, was that whites used the word indiscriminately to group involuntary workers such as Mars into a single social category along with black professionals and activists such as himself. Thus, by the late 1830s, the word nigger was alienating to people like Eason precisely because it blurred class distinctions within the race.

Some people of color claimed the word as their own, even as folks such as Walker and Easton bemoaned its use as a single racialized social class. For these African American laborers, at some point during the British North American colonial period, nigger became part of their vocabulary. It was a word that belonged to a group of people who understood that their claims to the United States as a home were impossible, even as they were born, toiled, loved, suffered, struggled, survived, and died within its topography of slavery and violence. It was a viable identification that imagined a community that was larger than an individual's immediate social networks and extended throughout the Atlantic World and across the diaspora. It is vital to think of nigger as part of a black vocabulary rather than as just a word and a violence thrust on people of African descent. Doing so helps to explain its vitriol—as opposed to less damaging racialized terms such as "slave," "African," "darky," "black," "sable," or "colored." But perhaps even more crucially, understanding the history of the word helps unlock the secret of its undeniable staying power in the vocabulary of African Americans into the twenty-first century.

At the root of both the word's discursive endurance and its perpetual violence is the fact that in American English nigger diverged and developed meanings among African Americans that were distinct from those of whites. Indeed scholars recognize that African-descended people had long developed their own vocabularies and ways of understanding language in the Atlantic world. In his discussion of colonial South Carolina, historian Peter Wood argues that enslaved people faced a "trauma of verbal isolation" that encouraged them to quickly acquire a common language in which they adopted some English words, but also retained African ones.[26] Historian John Thornton argues that commerce and social interaction between people of multiple ethnic backgrounds in the Atlantic World necessitated the creation of a lingua franca—a common language made up of the vocabulary of each.[27] Even as "broken" English allowed a common mode of communication between people of African descent and sailors, overseers, and slaveholders, this language and its vocabulary was never neutral, as historian Michael Gomez asserts. Gomez contends that when an enslaver forced an enslaved African to "repeat words associated with his captors" and "embrace concepts which further concretized his condition of social death," the enslaved person came to realize that language was in fact a political weapon. As an act of subversion, enslaved people responded by making the cadences and meanings of the master's language their own.[28] In this respect, the black use of the word nigger is just one example of what historian Shane White refers to as "style," meaning "the process by which objects . . . are taken from dominant culture and given a new meaning in the context of subculture." According to White, one of these objects was language.[29] Thus nigger emerged as a significant part of the lingua franca of African-descended people in British North America and the eventual United States.

As a result of this kind of African and African American cultural adaptation, the word nigger developed with distinctly different meanings depending on the speaker or the conversation. Depending on who spoke the word, the scope and tenor of its meanings reflected how Anglo-Americans felt about enslaved people on the one hand and how enslaved people felt about themselves on the other. African Americans built their own meanings around the word nigger and outsiders found these meanings opaque.[30] The black use of nigger beguiled white listeners. Indeed, African Americans kept the true significance of nigger hidden in plain view.

This is not an attempt to oversimplify the intentions of every black person every time she or he uttered the word nigger. At times, black usage indicated subservience or even class hierarchy. Certainly, Walker used it to demean black men who might be interested in interracial marriage for its own sake. But, in other instances, the word nigger disguised a range of complex meanings and intentions: when addressing whites, it might signal respect, manipulation, or dissemblance; when addressing other African Americans it could signal reproach, but more often it indicated a shared social identity. Indeed, as scholars such as James Scott and Darlene Clark Hine argue, interpreting the "hidden transcript" of a seemingly deferent people necessitates a careful listen to the low hum buzzing beneath the dominant discourse.[31] Consider the possibility that when African Americans spoke the word nigger to each other, they did so to articulate a sense of place within a land that was not their own. Historian Stephanie Camp argued that for enslaved people there were "alternative ways of knowing and using plantation and southern space that conflicted with planters' ideals and demands." She called these spaces "rival geographies."[32] In the same way that enslaved people, for their own benefit, laid claim to already existing sites within the plantation regime, so too did African Americans use the word nigger to stake out a verbal and social space of their own. In this way, the word, and really the social identity nigger, might be thought of as a point within the rival geography, an important site of linguistic contestation.

Identifying nigger as a significant part of the vocabulary and cultural identity of black laborers is not simply speculative but comes from several sources, including the writings of black activists, the 1930s Works Progress Administration (WPA) interviews of former slaves, and southern and northern slave songs. The most prolific evidence, however, exists in antiblack cultural productions that gained momentum as a source of entertainment in the North in the late 1770s and 1780s. These pieces mock the black usage of nigger and in so doing demonstrate that whites took note of the practice. As proto-blackface productions, they were the ancestors of antebellum minstrelsy. But unlike the stage performances that became popular in the 1830s, this blackface was of a literary variety and usually came in the form of letters to the editor in almanacs and newspapers.[33] Meant to be humorous, literary blackface usually worked in one of two ways. Either an editor purported to publish an authentic letter he personally received from an African American, or he published a letter from a person who claimed to have overheard and recorded verbatim an exchange between a white and a black person or between two or more persons of color. The satirists who actually wrote these items portrayed African American subjects who were almost invariably masculine, speaking in broken English, belying their slave roots.[34] Since these were caricatured performances, historians such as Shane White and Joanne Melish, in their studies of New York and New England, respectively, debate the value of relying on them as a source for real black speech. Whether the blackface literary productions were close renderings of real African American speakers, as White has argued, or a reflection of an increasingly fixed postrevolutionary racial ideology, as Melish has, the popularity of

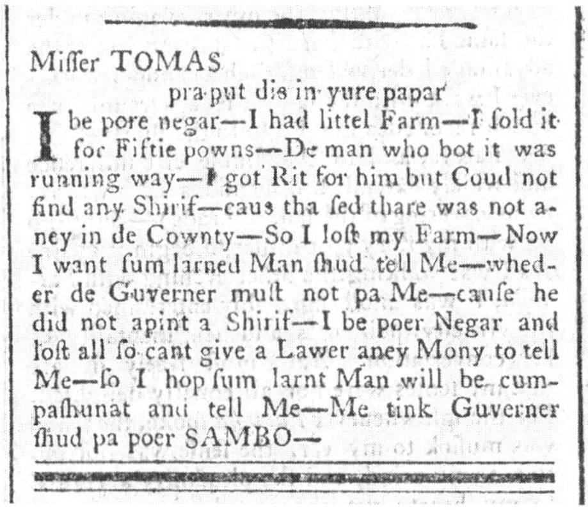

Miſſer TOMAS

pra·put dis in·yure papar

I be pore negar—I had littel Farm—I fold it for Fiftie powns—De man who bot it was running way—I got Rit for him but Coud not find any Shirif—caus tha fed thare was not a-ney in de Cownty—So I loft my Farm—Now I want fum larned Man fhud tell Me—whed-er de Guverner muft not pa Me—caufe he did not apint a Shirif—I be poer Negar and loft all fo cant give a Lawer aney Mony to tell Me—fo I hop fum larnt Man will be cum-pafhunat and tell Me—Me tink Guverner fhud pa poer SAMBO—

FIGURE 1.1 A letter from "Sambo," a "pore negar" to "Misser Tomas" in the *Massachusetts Spy*, 1788. Courtesy, American Antiquarian Society.

these items reveal what white satirists knew: depicting black characters who called themselves nigger made the portrayals believable.[35] In this way, the word nigger authenticated blackness for white audiences.

These blackface literary productions illuminated white anxieties about African American freedom and social mobility in the revolutionary age, even as the use of nigger within them was somewhat murky. On the one hand, the usage signaled the letter-writer's obsequiousness. On the other, it drew black characters who were sly and suggested that white listeners were suspicious of the outward subservience of black English, especially given the searing critiques in the letters of subjects such as slavery, property ownership, politics, and labor. The following examples all hail from northern newspapers. Therefore, it is important to note that when editors published them, slavery was still practiced in the North. In a letter written to the editor of Worcester's *Massachusetts Spy* in 1788, "Sambo" described himself as a "pore negar," but he was also a landowner (see figure 1.1). Although the satirist attributed the letter to a barely literate man, the subject dealt with how a swindler stole Sambo's property and also how Sambo proposed that the governor of Massachusetts should reimburse him for the theft.[36] Of course, black people had little recourse in the Massachusetts courts and even less of a chance of communicating with the governor, so the suggestion itself was part of the humor. At the same time, the very mention of such a gesture hints at the anxiety that whites harbored about the prospect of black freedom, property ownership, and political participation. The anecdote seemed to ask: how "poor" of a nigger might Sambo be if he (or any other person of color, for that matter) tried to use the system to benefit himself against the interest of whites?

As literary reenactments of postrevolutionary black identity, these anecdotes served to authenticate a caricature of blackness and of the African American subjects who spoke the word nigger. As highlighted above, the satirists imagined black people as innately subservient by coupling the word nigger with the adjective poor, a pointed modifier. In her discussion of white women during the revolutionary period, historian Mary Beth Norton argues that, in letters, white women who were facing hard times purposely described themselves in feminized ways. To emphasize their troubles, they would identify themselves as "poor" and "helpless," whereas men in similar dire circumstances self-identified as "unfortunate."[37] In the blackface anecdotes, the use of poor was therefore a decidedly feminizing gesture, meant to degrade black masculinity. Thus, in a letter published on 4 July 1789, a satirist mollified white fears of black emancipation by having a black subject called "Cuffe" refer to himself and others as "poor negers." This particular article was a facetious response to a report in Philadelphia's *Independent Gazetteer*. According to Cuffe, a previous article queried how the 600,000 enslaved people in the United States felt about their plight. Signaling how whites believed black people masked their true opinions, Cuffe was unwilling to share his own feelings on slavery but instead relayed a recent conversation he had with his friend "Pompey." Pompey warned that "by [and] by poor neger kik up a dus" and rise up. Moreover, he said that the abolitionists taught him that the "white man he no right to make slave de poor neger."[38]

Certainly, part of the message here was that blacks might seem docile, but insurrection was a real possibility. But it also revealed that, in the white imaginary, black people's apparent ignorance disguised dubious street smarts, challenging the social order even as it remained a source of ridicule. In the final analysis, the anecdotes posited African Americans as unintelligible not simply for their thickly accented speech patterns but for the sociopolitical identities encompassed by the label nigger, which rendered them homegrown foreigners.

WHEREAS BLACKFACE LITERARY PRODUCTIONS depicted African Americans who fawningly spoke the word nigger in earshot of white people, when real black people bandied it between each other, the tenor was quite different. They did so in recognition of a unifying social identity that positioned them as outsiders in white America but also as part of a viable inside group. One of the most useful examples of this comes from

Harriet Wilson's 1859 autobiographical book *Our Nig; or, Sketches from the Life of a Free Black, in a Two-Story White House, North.* . . . Wilson was a black indentured servant during the 1830s and 1840s who lived in Milford, New Hampshire, with an abusive white family. Literary scholars argue that the central character of the book, Frado, was Wilson's alter ego, and that the Bellmonts, with whom the character Frado lived, were likely the family of the abolitionist Nehemiah Hayward, whose wife and daughter brutalized Wilson.[39] According to Wilson's book, when she was six years old, her destitute white mother and equally poor black stepfather signed a contract of servitude, giving the child to the Haywards until she came of age, a process replicated by other impoverished black families throughout the North.[40]

At the end of this chapter, the discussion will return to Wilson's provocative title, *Our Nig*, and the multiple, even fractured, ways in which she used the word throughout the book. For now, it will suffice to say that Wilson's writing offered a rare and sympathetic glimpse into how African Americans spoke to each other. In the initial pages, Wilson imagined a conversation that took place before the main character Frado was born, between her real father, Jim, and his friend and landlord, Pete. In the exchange between the two men, Wilson positioned nigger as both neutral and culturally specific. This was emphatically different from how she would later depict her white characters speaking the term. Wilson portrayed Jim as "a kind-hearted African" who was part owner of a business hooping barrels. Jim fell in love with Frado's mother, the fallen and outcast white woman Mag. One day, Jim was in his workshop and muttering to himself about the prospect of marrying Mag when Pete, who was also black, startled him. Their exchange went as follows:

> JIM: Where you come from, you sly nigger!
> PETE: Come, tell me, who is't? Mag Smith, you want to marry?
> JIM: Git out, Pete! And when you come in dis shop again, let a nigger know it. Do n't steal in like a thief.[41]

This brief conversation demonstrated the easy way that Wilson imagined the term nigger fitting into the African American lexicon. Jim hollered it to Pete when annoyed, but he also used it to refer to himself. The word could tease, but could also express irritation and disdain. The simple interchange revealed a close relationship between the two men, a familiarity. Their use of nigger signaled a mutual recognition of a shared social identity. Although Wilson placed a class designation on the word by drawing Jim as unsophisticated and uneducated, she did not give it a negative value, indicating that its meanings were contextual and versatile.

If Wilson's example provides the richest contemporary evidence of the black use of nigger, the 1930s WPA interviews with former slaves offer the most compelling. The use of the word throughout the WPAs is worthy of further exploration and analysis. Yet, it is certainly anecdotally significant that almost seventy-five years after the Civil War, nigger remained a viable part of the vocabulary of many of the formerly enslaved. It is tempting to presume that in the WPAs, in which mostly white southerners interviewed former slaves in the Jim Crow South, the black informants used the word nigger to capitulate to white authority. A look at the Virginia interviews, in which many interviewers were African American, however, debunks this theory.[42] Instead, the Virginia WPAs demonstrate that black people spoke the word (during and after enslavement) and imbued it with meanings far more complex than simply mimicking the master's language. For example, Liza Brown used it casually when she described James Harrison's property in land and people, remarking that he "had a gra' big farm an' lots of niggers."[43] On the other hand, after revealing that her father, after far too many beatings, ran away to the woods, former slave Cornelia Carney proudly announced that her father and others were never caught because "Niggers was too smart fo' white folks to git ketched."[44] That enslaved people spoke the word among each other and used it in complicated ways is exemplified in the interview of Mrs. Virginia Hayes Shepherd who remembered that her enslaver allowed so much autonomy among his slaves that "we were called free niggers by slaves on other plantations."[45] Often African Americans used the word with a distinctly subversive tone, using it in a way that encapsulated the harsh realities of slavery. This was the case when Charles Grandy told the story of how an overseer tried to steal away an enslaved man's wife, and how her husband fought to the death to protect her. Importantly, throughout the story Grandy referred to the husband as a "colored man." But when the overseer wielded a gun and refused to stop shooting until the husband was dead, Grandy relayed, simply and solemnly, "Nigger ain't got no chance."[46]

The subversive qualities of the black use of nigger are also pronounced by an examination of southern slave songs. Sometimes enslaved people used the word defiantly, announcing their social differences from U.S.

whites. Such was the case with two secular songs that emanate a rebellious tone. In them, the character nigger was drawn as a trickster, a persona revered (and sometimes notorious) in African American folklore for his ability to win small and great victories from the enslaver.[47] This was the same usage adopted by Cornelia Carney when she used the word nigger triumphantly to reflect upon her father's escape. These songs demonstrate how by using nigger, African Americans could openly vocalize scathing cultural critiques of white supremacy and racial slavery.

> My name is Ran,
> I wuks in the sand,
> I rather be a nigger
> dan a po' white man

and

> Run, nigger, run, de patrollers will ketch you,
> Run, nigger, run, its almost day
> Dat nigger run, dat nigger flew;
> Dat nigger tore his shirt in two.[48]

Although each of the verses highlights a world in which nigger designated containment, neither suggests shame; rather, the word was an open acknowledgment of a shared experience that connected the singer to his audience. In the first verse, the black speaker flouted notions of white supremacy by declaring that he would rather be a slave than an impoverished white person. This was a usage echoed in the Virginia WPAs as when Charles Crawley compared his social condition to that of poor whites and unflinchingly remarked that "Ole Marster was mo' hard on dem poor white folks den he was on us niggers."[49] The second song juxtaposed the subject's captivity against his surreptitious flight; its rhythm is reminiscent of a somber chant in which still-bound slaves root for the success of a runaway. The African American trickster—who gets away with bold class analysis in the first verse and who takes his freedom in the second—was significant because of the challenge the always-male figure posed to prevailing values.[50] Unlike the "poor nigger" in literary blackface, these chants restored masculinity to the subject. For black laborers, the word signaled a flexible discourse that acknowledged the realities of racial identity in the Americas—including containment and servitude—but also bravado and resistance. Nigger was a laboring folk hero who defied notions of African American ignorance and subservience and was nevertheless called nigger by the people who admired him most. The usage announced that, as enslaved and degraded people, African Americans could take their punches and still develop a meaningful culture. They would make America their own.

African Americans appropriated the word nigger in the United States, eschewing it as a mere labor category and crafting it into a social identity recognized by people of color throughout the North and South. This self-proclamation was even found in northern slave songs. The following song was a product of African Dutch culture and was collected in Ulster County, New York.

Cold, frosty morning,
Nigger berry good.
Wid his axe on his shoulder,
And way to the wood.[51]

Blackface and the Making of an Epithet

Just as African Americans used nigger as a way to claim a unique identity as involuntary black laborers, whites developed their own version of the word, the trajectory of which kept pace with the northern transition from slavery to freedom. Significantly, when white northerners used nigger, they rarely thought of it as part of their own vocabulary, but instead they imagined themselves as quoting, imitating, and ventriloquizing black English. Nigger thus became an accusation that blamed African Americans for speaking the slur and therefore for being self-acknowledged niggers. In the early years of black emancipation, the white meaning of nigger expanded to include not just enslaved people but all free people of color and to flag them as backward and beyond redemption. The word denounced African Americans as people who occupied one immutable, racialized social class, incapable of achieving real freedom and citizenship. Crucially, the existence of this reenvisioned labor category nigger, one that was less concerned with work than it was with race, was necessary to define the very essence of what it meant to be white in the postemancipation North.[52] As historian David Roediger demonstrates, this was particularly true of white laborers in the early national period, who began calling themselves "white workers" to highlight the fact that they were "'not slaves' or 'not negurs.'" The rhetorical separation that rejected the terms "servant" or "master" was a move that both demeaned black laborers and also elevated the word nigger to a term of white working-class empowerment.[53]

In an effort to sustain white supremacy, as the region transitioned to freedom in the 1810s and 1820s, the legacy of slavery increasingly overshadowed all other features of black identity. Whites envisioned African Americans only within a context of their current, former, or imagined enslavement; black people were considered "slave," "free," or "fugitive." Being identified by one's proximity to enslavement carried a special weight in the United States, as Americans predicated republicanism on independence and therefore, as historian Leslie Harris argues, "slaves, as the property of masters, were symbolically and literally the inverse of the ideal republican citizen."[54] People of color were not only not citizens but were "anticitizens."[55] Unfettered, African Americans were dangerous to the institution of slavery as insurrectionists and as potential liberators of the enslaved. Free people of color were thus a distinct threat and, writ large, in need of sequestration as potential menaces to society.

This new, apoplectic version of nigger was more than mere name-calling. By the 1820s, it threatened real violence, especially to people of color who moved through public space independently. In particular, whites harnessed the word to prevent black geographic mobility and social aspiration. For example, in 1824, at the corner of Pearl Street and Broadway in New York City, three drunken white men attacked the African American owner of an all-night oyster house.[56] When the black man called for the night watch, the three men, described benignly as "rowdies," called out "kill the nigger!" After calling out the threat, one of the white men hit the black man on the head with a stone. Rather than take this level of violence seriously, the reporter who wrote it crafted the episode as comedy. The tag line of the piece made fun of the owner's head injury, asserting that "Ebony felt a fracture in his knowledge box." Demonstrating that such aggression was less an item for the police blotter than fodder for the joke section, the incident appeared in a Nantucket newspaper under the heading, "Light Readings."[57]

Whites invoked nigger to claim the northern streets as their own and to warn free people of color that the northern public was not their home. Whites summoned the word to vanquish the real black people they harassed and replace them with, in the words of one scholar's apt description of another racialized labor category, "a conglomeration of racial imaginings."[58] In blackface cultural productions, white actors and humorists insisted that nigger was black-only English, depicting African Americans as the sole and original source of the word. Through this process, the portrayals imagined black people as being too ignorant and too servile to know better than to use a word designed to contain them. In a move that is hauntingly similar to the excuses whites give for saying nigger in the twenty-first century, in the antebellum period, white Americans absolved themselves of the violence and rancor of the word by insisting that by calling black people nigger, they were simply repeating what African Americans said about themselves. Of course, such an assertion was disingenuous. Whites who verbally assaulted free African Americans with the epithet nigger were not reifying a shared social identity but instead inscribing black people as un-American. Between whites of all classes, the invocation of nigger was a social contract that united white Americans along racial lines. It was the violent call to arms of regional and ultimately national belonging and was radically different from the word that blacks used among themselves.

That whites reinvented the word nigger as black-only English was a sleight of hand that should not be underestimated. A search of digital databases of nineteenth-century newspapers demonstrates the frequency with which whites attributed the word to African Americans. From the postrevolutionary period and through the 1830s, editors and letter writers most often published it with quotation marks or italics. They thus attributed the word to black speakers through literary blackface productions similar to the anecdotes that first circulated in the 1770s and 1780s. For the next half-century of blackface cultural production, white humorists placed the word nigger into the mouths of black caricatures. They did this to make the black characters seem real.[59] When white satirists were not using the word in mockery, they rarely wrote it at all.

Within these performances, the black use of nigger was a smoking gun of African American backwardness that took direct aim at black people who moved through public space. To pose black citizenship as unimaginable, in hundreds of visual, theatrical, and literary cultural productions of the 1820s and 1830s, whites used the word nigger as a punch line to underscore racial difference. In one visual example, illustrator Edward Clay, in his "Life in Philadelphia" series, sketched a series of broadsides that juxtaposed black strivings against what he saw as a lack of black social etiquette.[60] Presumably, the artist observed each of the interactions he mocked in an urban, usually public, milieu. Dated circa 1830, plate #14 of his collection specifically expressed a gendered anxiety about black

FIGURE 1.2 Edward Clay, "Life in Philadelphia," Plate #14, published by S. Hart, 1830. The Library Company of Philadelphia.

upward mobility through the incongruous presence of a black woman, typically burdened by domestic chores, engaging in middle-class pursuits (see figure 1.2).[61] In this case, the woman and her male companion were browsing in a milliner's shop during the birth of American consumerism. It was only in 1827, a few years earlier, when builders and merchants in Philadelphia constructed the first mall-like retail structure in the city.[62] Partaking of the consumer culture, the woman shopped with her escort, a financially flush African American man called "Frederick Augustus," a grand name for a former slave and thus a source of comedy. Despite their show of wealth, the couple was outrageously overdressed and was depicted as so uncultured that they brought a dog into the store. Images such as this one asserted that economic achievement, rather than diffusing African American ignorance, merely afforded black people the resources to become a greater public nuisance.

Significantly, at the same time that Clay's "Life in Philadelphia" series belittled people of color for their social aspirations, it also revealed that African Americans, particularly those in Philadelphia, were developing a well-recognized and formidable political and public culture.[63] Such people posed a considerable threat to prevailing ideas about race and place, and, in the series, Clay's use of nigger was retaliatory against black people who infringed on public space. In #14 (per figure 1.2), the woman asked Frederick Augustus if he liked the oversized bonnet she tried on. He scoffed, "I dont like him no how, [because] dey hide you lubly face, so you cant tell one she nigger from anoder."[64] There are multiple levels to the intended humor here. The caricature played on the notion of nigger as an inescapable social class by asserting that African Americans were so incapable of individuation that not even a person of color could discern one black person from another. Most significantly, the commentary challenged black claims of masculinity that depended on the femininity of black women. By having the male figure refer to this woman by the animalizing phrase "she nigger," the caricature insinuated that black men were responsible for contradicting the possibility of black ladyhood. Unable to create the necessary circumstances to allow the black woman's social elevation, and even disparaging the woman in the process, Frederick Augustus denigrated himself, thus proving that no amount of riches could unmake a nigger.

In another Edward Clay piece from 1829, also from the "Life in Philadelphia" series, the artist used the word nigger to explicitly ridicule the geographic mobility of free people of color. He also insisted that nigger

FIGURE 1.3 Edward Clay, "Life in Philadelphia": *A Dead Cut*, published by S. Hart, 1829. Courtesy, American Antiquarian Society.

was a fixed racial category out of which no black person could rise (see figure 1.3). In the sketch, titled *A Dead Cut*, a man working as a boot-black recognizes an old friend, Caesar. Caesar, a colored traveler who has just returned to Philadelphia after a visit in New York, does not want to be recognized by the black laborer. Instead, Caesar fancies himself transformed by his travel and also his wealth, which is exemplified by his clothing. The joke lies in Caesar believing himself too good to know the other black man. His snobbery is drawn as ridiculous. When the boot-black shakes hands with Caesar, Caesar recoils. Caesar not only tells the other man that he has mistaken Caesar for someone else, but then goes on to expose his own impossible desires for racial dominance by calling the laborer a "black man!" A woman traveling with Caesar, most likely his wife, overly dressed in an outfit that belies her race and class, takes the verbal assault one step further. She asks her husband what the "impertinent nigger" means. The woman's malapropism—a misspoken cross between impertinent and impudent—is just part of a racial indictment that uses the word nigger as its anchor. The tableau not only asserts that black folks are outrageous for even trying to rise socially but also accuses the aspirational ones of being the very people who most demean lower-class blacks by calling them nigger. Furthermore, the illustration ostensibly absolves whites for doing the same. It is antiblack ventriloquism at its finest, and it had far-reaching impact. Hosea Easton complained that broadsides such as this one plastered the windows of popular bookstores, and the ceilings of barrooms and public houses were sometimes "literally covered with them."[65] Images such as these did important cultural work to negate and ridicule the possibility of African American social elevation (see figure 1.4).

Blackface representations, often depicted with black people calling themselves nigger, lampooned African American social aspiration, but they also cautioned against unrestrained black geographic mobility. This new iteration of antiblack cultural productions was largely a response to black freedom in the North and the interracial abolitionist movement. When activists organized the movement for immediate abolition in 1831, it garnered a swift and negative reaction.[66] Between 1833 and 1837, white mobs assailed African Americans and white abolitionists across the North, a demonstration of aggression that included thirty-five riots against abolitionists in the summer of 1835 alone. Antiabolitionists burned schools, pelted activists with eggs, beat people to a pulp, and shot at least one white abolitionist dead.[67] Antiblack cultural productions joined the antiabolitionist fervor. The most famous of these was the stage character Jim Crow. Made famous by white actor Thomas D. Rice, Jim Crow was violent, wild, and at times brilliant, but most significantly, he was a colored traveler who abused his freedom of movement. He crisscrossed the North and South, wreaking havoc along the way. Black sexual desire was palpable in Jim Crow's travels, as it was with other minstrel characters of the period. Male figures were overtly sexual and full of bravado, and female figures were highly promiscuous and fickle. This was evidenced in songs such as *The Nigger Wench Fight* or the minstrel opera *Oh Hush*, where a bootblack, a wood sawer, a coal scourer, and a chimney sweep all vie for the attentions of the "peerless Quasha."[68] According to these performances, African American bodily appetites needed strict regulation.

More daunting still was black male aggression, particularly against other African Americans, an anxiety made more obvious as the minstrel caricatures traversed the nation. Calling his rivals nigger, Jim Crow had

FIGURE 1.4 "Jim Brown." This Boston-based rival of Jim Crow traveled from Boston to Washington, D.C., bragging about his sexual prowess and threatening other African Americans along the way. He called himself and others nigger throughout. Image is circa 1832–1837. Courtesy, American Antiquarian Society.

a frenetic, primitive need to move, driven by lust, anger, and indiscretion, disrupting public decorum and endangering himself and others in the process. Consider several stanzas from the original Jim Crow song, popularized around 1832:

> I went down to de riber,
> I didn't mean to stay,

But dere I see so many galls,
I couldn't stay away
. . .
An den I go to Orleans
An feel so full of fight
Dey put me in de Calaboose,
An keep me dare all night.
. . .
I struck a Jarsey niggar,
In de street do oder day
An I hope I neber stir
If he didn't turn gray.
. . .
I met a Philadelphia niggar
Dress'd up quite nice & clean
Bud de way he 'bused de Yorkers
I thought was berry mean
. . .
But [Sambo] soon jumped up again,
An 'gan for me to feel,
Says I go away you niggar,
Or I'll skin you like an eel.[69]

As a colored traveler, Jim Crow moved seamlessly throughout the United States from New Orleans to New Jersey, Philadelphia, and New York. The innate violence and outlandish sexuality of characters such as Jim Crow ultimately endangered people of color because white audiences actually believed the social aggression enacted onstage was real. The fact that the actors onstage used the word nigger made their portrayals of black violence all the more authentic. In turn, whites could assert their own Americanness by defining themselves against the recalcitrant nigger who chased after women, landed in jail, and beat up and even threatened to stab other African Americans. According to onlookers, such uncontrolled African American behavior warranted, even necessitated, white discipline. Under the guise of ventriloquism, whites reenacted antiblack aggression in public spaces and regurgitated nigger in their impromptu performances. In so doing, they sought to eliminate a free black public presence and claim the northern streets as white-only terrain.

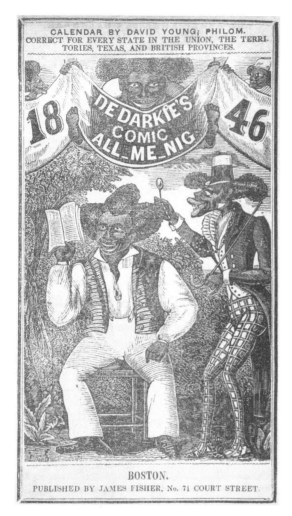

FIGURE 1.5
Demonstrating the ubiquity of antiblack sentiment in the antebellum North and its increase in the 1830s and 1840s, this mock-up of an almanac ridicules black dress, style, and habits but most emphatically indicts the presence of men of color in public space. From the cover of *De Darkie's Comic All-Me-Nig* (Boston: James Fisher, 1846). Courtesy, American Antiquarian Society.

Thus, nigger increasingly announced and symbolized the tense relationship that free people of color had with the United States (see figure 1.5). As historian Patrick Rael has meticulously detailed, by the 1830s, nigger had emerged as such a popular epithet that whites even deployed it against other whites to signal the moral and intellectual defects of their ideological enemies. For example, white abolitionists were "nigger lovers," and Republicans were members of the "nigger party."[70] Those Americans who loathed northern emancipation dubbed the region the "'free nigger' North," and New England specifically, "Free Nigger-dom."[71] One white abolitionist proposed a radical strategy of resistance to such attacks. In the spring of 1839, the editor of New

Hampshire's *Herald of Freedom*, Nathaniel Peabody Rogers, defiantly exclaimed, "'Nigger!' 'Nigger!' The hideous epithet is glorious to us. We wear it as a plumage in our crest. We glory in the badge. . . . We covet the appellation. It is full of the deathless honor to abolitionists, but of infamy and condemnation to this land."[72] In order to ameliorate the word's venom, Rogers proposed that (white) abolitionists adopt the term with pride.

Rogers must have quickly found that his African American peers were unconvinced by the strategy of reappropriation, because Rogers soon clarified his position "lest our frequent use of the hated word 'nigger' should have wounded our respected and beloved colored friends." He explained, "We use the term to put to shame the mean and ungenerous taunters, who continue to cast it on their fellow men. We hope our colored friends will esteem it and use it as we do. It is a weapon for them now to turn upon their unmanly enemies."[73] Notwithstanding his earnest enthusiasm and desire to detoxify the word and the violence that encircled it, Rogers failed to see the reality that as long as antiblack feeling proliferated in the North, nigger would never and could never mean the same thing when spoken by African Americans and by whites. When wielded as an epithet, it would always set the terms of racial inclusion and exclusion.

Black Activists Reject Nigger

Unlike with black laborers and even white abolitionists such as Nathaniel Rogers, nigger was not an easy word for black activists to vocalize. Instead, it remained a word that not only denoted race, as the word is understood today, but also invariably class. As early as 1776, a British ex-slave, Ignatius Sancho, who lived in England, showed his disdain for the word by describing himself as "one of those people whom the vulgar and illiberal call 'Negurs.'"[74] Sancho's rejection of the term mirrored his social mobility out of servitude and his class aspiration. As with Sancho, when black activists abandoned the word nigger, they did so as a discursive political tool that built on the conscious decision to create symbolic and intellectual distance between themselves and the condition of enslavement. They discussed nigger publicly not as a unifying status but as a harmful epithet. In the very process of rejecting the word, these activists made their own overt claims to citizenship and social entrée.[75]

The disassociation from the word nigger was in keeping with early strategies for social and political inclusion that hinged on explicitly proving that the categories of black and slave were not interlocked social identities. Starting with a seminal speech made by enslaved activist Jupiter Hammon to black New Yorkers in 1784, activists sought to combat the negative connotations of enslavement, such as immorality, ignorance, and dependence. To do so, they implemented a stringent practice of gender normativity and controlled public behavior, including piety, hard work, and good manners, for the purpose of presenting African Americans as people worthy of citizenship.[76] Far from passive, in lectures, writings, and church sermons, adherents of "moral improvement" emphasized the political significance of respectability when public perception of people of color was dangerously low. For example, in 1837, Samuel Cornish, editor of the African American newspaper *The Colored American*, grieved that whenever "one of the baser sort of our people commit a crime . . . the cry [among whites] is *the niggers! the niggers!!*"[77] For African Americans, this version of nigger denounced racial difference as a social transgression.

Among African Americans, the speaking of nigger came to denote a person's class. Thus, black writers rarely developed characters who spoke the word. When they did draw such characters, it was meant to highlight the writer's own social elevation. Usually former slaves themselves, these authors depicted the utterance of nigger as the insular vocabulary of people constrained by bondage but also by a lack of worldly sophistication. As with Harriet Wilson, the word emerged as a marker of class difference among people of color. For example, former slave William Wells Brown's 1853 novel *Clotel*, in part, told a story about the tragedy of racial supremacy wherein he critiqued color consciousness within enslaved communities. In one passage, Brown portrayed a privileged group of slaves who disparaged darker-skinned laborers as niggers. In another passage, a darker-skinned worker proudly declared in reference to himself: "Dis nigger is no countefit; he is de genewine artekil."[78] Both versions of the word show how it was multidimensional; it emitted contempt in one moment and audacity in the next. Yet, in either case, its use marked the speaker's lower-class standing. In her 1861 autobiography, *Incidents in the Life of a Slave Girl*, Harriet Jacobs, a self-liberated woman, likewise utilized the word nigger to infuse the language of her most provincial black characters in her narrative. In just two examples, an enslaved woman named Betty assisted Jacobs in her 1835 escape promising: "If dey *did* know whar you are, dey won't know *now*. Dey'll be disapinted dis time. Dat's all I got to say. If dey comes rummaging 'mong *my* tings, dey'll get one bressed sarssin from dis 'ere nigger." Later, while awaiting an inspection of the premises by a slaveholder, Betty cursed him and his family, saying, "Dis nigger's too cute for 'em dis time."[79] Like the black worker in Brown's novel, Betty's use of "this nigger" to describe herself was a conspiratorial wink to punctuate her autonomy and to indicate her ability to easily outwit the enslaver. It also marked her as just one member of a larger social identity.

One more example from *Incidents* helps illustrate the point that class was a paramount factor in the black use of nigger. The character of Linda Brent (Jacobs's pseudonym and alter ego in the memoir) only uses the word nigger once in the entire book and to pointed effect. To allay her grandmother's fears about the enslaver who relentlessly pursued her and to underscore his impotency, Linda assured her grandmother, "The mayor of Boston won't trouble himself to hunt niggers for Dr. Flint."[80] Even though Linda used the word facetiously to dismiss her pursuer, ultimately she and other black authors painted nigger as the vocabulary of a degraded social standing and a debased people. These writers acknowledged nigger as a viable social category but most emphatically one to which they, as free people of a certain social class, did not belong. By thus adopting a politics of respectability that included a rejection of the word nigger they made their own claims to the United States as home.

Clashes arose when certain activists imposed their vision of social identity and national belonging on black laborers in the North. Indeed, as the invocation of nigger attests, black workers also had a political consciousness and desired liberation, but they did not necessarily believe that adopting middle-class respectability would deliver them from their poverty or social ostracism. Most dramatically, conflicts between the classes centered on public behavior and presentations of blackness. Advocates of moral improvement urged "respectable" men not to visit grog shops and "frolics" because public drinking, in particular, was "more ruinous to the lower class of our colour, than any other vice."[81] Other activists bemoaned the practice of dandyism, a reference to those people who some believed spent their money frivolously on clothing, gambling, and entertainment rather than on education. Activists also debated the boundaries of acceptable work; some considered domestic labor of any kind proof of servility, whereas others deemed it viable and sustaining employment. In 1852, in a gendered rant, Martin Delany argued that if African American men continued to allow black women to hold servile occupations, citizenship would be impossible. He urged that "until colored men, attain to a position above permitting their mothers, sisters, wives and daughters, to do the drudgery and menial offices of other men's wives and daughters . . . it is pitiable mockery, to talk about equality and elevation in society."[82]

At the same time, African American laborers pushed back against respectability politics and continued to assert that their own jobs, values, and social identities were valid, a fact that activist complaints made plain.[83] In one instance, a Boston-based correspondent for the first African American newspaper, *Freedom's Journal*, lambasted a black woman he called "Mrs. G" and described her as a female "dandy" for scandalously speaking ill of "our most respectable coloured families." Writing in 1827, the correspondent was most angry that Mrs. G described those families as snobs and as people who lived beyond their means. Suggesting that some working-class folks saw formal education as a barrier to racial unity, Mrs. G confessed the she found black people aspiring to attain middle-class success to be "too great for me, they have too much learning."[84] Between middle-class blacks and the laboring poor, the speaking of nigger was another fault line along which intraracial class conflict played out. When black laborers called Walker and his followers nigger, Walker denounced their language as "aggravating."[85]

We Don't Allow Niggers in Here!

For elite colored travelers, nigger came to signify a concerted assault against free people of color in public space. Therefore, by the late 1830s, transatlantic black abolitionists began using the word in their writings and speeches to emphasize their growing sense of alienation at home. This was a strategic maneuver meant to lay rhetorical claims to the country of their birth. These black activists exposed the word's vitriol, debunked the frivolity it conveyed in blackface performance, and told a community of international abolitionists how nigger encapsulated African American degradation and white supremacy in the United States. In an 1843 lecture before the World Anti-slavery Conference in London, black abolitionist J. W. C. Pennington outlined the myriad impediments that confronted newly freed African Americans in their quest for equality and citizenship. But before he launched into his discussion, Pennington described what he felt was a commonly held belief in "all countries" that free people of African descent were destined to remain niggers because they stubbornly refused to better themselves. He showed the particular dominance of such thinking in the United States by provocatively quoting a stanza he heard from a "Jim Crow" performance: "Do what you will, the nigger will be a nigger still." Lest his international audience believe that such language was only the purview of white workers and not gentlemen, Pennington made plain the multiclass appeal of such cruel prejudice. He confessed that he often heard "from the lips of respectable white people" the following, "Take a nigger, cut off his head, boil him, broil him, throw him into an oven, roast him, he will be a nigger still."[86]

Reluctantly, Pennington repeated the verses to expose the racism beneath the comic façade of antiblack humor. His examples powerfully detailed the disingenuousness of white racism that accused African Americans themselves of occupying the reviled social status of nigger. He made clear that nigger was not simply a benign word that black laborers used but also a uniquely violent American racial profanity. His repetition showed how each childish-sounding rhyme belied a vicious mode of thinking. The verses addressed an invisible white person who exasperatedly tried to dislodge a black person from his slave roots, but to no avail. Despite this white person's valiant efforts, an African American was still a nigger. Indeed, under this logic, the social class nigger was not only the fault of people of color but was also immutable by black design. Moreover, black people's belligerent poverty and ignorance entitled whites to meet them with aggression. As revealed by the casually cannibalistic language of the second poem, violence crackled around the edges of the nigger accusation. It rendered the black body unsafe from such brutalities as dismemberment and lynching. By insisting that the word was white-only speech and an antidemocratic epithet, Pennington broadcasted its ubiquity, its violence, and the obstruction it caused to the mobility of African Americans in their rightful home.

In an effort to situate themselves as a people with legitimate political and social claims to the United States, activists such as Pennington publicly enacted a type of literary and discursive "white face" in which they, too, ventriloquized the word nigger.[87] Like white Americans, African American activists spoke and wrote the word to quote their enemies. Only this time, black people branded the word as *white*-only English. Importantly, the stakes were high for international black activists who spoke the word nigger, even for the sake of exposing white racism. By doing so, they chanced being categorized as part of the immutable social class out of which they aspired to rise. Therefore, among early activists, the word was verboten. It did not appear in the first African American newspaper, *Freedom's Journal*, which ran from 1827 to 1829, nor was it credited to a black activist in *The Liberator* until the mid-1830s.[88] The reluctance of early activists to repeat the word brings into stark relief the magnitude of David Walker's use of the word in his 1829 *Appeal*. When Frederick Douglass traveled to the British Isles from 1845 to 1847, he engaged in a rare instance of using the word casually. He wrote to white Boston abolitionist Francis Jackson that, "It is quite an advantage to be a 'nigger' here." He went on to describe that he was not quite black enough for the British, but as long as he kept his hair "wooly," he could "pass for at least a half a negro at any rate."[89] Yet, even as he playfully conjured the familiar pejorative in his letter, he made sure to use quotation marks to indicate that he was quoting U.S. whites and/or racist Britons.

By the latter part of the 1830s, colored travelers strategically used the word nigger in their writings and speeches, arguing that in the United States people of color were not somehow uniquely constituted for enslavement and containment. Instead, they asserted that white Americans demeaned and alienated black people through the ideology that the word represented. Transatlantic abolitionists consistently linked the white use of the word to attacks on black social mobility. In his famous 1845 *Narrative*, Douglass depicted the word as representative of racial violence and oppression, demonstrating one memorable instance where his enslaver spewed the word nigger several times to prevent Douglass's education.[90] When Douglass traveled to the British Isles, he even more passionately detailed how whites in the United States deployed the word nigger to obstruct independent black movement, especially at the thresholds of public space. In a letter Douglass sent from Ireland to white abolitionist William Lloyd Garrison in 1846, he made clear that slavery was not the sole cause of his consistent alienation. He told how in the North both poor and middle-class whites seethed at the prospect of his inclusion in an array of public venues, including steamships, omnibuses, stagecoaches, inns, zoos, and lyceums. Describing the "fiendish hate" he confronted as a man of color attempting to navigate the antebellum North, Douglass repeated nine times the fierce mantra of his white countrymen, *"we don't allow niggers in here."*[91]

Ultimately, black activists made it known internationally that the word nigger and all it represented was a central dictum in the development of African American social identity in the United States, particularly in the North. They reiterated that nigger was what home sounded and looked like. Whether laborers of color incorporated the word into their own vocabularies to signal a shared social experience or middle-class activists brandished it as a sword to fight slavery and prejudice, nigger was a constant companion. Its virulence was a nasty mockery of the culture that people of color built for themselves in the postrevolutionary United States. In the 1830s, when blackface cultural productions reached their height of popularity and white parents used nigger as a centerpiece for antiblack instruction, the word gained a violence and omnipresence from which it has never recovered. Nevertheless, when colored travelers used it, they did so to insist that, despite white attempts to exile and banish them, the United States was still their home. They exposed nigger and the sentiment it fostered as impediments to their freedom. By presenting themselves internationally as gentlemen and ladies who reluctantly conjured the word nigger to unmask white racism, they made it the verbal symbol of their ostracism in the country of their birth.

I'd like to say a final word about nigger. Not all African American laborers built a healthy social identity around the black version of the word, tellingly demonstrating that home remained a dangerous and unwelcoming place even after the transatlantic abolitionists traveled abroad. Not all black activists in the North were people who had the opportunity or the resources to escape slavery, involuntary labor, or poverty and thereby transcend the repression of the word nigger. Certainly, only a limited number of activists ever acquired the patronage to travel at all, let alone to foreign shores. For those who reviled the white racism that nigger symbolized but lacked the capital and/or wherewithal to move independently, the word came to represent their lack of options and the very real fact of their containment. Harriet Wilson was one of these people. Driven by poverty, disability, homelessness, and motherhood, she self-published the book *Our Nig* to raise money for herself and her child. Although the autobiographical work showed how the word nigger signified a shared social identity and offered countless examples of the cruelty and violence of her white characters who used it, more importantly, it demonstrated how it was capable of fracturing Wilson's own self. No doubt, the book's title, *Our Nig*, referenced the Bellmonts' sense of ownership of the child. Yet, in a rhetorical slippage

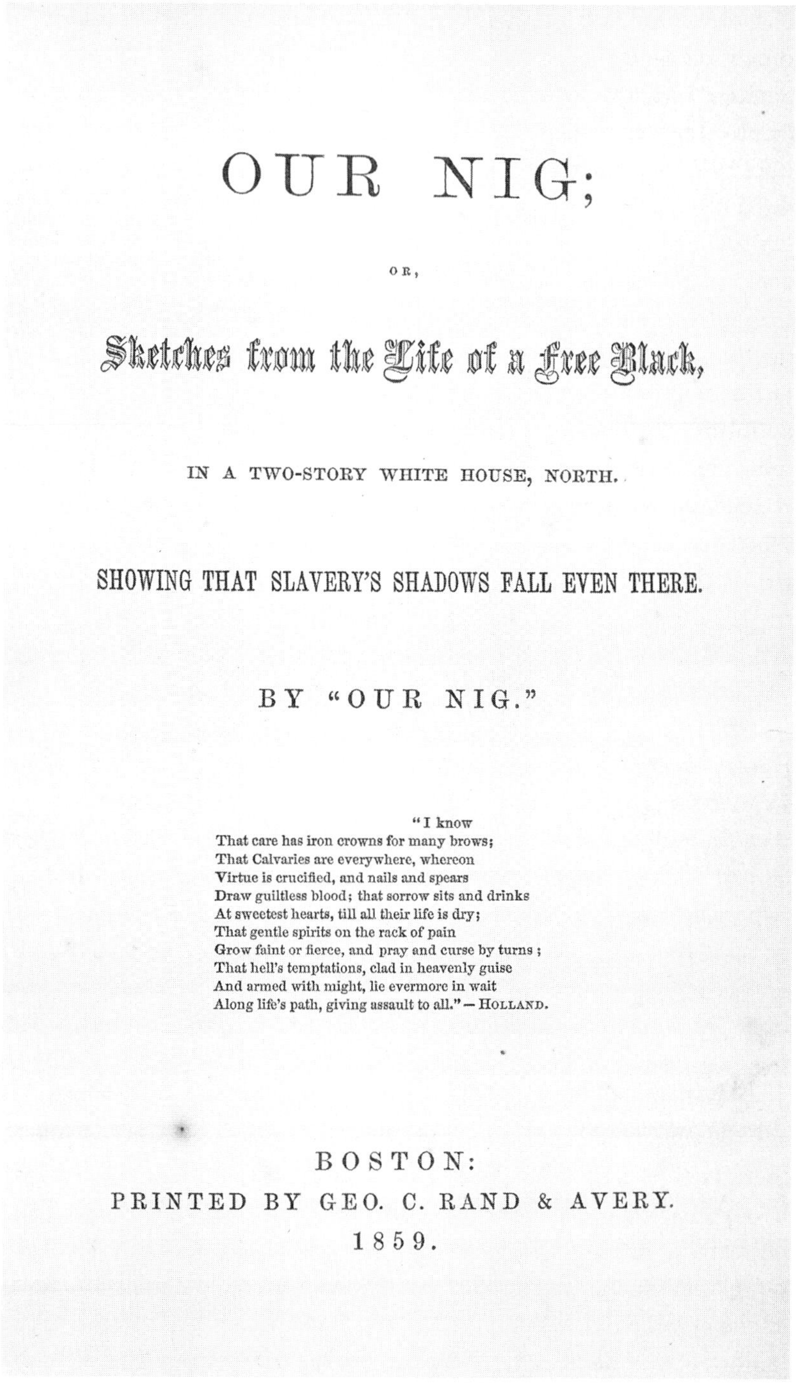

OUR NIG;

OR,

Sketches from the Life of a Free Black,

IN A TWO-STORY WHITE HOUSE, NORTH.

SHOWING THAT SLAVERY'S SHADOWS FALL EVEN THERE.

BY "OUR NIG."

"I know
That care has iron crowns for many brows;
That Calvaries are everywhere, whereon
Virtue is crucified, and nails and spears
Draw guiltless blood; that sorrow sits and drinks
At sweetest hearts, till all their life is dry;
That gentle spirits on the rack of pain
Grow faint or fierce, and pray and curse by turns ;
That hell's temptations, clad in heavenly guise
And armed with might, lie evermore in wait
Along life's path, giving assault to all." — HOLLAND.

BOSTON:
PRINTED BY GEO. C. RAND & AVERY.
1859.

FIGURE 1.6 Title page from Harriet Wilson's *Our Nig* (Boston: Geo. C. Rand & Avery, 1859). Mortimer Rare Book Room, Smith College.

that is repeated throughout the book, the narrator interchangeably called the central character "Frado" and "Nig." For example, when the petulant and violent Bellmont daughter moved away, the narrator commented on Frado's relief, remarking that "Nig went as she was told, and her clear voice was heard as she went, singing in joyous notes." Did Wilson think of herself as a nigger, and in the most degraded sense of the word? Did she utilize the epithet to highlight the horror of her degradation? The book's title page raises even more questions. Wilson credited the authorship of the book not to herself but instead simply to "Our Nig" (see figure 1.6). Whereas the title of the book was an obvious indictment of the cruel family that indentured her and the society that allowed it, by calling the author of the piece "Our Nig," Wilson was doing other important work as well. Her anonymity and invisibility here announced a racial alienation that declared that, despite her birthright, the white North could never fully be her home.[92]

CHAPTER TWO

Becoming Mobile in the Age of Segregation

In 1840, after attending the first World's Anti-Slavery Convention in London, African American delegate Charles Remond revealed the details of his harrowing transatlantic journey to a large audience at London's Exeter Hall.[1] In his speech, he outlined how the system of slavery in the United States corrupted the value of American liberty, even in the "non-slaveholding" states. He described prejudice as a "hydra-headed personage" that relentlessly popped up throughout the North.[2] Yet, he confessed that his most humiliating experience took place not in Massachusetts or New York but over the depths of the Atlantic Ocean. As he told his abolitionist audience, the captain of an American-owned ship forced him to spend every moment of the three-week transatlantic voyage outside on the exterior deck of the boat. Unlike his white traveling companions, who ate and slept within the safety of the ship's cabin, for twenty-one days, Remond's only protection from the weather and the waves was a lean-to covering his makeshift bed. Of his 1840 voyage, Remond quipped that he was "in America all the time he was on the water."[3]

By the 1840s, stories such as Remond's were commonplace. By the time Remond set sail for London, it was the custom—although not yet the official rule or legal code—for transportation proprietors to segregate or refuse service to free African American passengers during travel. In the United States, it was the dawn of the age of segregation. As black people became free, white northerners fashioned racial boundaries in public space, color lines designed to maintain white supremacy. Public vehicles were ripe settings for this contest over race, space, and mobility. They were the sites of vast technological growth, encompassing changes that took place between the 1790s and the 1860s. Scholars call these shifts a "transportation revolution," an historical moment that included improvements in infrastructure, the building of roads and canals, and the harnessing of steam power, all of which created inexpensive, fast, routinized, and publicly available modes of transportation.[4] Often called "public conveyances," the most accessible transportation vehicles were privately and/or corporate owned and were sometimes government-chartered mail carriers that had room for a limited number of passengers.[5] The

American public could access these vehicles for a fee, and such vehicles included stagecoaches, steamships, and railroads, and later the passenger-only streetcars and omnibuses of the urban milieu. Folks who gained entrée were afforded a hitherto unrecognizable geographic breadth that in turn allowed the expansion of their social, political, and economic capital. Americans increasingly saw these vehicles as essential to modernizing the nation.

In order to keep these vehicles modern, U.S. whites worked hard to prevent African Americans, the people they imagined as niggers, from gaining equal access to public conveyances. They criminalized black travel by making it appear illegal, suspicious, unconscionable, inappropriate, and anathema to American identity. As part of this criminalization, northern whites deemed it aggressive and dangerous for free people of color to enter public vehicles as equals and thus partake of travel's promise. Whereas the epithet nigger was a discursive weapon meant to stunt black social mobility, public conveyances became spaces that prohibited black geographic mobility. Such exclusion was significant because both white and black people understood that travel was a vital mechanism for citizenship. Thus, public conveyances quickly became sites of racial and, by default, political struggle. To assert white authority in these spaces, stagecoach drivers, steamship captains, railroad conductors, and white passengers threatened, insulted, and forcibly ousted colored travelers to insist that access was white-only domain.

At the same time, early black activists believed they deserved the fruits of modernity and as a result fought for equal access to public vehicles. Colored travelers understood that the stakes of gaining equal entrée were enormous. They impacted a traveler's economic livelihood, church affiliation, familial ties, organizational strength, physical safety, emotional well-being, and ultimately citizenship. It was in response to ill treatment on public vehicles and in defense of their civic and commercial inclusion that colored travelers planted the seeds of a long-lasting protest tradition. As historian Robin D. G. Kelley argues, as a result of black protest, public conveyances emerged as "moving theaters." They were at once theaters of drama where colored travelers performed and enacted citizenship but also theaters of war in which they fought hard battles over the right to travel freely and equally.[6] Through such performing and warring, activists in the antebellum period made access to public conveyances the perennial symbol of freedom and equal rights in the United States.

Criminalizing Black Mobility

Even before white northerners used stagecoaches, steamships, and railroads to carve out racial boundaries, travel had long been imagined as the purview of U.S. whites. Black mobility was under tight scrutiny, and American law along with popular culture trained white people to distrust any person of color traveling or venturing into public space. This process criminalized black mobility and had far-reaching implications for free people of color in the United States.[7] Born out of the system of slavery, it rendered suspicious any black person who moved of his or her own volition. Such thinking not only supported laws against independent movement but also fostered antiblack vigilantism. Indeed, the notion that African Americans who traveled on their own were doing so unlawfully and were thus dangerous created an attendant system of surveillance that deputized all white Americans—slaveholders and nonslaveholders alike—to interrogate, harass, arrest, seize, and discipline people of color who dared to move outside of those spaces designated for black use by whites. Slavery was about confining black laborers within prescribed locations, and the mission of slaveholders and lawmakers was to restrict people of color within those physical spaces. This style of captivity relegated African Americans to occupy those sites that reinforced their servitude and included slave ships, coffles, auction blocks, slave pens, plantations, big houses, farms, kitchens, factories, chain gangs, sailing vessels, and the countless work environments of forced labor. Cultural theorist Katherine McKittrick calls these spaces "black geographies," locations that are at once sites of confinement and terror, but also of resistance and humanity.[8] Likewise, the work of historian Stephanie Camp convincingly conceptualizes antebellum southern enslavement as a "spatial impulse: to locate bondspeople in plantation space and to control, indeed to determine, their movements and activities."[9]

There is no doubt that the desire to confine enslaved people elicited a vigilante culture aimed at disciplining black mobility. Efforts to keep black people cordoned predated the writing of the U.S. Constitution, as evidenced by a slave pass system that flourished in the southern colonies by 1715. This method of containment enlisted white men to act as patrollers who guarded against escape but who also sought to curtail enslaved people's autonomous use of space and time.[10] As a result, patrollers tried to prevent any type of truancy, including visiting friends and relatives on neighboring plantations, taking unauthorized vacations and holidays, and socializing without the express permission of the slaveholder, a restriction designed to quash black resistance.[11] The slave pass system was a colonial strategy of sequestration that lawmakers eventually folded into state law.

Importantly, methods that regulated mobility were interregional and not just a peculiarity of the South. In the colonial North, where slavery also reigned, curfew laws emboldened white citizens to practice antiblack and antinative vigilantism. In Connecticut, a 1723 act "to Prevent the Disorder of Negro and Indian Servants and Slaves in the Night Season" empowered "any person" to capture a laborer if she or he ventured out past nine "without special order." An earlier 1703 Rhode Island statute targeted not just slaves and servants but all people of color, making it illegal for "any negroes or Indians, *either free men, servants, or slaves*" to walk within the colony after nine at night. If African Americans or Native Americans broke curfew, the law empowered whites to detain and arrest them.[12] The significance of these laws should not be underestimated. They not only institutionalized the mechanics of racial containment but also deputized whites to police the movement of any nonwhite people throughout the colonies.

The drafters of the nation's foundational legislation precluded black domestic travel by codifying the right to unlimited domestic travel as a privilege of free white men only. The 1777 Articles of Confederation explicitly outlined travel as a means to foster commerce and trade and thus "secure and perpetuate mutual friendship and intercourse among the people of the different states."[13] The authors promised that right to "free citizens," a group synonymous with white and male.[14] The Articles assured those white citizens safe travel between states while at the same time denying safe passage to "paupers, vagabonds, and fugitives from justice."[15] Here, the drafters criminalized poverty along with African American self-emancipation, making explicit their understanding of how the rights of citizenship and the rights of migration were directly connected. Of course, these were gendered logics as well and prohibited the autonomous movement of white women, who were imagined as people dependent on a husband or a father. Thus, the Articles of Confederation understood gender, race, citizenship, and mobility as ideologies that were inextricably intertwined.

That travel was meant to be a free white masculine domain was a notion reiterated in the 1787 U.S. Constitution, a document that explicitly prohibited African Americans from freedom of travel by decreeing running away from involuntary servitude a federal crime.[16] A few years later, Congress followed up with the 1793 "fugitive slave law," an amendment that detailed enforcement and threatened a $500 fine for anyone who harbored "fugitives from labor."[17] Although not all people of color were enslaved at the time the Constitution was written, Anglo-Americans conflated African descent and dark skin with involuntary servitude. As a result, the drafters defined the right to domestic travel racially, with whites as mobile beings and African Americans as static ones.[18] Therefore, when people of color moved of their own volition, they not only defied masters, slaveholders, and legislators but also breached deeply held precepts about race and travel in the United States. By marking all African American movement as fugitive behavior, the drafters defined independent black travel as illegal and, perhaps more critically, made all whites responsible for keeping watch over black travelers.

The emancipation of African Americans after the Revolutionary War intensified vigilante culture. During gradual abolition in the North from the 1780s to the 1860s, lawmakers formally criminalized free black mobility in state and national laws by debating and often passing legislation designed to block the migration of free people of color into certain states.[19] Even those opposed to slavery imagined black migration as dangerous. In 1805, Thomas Branagan, a former West Indian slaveholder who converted to the antislavery cause, wrote a treatise about the problem of people of African descent living in his adopted home state of Pennsylvania. He argued that any further northward migration by former southern slaves threatened the fabric of Philadelphia society, describing the formerly enslaved as people who "generally abandon themselves to all manner of debauchery and dissipation" and even posed serious sexual threats to young white girls.[20] Throughout the decades, debates over African American migration continued in several states, including Massachusetts, where, in 1821, state legislators feared that black emigrants would increase the number of "convicts and paupers," inundate large towns with "an indolent, disorderly and corrupt population," and also threaten white jobs.[21]

At their core, these anti-immigration laws deputized all whites to surveil black mobility. Even though laws targeting free black people failed to pass in some northeastern states, such as Pennsylvania and Massachusetts, they did become law in several northwestern states, including Ohio, Indiana, and Illinois. For example, an 1853 Illinois law threatened to sell into slavery "any negro, or mulatto, bond or free" who tried to take up residence in the state.[22] Although the laws were not strictly enforced, the sentiment behind them sent the message that it was the duty of all U.S. whites to keep track of black people in motion. Moreover, several other southern and northern legislatures required people of color to carry manumission papers in order to cross over their borders, again beckoning all whites to scrutinize the travel of black people. Such laws were particularly deplorable to free people of color in New York, who were outraged by the 1837 antitravel laws passed in New Jersey—still a slave state in that year.[23] The editors of the black periodical *The Colored American* believed that the New Jersey legislature approved the enactments "to degrade her colored population to the level with brutes." The activists were particularly frustrated because, having never been in bondage, they had no free papers and were therefore penalized under this statute for being born free.[24] They recognized that state lawmakers were working tirelessly to fashion the United States as a racially homogenous and white supremacist nation.

Laws such as these reflected a U.S. racial project in which most Americans viewed anybody who was not "white" as fundamentally un-American. Within this racial order, Native Americans had to be excised from their territorial homelands. Most famously, U.S. politicians devised ways to remove Native Americans from their lands in the southeast, indicating how racial separatism was a fundamental ideology of the United States.[25] Independent organizations intermingled with separatist legal codes forwarded the agenda of racial removal. The American Colonization Society (ACS), founded in 1816, espoused the idea that Americans could avert a racial apocalypse by sending newly freed African Americans to colonies in Africa.[26] They could not imagine citizenship as belonging to anyone other than whites. In 1829, U.S. Secretary of State Henry Clay, a member of the ACS, addressed an organizational meeting and advocated removal by frightening his audience with his theory that of all people in the United States "the free people of color are, by far, as a class, the most corrupt, depraved and abandoned."[27]

In the 1840s, the U.S. Congress reiterated the notion that there was something uniquely criminal about free blacks, and they had to be contained because of it. Congress began seriously debating black removal, a fact evidenced by discussions surrounding the annexation of Texas that included arguments for statehood that reasoned that Texas could become a colony in which to quarantine free African Americans.[28] Undeniably, the most egregious law to pass Congress regarding free black mobility was the 1850 Fugitive Slave Law, which stripped African Americans accused of being runaways of the right to launch a legal defense. This gave southern slaveholders and slave catchers wide latitude to come to the North and accuse, adjudicate, and thereby enslave black people who claimed their freedom.[29]

The criminalization of black mobility played out on city streets, often with brutal results for free African Americans. Historian John Sweet illustrates this violence in his description of the causes of an 1824 race riot in Providence, Rhode Island. Sweet explains that the streets of Providence were undeveloped and muddy, and therefore it was cleanest and safest to pass away from the middle of the road and nearest to the buildings on the "inside walk." When, in 1824, several African American men did not step aside and allow a group of white men to take the inside walk, tempers erupted and fighting ensued. In Sweet's words, this was an insult to a "widely shared sense of racial honor."[30] Black people, while free, were not, in fact, free to occupy public space without deferring to whites. Similarly, in 1828, when a group of black men and women in Philadelphia attended a subscription ball in fancy dress and arrived at the event in carriages driven by white men, a group of white city boys attacked the black partygoers, hitting them, tearing their clothes, and calling out racial epithets as they alighted the vehicles. Rather than describe the incident as an antiblack assault, the editor from *The Pennsylvania Gazette and Democratic Press* blamed the black ball attendees for the skirmish. The editor suggested that the partygoers had committed a crime of racial inversion. He cautioned, "it may be well to inquire, if matters progress at this rate, how long it will be before masters and servants change places."[31] The stakes were high for African Americans who moved about freely in the North. Doing so threatened to unravel the existing racial order.

While state and federal laws taught white Americans that black mobility was criminally suspect and white northerners fought back against black travel in city streets, popular culture deployed a visual companion that helped to foster white vigilantism: the portrait of the runaway slave, which flourished from the 1760s until the end of the Civil War (see figures 2.1 and 2.2). Runaway slave advertisements in circulars, newspapers, broadsides, and handbills appeared as early as 1704 as tools for slaveholders to retrieve recalcitrant slaves.[32] The announcements offered rewards, detailed slaves' attributes—including birthplace, languages spoken, skin color, height, scars, disabilities, personality, work skills,

10 Dollars Reward!

RUNAWAY from the subscriber, on Sunday the 14th inst. a Negro fellow called JACK, about 20 years of age, a tall well set fellow, with large thick lips, his head sheared,---speaks good English.----Broke open his master's desk, and took out upwards of twenty dollars, in dollars and crowns, with small change, and a pair of money scales.---- Broke open a chest, and carried with him, three white and six striped shirts---one pair Nankin overalls---one pair black velvet breeches and jacket---one pair dark queens cord, and one pair jane breeches---one callico, and one thick cloth jacket not lined ---two pair thread stockings---one new pair thin shoes---one large coarse homespun handkerchief---one pair plated buckles--- one gun and two bayonets, with powder and shot---a large water dog, dun coloured and long tail.----Whoever will take up said Thief and Runaway, secure him, and give notice thereof to the subscriber, shall receive the above Reward, and all necessary Charges by applying to
ZEBEDEE GRINNELL.

N. B.—He also took one or two newish kersey bags marked Z. G. with ink, something dull, an old silk purse, and several other articles.   ☞ All masters of vessels and others are forbid, on the penalty of the law, from harboring or carrying off said fellow.   Z. G.

Littlecompton, State of Rhodeisland,
June 15th, 1795.

Glocester, July 19, 1769.

RAN-AWAY from me the Subscriber, of Glocester, last Night, a Negro Man named *Titus*, about 21 Years of Age, of a middling Stature, stutters considerably when he speaks, and hath lost Part of his great Toe on one Foot ; had on when he went away, a striped Jacket, a striped woolen Shirt, and a Pair of sheep-skin Breeches, (no Hat nor Cap, Shoes nor Stockings) : It is supposed he will change his Cloathing if he has Opportunity.---- Whoever will take up said Negro, and him safely keep, or convey him to his said Master, shall have EIGHT DOLLARS Reward, and all necessary Charges paid by me the Subscriber.----Said Negro is the same that ran away from me the first of June.   THOMAS JAQUES.
N. B. All Masters of Vessels and others are hereby cautioned against harbouring, concealing, or carrying off said Negro, as they would avoid the Penalty of the Law.

FIGURES 2.1 AND 2.2 Two eighteenth-century examples of runaway slave advertisements with the figure of a black person running and holding a staff. Courtesy, American Antiquarian Society.

and possible destination—and also threatened "full penalty of the law" for those who harbored or enticed "said runaway."[33] Yet it was not until the printing boom of the Revolutionary Era that printers enhanced the advertisements with tiny depictions of a running individual. Sometimes this was a white figure representing an escaped apprentice or indentured servant, but most often it was a fleeing black figure who was traveling alone and headed toward an undisclosed destination. By the 1830s, the iconic wood or metal cut imprint of the runaway slave—also known as a stereotype cast—was so commonly used in newspapers in both slave and free states that it became standardized, part of the stock-in-trade of the printer's repertoire (see figure 2.3).[34]

FIGURE 2.3
Specimen and printing types and ornaments, cast by Johnson & Smith (Philadelphia, 1834), including depictions of runaway slaves for printers. Mortimer Rare Book Room, Smith College.

The fact that printers standardized the image of the runaway slave for repeated use demonstrated that one black transgressor could stand in for the next; the criminalized African American body was fungible, and the portrait of the black suspect, in the most literal sense, was stereotyped.[35] Importantly, these imprints most often depicted a figure of a black male runaway, and therefore there was not a large cast of a runaway woman in the specimen books. Needless to say, women did run away, as the famous self-emancipation narratives of Ellen Craft and Harriet Jacobs, and even the story of Harriet Tubman, suggest. Nevertheless, the figure most often criminalized in advertisements was the black male body, even as the actual sight of an African American woman traveling of her own accord was more likely to draw suspicion. In the slave economy, black men more often worked in cities and towns as carpenters, drivers, shipbuilders, sailors, and other professions, and were therefore less conspicuous than women when out and about in public space. Moreover, when men and women had "abroad marriages," it was men, whether they had a pass or not, who were more likely to visit their wives on neighboring plantations while the women stayed put.[36]

The image of the runaway slave was so pervasive in antebellum U.S. culture that even white abolitionists, in the name of the cause, conflated the image of a free black person with a fugitive. In the 1830s, the American Anti-Slavery Society's periodical, *The Anti-Slavery Record*, devoted an entire issue to telling the self-liberation stories of several African Americans. The cover of the July 1837 issue showed the standard portrait of the runaway slave, a move meant to indict printers who manufactured the stereotype cuts in New York City as well as slaveholders in the southern markets, who used the image to catch fugitives (see figure 2.4). Even as the usage was decidedly antislavery, however, the portrait of the runaway also served to publicize the contents of that particular issue of *The Record*. Using the image as an indictment of slavery and simultaneously as an advertising ploy was a slippage that demonstrates how abolitionists imagined people who emancipated themselves as symbols of enslavement rather than as individuals. Likewise, the idea that every self-liberated person made their way to freedom on foot with a bundle tied to a stick infiltrated the thinking of even the most radical white abolitionists. In 1845, the reformist ensemble known as the Hutchinson Family Singers wrote a song called "The Fugitive's Song" and dedicated it to Frederick Douglass. The cover of the sheet music depicted the standard runaway, only this time with Douglass's face superimposed on the picture (see figure 2.5). Perhaps it was not important for the Hutchinsons to accurately note that Douglass escaped not by foot but via railroad, ferry, another railroad, and a steamship, all while disguised as a sailor and carrying (false) identification papers.[37] The Hutchinsons likely intended to use the portrait to exploit the image of the runaway in popular culture and to appropriate the ubiquitous stereotype cut to

ANTI-SLAVERY RECORD.

VOL. III. No. VII.   JULY, 1837.   WHOLE No. 31.

This picture of a poor fugitive is from one of the stereotype cuts manufactured in this city for the southern market, and used on handbills offering rewards for runaway slaves.

THE RUNAWAY.

FIGURE 2.4 Even white abolitionists deployed the runaway slave advertisement although admittedly in the interest of antislavery. From the cover of *The Anti-Slavery Record*, July 1837. Courtesy, American Antiquarian Society.

advocate for the plight of the enslaved. The effect, however, was to draw on a trope—the portrait of the runaway—that accused and therefore endangered all black people traveling, no matter their reasons. It perpetuated the notion that black mobility was suspicious, encouraging whites to be wary of African Americans who were in transit independently.

FIGURE 2.5 Frederick Douglass representing all self-liberated people on the cover of sheet music from the Hutchinson Family's 1845 song "The Fugitive's Song." The Library Company of Philadelphia.

Self-Liberation on Public Conveyances

In the early nineteenth century, the idea that people of color could be travelers contradicted popular notions of black mobility as criminal and fugitive. Complicating matters, some of the most harrowing stories of enslaved people's self-liberation involved people who clandestinely hitched a ride. These were folks who harnessed an ever-expanding

FIGURE 2.6 John, the man portrayed, was nineteen years old and enslaved in Alabama when he escaped via railroad to reconnect with family in Virginia. He traveled on the tops of the cars by night and hid in the woods by day. See Still, *The Underground Railroad*. Courtesy, American Antiquarian Society.

network of steamships, stagecoaches, and railroads to make speedy getaways from slavery (see figure 2.6). These travelers coupled ingenuity with opportunity, making their escape by taking advantage of the preponderance of black servants and laborers who worked on and around public vehicles in the North and South. By sneaking onto a railroad, for example, a person could slip away in plain view. Some of these runaways would try to pass as free, but perhaps more cleverly, others would pose as slaves on errands for fictitious masters. In 1804, a slaveholder from Natchez, Mississippi, griped that Lewis, age seventeen or eighteen, had deserted and likely "descended the Mississippi River in character of a free man, *or as the body servant of some person.*"[38] When Henry Bibb made his escape from Kentucky to Ohio in 1842, he pretended to be a valet to a fabricated master, purchased a traveler's trunk, and theatrically heaved the empty luggage onto a northbound ship as if it were full, thereby slipping onto the ship unnoticed (see figure 2.7).[39] The fact that self-emancipated African Americans escaped disguised as slaves demonstrates what enslaved people surely recognized: the slave economy made it necessary for enslaved people to have some autonomy and, in urban environ-

FIGURE 2.7 From Kollner, *Common Sights on Land and Water*, an 1852
instruction book designed for young children. A black servant carries a heavy
trunk across the docks of a major city for a white family who has just returned
home from a journey. Although it depicts a scene from the North, this image
conveys how common it was to see a black servant in public space throughout
the United States and helps to illustrate the ingenuity and utility of Henry
Bibb's daring plan. Courtesy, American Antiquarian Society.

ments, the independent movement of free blacks was often more closely
scrutinized than that of slaves.[40]

Significantly, it was much easier for men to make their escape on public conveyances than it was for women. The gender proscriptions that
governed the division of enslaved labor made it that much harder for
black women, most of whom had limited experience venturing beyond
the workplace, to feign a reason for traveling alone.[41] Some enslaved
women turned the gendered nature of travel against itself by disguising
themselves as men to escape. In the 1830s, Harriet Jacobs blackened her
face with charcoal, put on sailor's clothes, and walked "boldly through
the streets" of Edenton, North Carolina, dressed as a male seafarer; she
went entirely undetected.[42] Similarly, Ellen Craft exploited gendered expectations in 1848 when she escaped from a plantation in Macon, Georgia, to Philadelphia with her future husband, William, relying on public
conveyances to do so. Ellen was what abolitionists called a "white slave,"

ELLEN CRAFT.

ELLEN CRAFT.

FIGURES 2.8 AND 2.9 First pictured out of costume, Ellen Craft and her husband, William, escaped from Georgia in 1848. See Still, *The Underground Railroad*. In order for Craft, who was not literate, to fully perform masculine whiteness, she also masqueraded as a man with a disability, wearing a sling on her arm and, sometimes, a "poultice" tied to her cheeks so she did not have to speak. See Siebert, *The Underground Railroad from Slavery to Freedom*. Courtesy, American Antiquarian Society.

an enslaved woman with fair enough complexion to appear white.[43] To escape, she wore men's clothing and pretended to be an injured male slaveholder traveling with his black valet (William). The two ingeniously sailed and rode to freedom via steamship and railroad in just three days (see figures 2.8 and 2.9).[44]

Jacobs and Craft were not the only women to adopt masculine garb to make their escapes. William Still, conductor and historian of the Underground Railroad, documented several cases of women dressed up as boys or men in order to pass publicly from the South to the North. One of these was Ann Maria Weems, who at fifteen years old fled in the guise of a male carriage driver called Joe Wright (see figure 2.10).[45] Although

MARIA WEEMS ESCAPING IN MALE ATTIRE.

the abolitionist press counted such stories as victories, and they no doubt were, such anecdotes fortified the white belief that any colored traveler was a potential fugitive and, in the minds of many white northerners, a nigger in need of discipline and containment.

The Stakes of Mobility

For all people in the United States, the ability to travel made American freedom visceral and thus lubricated the cogs of citizenship.[46] First and foremost, public vehicles shrank the country. By 1838, a 220-mile trip from Boston to New York was shortened from what had once been a journey of six to seven days to just sixteen hours. To accomplish this feat, travelers availed themselves of an ever-expanding transportation infrastructure that linked turnpikes, railroads, and waterways and involved steamships, locomotives, and stagecoaches to complete a single trip.[47] Moreover, at just $4, the trip from Boston to New York had become relatively inexpensive, costing less than it had forty years earlier.[48] Inventors, entrepreneurs, corporations, and state legislators throughout the United States, especially in the North, replicated these improvements from route to route, enabling travelers—mostly middle-class white men— to freely conduct business, attend annual meetings, visit faraway relatives, tour the country, and, as historian Walter Johnson has recently argued, shift "the terrain of conquest," allowing planters and settlers to fulfill their imperialist dreams and claim ownership of Indian lands in the interior of the nation.[49] Importantly, these spaces were gendered male and raced white, although by the 1850s, as one historian contends, streetcars were accessible to white and sometimes black women, offering each "a way to move inconspicuously through public space."[50]

Importantly, these early nineteenth-century public conveyances were different than the modern mass transit, on which working folks have come to rely in the twentieth and twenty-first centuries. In 1800, not only could a fifty-mile stagecoach ride from Baltimore to Alexandria take a full day, but also at $4 it would effectively price out an unskilled male laborer who unreliably earned just $1 a day.[51] When poor and working-class men and women did use public vehicles, they were often segregated in the same way that colored travelers were, a point to be illuminated in a moment.[52] Conversely, members of a burgeoning middle class rode in "first class," or more accurately the interior spaces of the vehicles, allowing them to flaunt their respectability and their class standing. Middle-class women who traveled either alone or with a male chaperone, especially on steamships, likewise benefited from access to a space constructed exclusively for their protection. As historian Patricia Cline Cohen outlines, the "ladies' cabin," a site invented by shipbuilders on early canal boats, shielded white middle-class women from possible male seduction and potentially even rape.[53] And these cabins were meant only for women of a certain race and class. As Evelyn Brooks Higginbotham argues, the very conjuring of the term "lady" in the naming of the separate space evoked class difference.[54] Neither proprietors nor white passengers designated a protected space for the exclusive benefit of working-class women of any race. For example, an 1836 etiquette book instructed men to be discerning before giving up one's seat to women who did not hail from the middle class. The writer cautioned, "If the women are servants, or persons in a low rank of life, I do not see upon what ground of politeness or decency you are called upon to yield your seat."[55]

Like their middle-class white counterparts, however, free and flush people of color wanted equal access to the geographic and capitalist promise of public conveyances. Being able to partake of the undeniable opportunity that travel afforded was vitally important to any American with middle-class aspirations, but particularly to people of African descent, for whom movement had long signified diaspora—forced migration, separation from family, and servitude. The story of Paul Cuffe, a Massachusetts-born sea captain of African American and Native American descent, exemplifies how travel proved essential to economic independence and fostered citizenship for people of color. In 1812, Cuffe used a trip from Rhode Island to Washington, D.C., to help resolve a dispute with the U.S. government, saving his small sailing business. Earlier in the year, the fifty-one-year-old captain had returned from a voyage to Sierra Leone when a customs officer in Newport, Rhode Island—wary of the ongoing war with the British and thus suspicious of the contents of Cuffe's cargo—confiscated his ship. To get the ship and its cargo back, Cuffe, who had many influential white friends in Rhode Island, arranged meetings with the president of the United States, the secretary of state, and the U.S. Congress. He started out from Newport on 27 April and reached Washington by stagecoach in six days, and after successful meetings and some socializing during his return, he was back in Newport by 22 May to retrieve his ship and resume his business.[56]

Cuffe's access to public vehicles not only allowed him to save his ship and its cargo but also afforded him social and political capital. On the way home from Washington, Cuffe found himself enthusiastically greeted by the U.S. senator from Rhode Island, who "Was Very free and Conversant." That encounter caught the attention and changed the attitude of a man who had confronted Cuffe earlier in his journey. Cuffe wrote in his journal about a "powder headed man With Starn Countenance" who had at first reacted to the sight of a colored traveler with "much Evel Contempt," but after observing Cuffe's popularity with a national politician suddenly "became Loveing."[57]

Even though it ended up well for Cuffe, the skirmish between him and the "powder headed man" was a style of conflict that became common for colored travelers who wished to ride in and on public conveyances—Cuffe wished to sit in the stagecoach, and the white passenger emphatically resisted. Like other black activists, Cuffe believed it was his right as a U.S. citizen to gain equal access to the vehicles, and therefore he quietly refused to back down. Colored travelers recognized that getting from here to there was only part of the African American travel story. In order to reap the full benefits that modern transportation vehicles afforded, free people of color needed to rely on vehicles not only to get them from one place to another but also to use the interior spaces of public conveyances to affirm their class and gender standing and ultimately their equality. To this end, when they could afford it, colored travelers sought to occupy the best accommodations, insisting that fellow passengers, drivers, captains, and conductors treat them as gentlemen (and lady) patrons and not as upstarts or interlopers.

When proprietors and passengers refused to allow men and women of color to travel as equals, the stakes of segregation were high. Although it was important for colored travelers such as Cuffe to travel on equal terms with whites, the alternative was not just insulting but threatened real, physical dangers in brutal travel conditions. On stagecoaches, segregation entailed riding on the top of the stage next to the driver and the luggage. This position exposed people of color to the weather as well as an occasional drunken or racist driver. In 1835, abolitionist Henry Highland Garnet traveled on top of a stagecoach for days on a trip from Providence to New Hampshire only to arrive with his clothes in tatters and his body damaged.[58] On a steamship or canal boat, segregation meant sailing on the decks of the ship—just as Charles Remond had done—no matter the season, the weather, or the duration of the voyage. In 1832, two colored travelers publicized an incident where the captain refused them entry into the cabin and thus required them to "walk the deck all night." Even when a driving rain bombarded the ship and drenched the men, rather than allow them to enter the cabin, the captain forced them to lay "amongst the pots in the kitchen."[59] One colored traveler, writing about his experience on a Nantucket steamboat, confessed that sometimes he shared space with "four-footed beasts."[60]

As with steamships, segregation on the railroads was equally dangerous, dirty, and demoralizing. Conductors often forced colored travelers into a separate railroad car that was eventually dubbed the "Jim Crow car." As the next chapter will show, conductors and their posse had the railroad company's sanction to bodily and viciously push colored travelers into this separate car. Meanwhile, when black women traveled, they faced uniquely gendered dangers on ships because the spaces were decidedly masculine and, by refusing black women access to the interior or ladies' cabin, proprietors and captains exposed them not only to the elements but also to the unsupervised overtures of strange men. In this respect, travel personnel treated African American women not as female but as people undeserving of the protections afforded to middle-class white women.

Segregation was physically harsh and also psychologically taxing. For colored travelers, depots and stations were dangerous as venues of insult and injury, where supercilious ticketing agents could either refuse to sell a ticket or, in one of the most frequent complaints made by colored travelers, overcharge free people first-class fees to ride on decks, on top of the luggage, or in separate cars. Platforms and docks were points of anxious anticipation at which a colored traveler learned whether a captain or a driver would foil or allow a scheduled trip. Compartments, cabins, and cars were potential sites of conflict and insult or, at their worst, physical violence. Even the fact that some proprietors chose to ignore the custom of segregation and allow colored travelers equal entrée only served to emphasize the arbitrariness of the practice and the complete power of any white individual in dictating the mobility of a free person of color. For a colored traveler, riding in public conveyances was dangerous, stressful business.[61]

Maddeningly, whites most often used racial segregation as a weapon against free rather than enslaved people. Indeed, transportation proprietors allowed enslaved and free black servants who accompanied whites to travel without impediment. Thus, as enslavement came to an uneven end in the northern states, the age of segregation commenced in the region. In fact, scholars note that segregation was invented in response to emancipation, a method of "semi-porous" racial boundaries that allowed African Americans to cross into white-only sectors of society when that movement benefited white supremacy.[62] This was a practical edifice of segregation; servants could move freely when in service to whites, but other people of color needed to stay out of public space. Self-liberated woman Harriet Jacobs critiqued this practice after settling in New York City in the 1840s. When she secured a job working for a prosperous white family as the caretaker for their child, Jacobs found that railroad conductors and stagecoach drivers recognized her status as servant and thus permitted her to ride first class with the child. When Jacobs traveled for her own purposes, however, proprietors ousted her from the first-class car. She described these episodes as demoralizing, remarking how each incident "so discourages the feelings, and represses the energies of the colored people."[63] Making exceptions for servants of color was a practice that continued throughout the nineteenth and twentieth centuries.[64] When a colored traveler circumvented the customs of place to move independently, whites quickly rallied to remove the black threat. Such was the case when prominent African American New Yorker Thomas

Van Renselaer traveled from Boston to Providence via steamship in 1838. After Van Renselaer went below the ship to enter the berth for which he had paid $3.50, a white man approached him, asking "whose servant are you?" When Van Renselaer replied "I am my own, sir," the man insisted the colored traveler go to the deck because "you ought to know your place." Indeed, keeping people of color within a proscribed place was a crucial component of the developing segregation policies on public vehicles. In Van Renselaer's case, the white traveler eventually rallied the captain to keep the black abolitionist out of the berth for which he had already paid.[65] For colored travelers, this outcome was far too familiar.

Black Respectability and the Politics of Exclusion

Riding as an equal on a public conveyance offered a passenger tremendous geographic mobility and also represented the possibilities of U.S. citizenship. Still, it was the sharing of the tight space of public conveyances and the intimacy of those interactions—strangers pressed together, unavoidable touching, the smell of another's body, awkward conversation, and an arduous journey for all involved—that elevated public conveyances to a site of struggle. A glimpse into nineteenth-century stagecoach design illustrates the point. In the late 1820s, the most commonly used stagecoach was the Abbot-Downing Company's Concord stage—a vehicle built with one cabin, drawn by four horses, and seating nine passengers, who knocked knees and elbows with fellow travelers (see figure 2.11).[66] Passengers often grumbled about the closeness of the quarters. Of the experience, white abolitionist William Lloyd Garrison vented that a stagecoach ride was akin to incarceration, "wedged-packed-consolidated."[67] A humorist writing in 1825 peppered his complaint with sexual innuendo, whining that the space was so tight that an overweight man had "a spyglass in his pocket, which made no small impression on my ribs."[68]

The obvious sexual humor of the spyglass innuendo was no fluke. The intimacy of public vehicles made them sites where sex, sexuality, and the politics of respectability came to shape both white panic over the presence of colored travelers and black resistance to segregation. Indeed, one of the central ways that white men criminalized the mobility of free people of color was to accuse black male travelers of sexual licentious-

FIGURE 2.11 Concord coach, 1886, Abbot-Downing Company, Concord, New Hampshire. The Long Island Museum of Art, History & Carriages. Gift of Webster Knight II, 1962.

ness and impropriety toward white women while en route. Looking once again at Paul Cuffe's trip in 1812, Cuffe noted in his diary that the powder headed man first became irate when two white women were about to enter the stagecoach (see figure 2.12). Although the white traveler demanded that Cuffe move from his seat, Cuffe refused. The conflict between the men spoke to racial and sexual mores of the nineteenth century as well as to the physical intimacy of the space.

Of course, the notion that a colored traveler within this intimate space was somehow more dangerous to female passengers than any other male was a figment of the white imagination. This mode of thinking was profoundly insidious and excused a large swath of antiblack violence. It pathologized black activism by conflating the desire for equality with sexual desire, reasoning that black men who wanted first-class accommodations cared little about public access. Instead, it suggested, they were actually striving for physical, and ultimately sexual, intimacy with white women. By the 1830s, the enemies of black freedom came to call this process "amalgamation" (see figure 2.13).[69] Colored travelers recognized the folly behind this accusation and exposed it as subterfuge meant to specifically target free people of color with demonstrated social standing.

NEGRO EXPULSION FROM RAILWAY CAR, PHILADELPHIA.

FIGURE 2.12 As evidenced by Paul Cuffe's experience, the accusation that black men on public conveyances threatened white women was a common rebuke during the antebellum period. This sketch from *The Illustrated London News* in 1856 depicted the struggle over the Philadelphia streetcars that started in the 1850s and continued into the 1860s. It portrays a black man who is imagined as disorderly and disruptive because he takes up too much space while a white woman and her infant are forced to stand. The illustration suggests that the conductor had no choice but to loudly intervene on behalf of the white woman. The Library Company of Philadelphia.

In 1838, one traveler remarked that on public conveyances cries of amalgamation only arose when a person of color was "given a berth and a comfortable place in a Steam Boat cabin, or an inside passage in a Rail Road car or a stage coach."[70] To defend themselves against the charge, black men and women relied on their sense of themselves as respectable Americans. Back in 1812, Cuffe wrote of the stagecoach incident that although he refused to interact with the passenger who insulted him, he did make room for the white women, announcing, "We always gave away to accomadate [*sic*] the Women."[71]

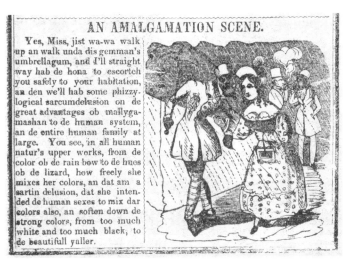

FIGURE 2.13 "An Amalgamation Scene" from the 1846 *De Darkie's Comic All-Me-Nig* depicts an African American man who, in a rainstorm, lecherously offers to share his umbrella with a white woman just to get close to her. The image reflects the perceived dangers of allowing black men freedom of mobility and equality in public space. Courtesy, American Antiquarian Society.

Despite black protest, whites enacted exclusion in increasingly aggressive ways that highlight how the white supremacist ideology fostered vigilantism. Most often, white passengers and proprietors blocked entryways to public vehicles by yelling, screaming, pushing, and spitting out "many infamous epithets and the most violent language."[72] In this way, whites wielded the antiblack mantra to which Frederick Douglass had grown accustomed by 1846—"we don't allow niggers in here." It became a rallying cry, a verbal assault that reiterated the idea that people in dark skins were unfit for social inclusion. In 1833, a Boston stagecoach driver refused to carry two Liberian missionaries because he "would not carry *Niggers*! unless they would take an outside seat!" Likewise, a white steamship passenger lambasted a captain in 1837, shouting incredulously, "do you allow *niggers* to eat in your cabin?"[73] Interestingly, each of these cases of white fury was less focused on the actual mobility of the independent black traveler than the prospect of the travelers' equal treatment—the Liberians sitting inside the stagecoach and a black passenger eating within the ship's cabin—indicating that citizenship rather than intimacy was really at the root of white complaints.

During the antebellum period, Douglass and other activists of color argued that it was their very claims of respectability and citizenship that made them the specific targets of segregation. Douglass reasoned that as long as a black man "is drunken, idle, ignorant and vicious," whites welcomed him and dubbed him "a source of amusement." But when a man of color sought sobriety, industry, intelligence, and respectable employment, those same whites ousted him with the "fiercest hatred." In a scathing 1850 editorial, he wrote,

> While we are servants, we are never offensive to the whites, or marks of popular displeasure. We have been often dragged or driven from the tables of hotels where colored men were officiating acceptably as waiters; and from steamboat cabins where twenty or thirty colored men in light jackets and white aprons were frisking about as servants among the whites in every direction.[74]

One particularly frustrating aspect of segregation was that whites rarely acknowledged that their intentions were in fact political. Instead, they often argued that segregation was a necessity to protect white travelers from black bodies. Most commonly, white northerners accused black people of having uniquely offensive body odor, a charge with sexual undercurrents. In 1845, a white railroad passenger wrote an editorial advocating for racially segregated seating, based on a recent experience he had on a railroad car in Maine. To make his point, he blatantly sexualized the presence of an African American woman during his trip, describing her as a "fat, strapping negro wench" and suggesting that she disturbed others when she and several white men who accompanied her, in a demonstration of "practical amalgamation" sat within a first-class car. The disgruntled passenger insinuated that the woman's relationship with her traveling companions was a sexual one by suggesting that, in order to sit closely to her, the men had to have a "peculiar taste in odors." The editorial also claimed that the woman's stench was so unpleasant that it caused other passengers to cough and sneeze and that "ladies curled their pretty lips."[75] It's hard to imagine the humiliation that this woman must have felt in the face of such open hostility, but such rhetoric was more than insulting. It reflected the nineteenth-century belief that foul smells indicated the presence of miasmas and, later in the century, germs that carried disease.[76] By imagining free people of color as harbingers of contagion, whites likened blackness to an illness capable of infecting the white public. Therefore, in keeping with this thinking, independent black travelers posed a veritable health crisis. Significantly, post–Civil War emancipation only served to intensify critiques of African American odor, suggesting that unregulated and free black bodies posed a greater sensory threat than those of slaves.[77] Ultimately, whites did not fear black people as much as they feared black freedom.

Even as whites wielded the accusation of black odor, activists and their white abolitionist allies identified the complaint as a politically motivated assault on racial equality and black citizenship. In 1837, an English traveler commented that "Americans say . . . [blacks] stink . . . if they did, the noxious effluvia arising from them" would make the odor of the South unbearable. He went on to argue that people of color "do not stink as Slaves but Freemen—why—Because liberty ever stinks in the nostrils of a tyrant."[78] Likewise, a series of antiblack racial incidents on the Eastern Rail Road of Massachusetts in 1841 encouraged one observer to remark, "There is no 'offensive odor' to a servant or a slave, but the colored freeman emits an intolerable stench."[79] Activists recognized that accusations of black rankness articulated a need for greater restraint over black equality. Activists agreed that the resistance they faced on public conveyances was not only a problem of color but also most emphatically an assault against emancipation. As one African American traveler acknowledged, "the colored person to be excluded must also be *free*!!"[80]

Travel as Citizenship

Colored travelers well understood that the freedom to travel was a core American value, and they protested segregation as a fundamental violation of their equal rights. First and foremost, black activists fought segregation by claiming their respectability. In keeping with the philosophy of moral improvement, they insisted that their proper public etiquette, class standing, and religiosity merited inclusion, as it so clearly did with middle-class white Americans. They argued that exclusion was simply white supremacy in action. In the early days of northern protest— between 1812 and the early 1830s—colored travelers withstood countless humiliating episodes and boldly publicized these incidents in newspapers, lectures, pulpits, and letters. Their message was clear: access to public conveyances was an essential social and economic tool, and equality within the vehicles was crucial to their sense of themselves as Americans.

Most emphatically, activists of color used the black and abolitionist press to highlight how segregation was not an ethical business practice. In addition to overcharging, proprietors also interrupted service in the name of preserving white supremacy. Frederick Douglass told how in 1841 a steamship captain on the route from New Bedford to Nantucket held up his boat for two hours rather than allow white and black abolitionists to travel together in the cabin.[81] Historian Geoff Zylstra, who studies segregation in 1850s Philadelphia, notes that "conductors and drivers frequently considered race to be more important than efficient transportation, so when blacks boarded streetcars the conductors often stopped the vehicles in the middle of the street."[82]

In their protest letters to editors, colored travelers also fought segregation by asserting their respectability and layering it with a sense of class entitlement. In 1854, after a New York City streetcar conductor brutally tossed out African American activist and music teacher Elizabeth Jennings, she fought back. She confronted the conductor and demeaned him, telling him that she was a U.S. citizen, born and raised in New York, and inquired if the man she recognized as a person of Irish descent was likewise born in America. Then she attacked his sense of morality by scolding that "he was a good for nothing impudent fellow for insulting decent persons while on their way to church."[83] According to Jennings, her birthright coupled with her claims to a middle-class identity should have trumped the foreign-born conductor's whiteness. In 1855, a correspondent to the Afro-Canadian periodical *The Provincial Freeman* reported that "colored travellers" while seeking a stagecoach "have met with resistance from upstart drivers."[84] For these travelers, the people who threatened their equality most were members of the white working class, who they deemed their social inferiors.

Black male travelers also emphasized their middle-class masculinity, a quality that lay at the heart of much antisegregation activism in the antebellum period. They presented themselves as the protectors of their communities and tried to show how the practice of exclusion and exile threatened African American women and mothers. They made heart-wrenching appeals to whites for equal treatment. They called for "polished Republicans" to join them in safeguarding the most vulnerable of the race. On 23 March 1827, Samuel Cornish and John Russwurm, the co-editors of the first black weekly, *Freedom's Journal*, reported the recent death of Betsey Madison. Madison was a self-liberated woman who suffered a "lingering sickness" after a steamship captain forced her to sail from New Orleans to New York on the deck of a ship. Seeing her death as an entirely avoidable tragedy, Cornish and Russwurm blamed her passing on white shipworkers. The co-editors identified captains and officers as the culprits because they consistently endangered the "health and lives of delicate females and infants, so unfeelingly exposed."[85]

Black male activists often used intersectional arguments of class and gender in their push for equal rights, relying on middle-class tropes that deemed a true woman as fragile and domestic. For example, in 1831, a white passenger cursed at and refused to sit with a black clergyman who traveled with his wife and "two respectable, pious females" from Nantucket to New Bedford during the chill of the late fall.[86] The captain of the boat eventually acquiesced to the angry passenger's demands and forced the clergyman and his companions to sit outside on the rain-soaked deck. According to the editorial, the unprotected seating, given the nasty weather, made the clergyman's wife sick.[87] As with the case of Betsey Madison, segregation was emerging as a crime against middle-class black women's health. Similarly, the Reverend Theodore Wright, a leading black activist from New York City, pleaded with abolitionists at the 1837 annual meeting of the New York State Anti-Slavery Society to recognize slavery's impact on free people in the North, particularly on women and the elderly, whom he deemed the most vulnerable colored travelers. After telling how the journeys of several black travelers ended in death, Wright devastatingly confessed that in 1828 his own wife had died from an illness after traveling on the deck of a New York steamship when the Hudson was icy and the weather cold.[88]

No doubt, segregated travel, particularly on the decks of ships, was dangerous or even deadly, especially for black women, whose clothing offered less protection than men's. At the same time, Wright and other male activists used black women's victimization strategically to emphasize women's frailty, to show that black women had identities beyond their labor capacity, and that black men, as fully realized masculine men and U.S. citizens, sought to shield them. In so doing, male activists sought to produce a gendered outrage on the part of white northerners. Unfortunately, northern whites did not respond as activists had hoped. When the transportation industry denied men of color entrée despite their respectable attributes—the vulnerability of their ladies, their prosperity, their good manners, and their clean appearance—the snub shook the foundation of black strategies for racial uplift to their core.

As the insults and dangers of travel grew more and more pervasive, black activists increasingly articulated segregation and exclusion as violations not only of their person but also of their rights. In 1831, a man from Bridgewater, Massachusetts, directly connected segregation to a type of civic fraud when he wondered why "Stage Proprietors of the city of Boston wickedly combine in agreement to prevent colored citizens from being accommodated like other citizens."[89] In an unusual public letter from a black woman in the mid-1830s, schoolteacher and activist Susan Paul wrote passionately about how exclusion was a direct assault on black upward mobility. In 1834, after a stagecoach driver denied a ride from Boston to Salem to Paul and several children from the youth choir she organized, Paul reasoned that exile was far more damaging than the mere obstruction to geographic mobility it caused. She described her ousting as political, an example of the "cruel prejudice which deprives us of every privilege whereby we might elevate ourselves" and then "absurdly condemns" people of color for not having made more social progress.[90] Likewise, Charles B. Ray exposed segregation as a mere excuse for whites to enact undemocratic racial maneuvers. In 1838, after a proprietor mistreated him, Ray noted that a "white black-leg"—a reference to a swindler—"with their cards, their guns and their dogs" could travel unimpeded, whereas a "colored gentleman of education, wealth, and piety" could not.[91] In other words, if the most dangerous and degraded whites traveled unobstructed, then segregation was not about the quality or potential danger of the traveler but was simply a method of preventing black social, economic, and political inclusion.

Whereas black male activists wrote letters and appealed to the gentility of white men, African American women employed their own strategies for inclusion in travel. Many claimed their right to be passengers on public conveyances by slipping unnoticed onto stagecoaches, steamships, and railroads, defying convention and simply seizing the opportunity to catch a ride. Importantly, the only proof that free women of color traveled covertly comes from anecdotal evidence. Nevertheless, these stories, ones that largely focus on stagecoach travel in the 1820s and 1830s, highlight white anxieties about the possibility of black female travelers sharing the intimate quarters of public vehicles with white passengers. In 1837, white abolitionist Lydia Maria Child told just such a story by recounting how a young woman of color with "sallow complexion" slid into a stagecoach unimpeded because the other passengers believed she was white. At the end of the trip, the woman's race was revealed

FIGURE 2.14 This image of two veiled black women depicts a slaveholder searching for a self-liberated woman on a railroad car. It also illustrates how vulnerable black women were when traveling, even if hiding their race. From Still, *The Underground Railroad*. Courtesy, American Antiquarian Society.

when her dark-skinned and clearly African American husband met her at her destination. According to Child, the woman's fellow passengers "were at once surprised and angry to find they had been riding with a mulatto—and had, in their ignorance, been really civil to her!"[92] As legal scholar Ariela Gross argues, anger was a consistent reaction to this type of racial discovery because "the greatest blow to a white man's honor was to be deceived into bestowing the privileges of whiteness on a 'negro.' "[93]

In another version of this mistaken-identity trope, the anecdote served as comic fodder, demonstrating how the prospect of sexual violence against black female travelers was not only pervasive but also good for a laugh. According to one frequent traveler in upper New York State in the 1820s, stagecoach passengers often "amuse[d]" themselves with the story of "what happened to Mr. John C. Spencer." According to the story, on a rainy night when the nine-person stagecoach was full, "a lady, closely veiled," urgently needed transportation (see figure 2.14). Although eight of the passengers in the packed compartment demurred, a ninth, Mr. Spencer, offered his lap, lewdly insisting that "a lady ought not to be refused passage." But the joke was on Mr. Spencer. When the "lady" exited the stage and stood under the light, "a very ebony colored individual of the female gender" appeared in her stead.[94] In the author's description, the black woman traveler quickly devolved from lady to specimen, belying the racism of the anecdote. Yet this story was funniest because of the way sexual innuendo crackled around its edges as Mr. Spencer dubiously offered up his lap for a lady to gyrate there, only to discover that he had been duped. Wasn't this really the joke? That Mr. Spencer's overture resulted in his own seduction?

Even though the story is largely hearsay—a type of urban legend retold for comic effect—it makes clear that the unregulated movement of colored travelers, especially black women, ignited white male sexual fantasy but also, and more importantly, made women of color exceptionally vulnerable when on the road. Indeed, if black women joined their husbands or a black male chaperone, whites might unceremoniously cast them out of the interior spaces of public conveyances. If black women traveled alone, they faced the potential of ridicule, insult, and sexual assault. Women who traveled, such as the acquaintance of Lydia Maria Child and the woman from the John Spencer story, had few resources to protect themselves in transit. These stories shed light on a strategy of resistance clandestinely employed by women of color who, to protect themselves, ignored custom to get where they needed to go in the most efficient manner possible. In so doing, black women braved multiple violations to assert themselves in defiance of de facto segregation.

Whether they wrote outraged letters or passed onto vehicles unnoticed, the methods of early activists did not end segregation. Their strategies, however, did lay the groundwork for later activism and created a rhetoric that likened exclusion from public conveyances to exclusion from the body politic. That early protesters did not have a more profound impact was in part caused by their failure to identify a central villain in transportation discrimination against whom they could rally. The challenge in gaining widespread support rested on the fact that segregation on public vehicles concerned only an elite group of colored travelers who could afford first-class passage. Other people of color either walked or accepted segregated seating because it was all they could afford. In the final analysis, the strategy of moral improvement could not offset the presumption that free people of color on the move, especially those who sought equal entrée into public conveyances, must be breaking a law. The criminalization of black mobility undoubtedly threatened the independent movement of free people of color and encouraged a dangerous white vigilante culture meant to guard against black entrée into public space. This criminalization, the segregation it engendered, and the black protest it inspired ultimately planted the seeds of the nineteenth-century equal rights movement.

CHAPTER THREE

Activist Respectability and the Birth of the "Jim Crow Car"

In early August 1838, a twenty-eight-year-old black New Yorker named David Ruggles dashed off a letter to *The Providence Courier* and a follow-up to *The Colored American*. Like other black activists in the antebellum North, Ruggles used his letter to expose injustice on public conveyances. He told how representatives of the Boston and Providence Railroad had swindled and assaulted him during a trip from New York to Boston by way of steamship and railroad via the Stonington (Connecticut) Line. On the first leg, Ruggles bought a full-priced, full-access ticket for the steamship *Rhode Island*, but the clerk handed him a cheaper, deck-only ticket, preventing him from gaining entrée to the interior cabin during any part of the fourteen-hour journey (see figure 3.1). Ruggles was furious, but unlike most colored travelers, who customarily wrote outraged letters to sympathetic editors after the fact, he addressed the issue with transportation personnel during the trip itself. When he transitioned in Stonington from the steamship to the railroad, he entered the first-class train car, complained to the conductor, and insisted on being reimbursed. Instead of refunding him the money, however, the conductor charged Ruggles another $.50 and directed him to leave the first-class car in order to ride in a separate, smaller car reserved for black people and the poor. Ruggles refused to move to the inferior accommodations, a decision that prompted the conductor to summon three other men to aid in Ruggles's removal. The four railroad men overpowered Ruggles, called him a "[damned] abolitionist," and pushed him bodily into "what [railroad workers] call the pauper (or jim crow) car."[1]

Aside from publicizing the violence he endured at the hands of railroad personnel, Ruggles made visible the existence of "the jim crow car," flagging a significant shift in both racial segregation and the fight for black equality. Ruggles's letter marked one of the first times that U.S. newspapers printed the term "Jim Crow" to denote a physical space, a separate railroad car. In exposing this usage, Ruggles revealed how workers on the New England railroads linked popular culture to racial exclusion. The reference Jim Crow came from an antiblack, comedic

76

STEAMER RHODE ISLAND of the STONINGTON LINE IN 1836

FIGURE 3.1 This commemorative postcard shows the Stonington Line's steamship *Rhode Island* riding rough seas. In 1838, the captain forced David Ruggles to spend fourteen hours on the deck rather than allow him to enter the segregated interior space of the cabin. Courtesy, American Antiquarian Society.

stage performance. By the late 1830s, the Jim Crow caricature was iconic at home and abroad, especially among working-class whites.[2] Antebellum railroad workers in New England were the first to connect the stage persona to racial segregation in a concerted attack against colored travelers, largely abolitionists, with the desire and the means to ride in the first-class cars.[3]

The Jim Crow car was an attempt to foreclose on black mobility, an assault made just as activists of color began to more vigorously demand equality on public conveyances. Most significantly, with the advent of this car, the antebellum northern railroad companies institutionalized segregation and its enforcement as no method of transportation had before. The corporate representatives of the railroads so rigidly imposed separate seating that they deputized in-house enforcers made up of conductors, brakemen, firemen, and others to brutalize black folks who defied their authority.

In response, black activists such as Ruggles, Frederick Douglass, and black New Yorkers Samuel Cornish and Charles Ray urged colored travelers to defy conductors on the scene in real time. They publicized their willingness to speak out, to stand up, to refuse banishment, and to take some blows and, if necessary, return them. This next generation of black activists embraced aggressive and masculine tactics, schooling colored travelers throughout the North in the art of direct confrontation. By doing so, activists identified a new geography of protest in which the vehicles of transportation, particularly the railroads, had become the front lines for the battle over equal rights.

This backdrop marked the moment when the age of segregation gave way to Jim Crow. This origin story begins with the launch of the Massachusetts railroads in 1835 and ends in 1843, when, as a result of black activist and white abolitionist pressure, the New England railroads abandoned their formal endorsement of segregated seating. Although these eight years did not signal an end to segregation on public conveyances, they marked a watershed in black activism. As railroad and streetcar workers throughout the Northeast bloodied the bodies of black men and women (and even white male allies), black radicals used new methods to assert their right to public space. To seek justice for their many assaults, black activists took conductors and their posses to police courts and, eventually, in February 1842, the Massachusetts General Court heard testimony regarding the violence. By examining the confluence of technology and race, the changing shape of what is best called black activist respectability, and the tightening segregationist grip of the railroads, this chapter redefines Jim Crow not merely as an oppressive custom but also as a contest between black radicals and their white detractors over race, space, and citizenship before the Civil War.

Rules and Regulations

When in 1835 the Boston and Providence Railroad (B&P) inaugurated the first steam-powered passenger railroad in Massachusetts, its cars offered ripe soil for segregation to take root. Between the late 1820s and early 1840s, state and city boosters across the East raised money to lay tracks for short-range railroads, the tracks extending anywhere between fourteen and forty miles.[4] In 1834, there were three different railroad lines running through Massachusetts, but by 1840 that number had quadrupled to twelve.[5] Dotting the eastern seaboard two generations before the Transcontinental Railroad connected the Atlantic coast to the Pacific Ocean, short-range railroads were powerful examples of U.S. prosperity. Their speeds and routinized schedules quickly made them popular. They raced across land at twenty miles per hour.[6] Members of a black elite were as anxious as whites to make use of this technology, particu-

FIGURE 3.2 A depiction of a train with engine, a cargo boxcar, and two passenger cars from a party invitation, Detroit, 1838. The cargo boxcar was sometimes called "the refuse," "the pauper," or "the dirty car," and eventually the "Jim Crow car." It was the space in which railroad officials expected poor whites and all African Americans to ride. Courtesy, American Antiquarian Society.

larly in Massachusetts, where radical abolitionists and black activists traversed the state and the region to speak out against slavery. Many activists of color relied on such transportation to bring them to Boston, the hub of abolitionism.[7] They came from reformist enclaves such as Salem to the north, New Bedford to the south, and, of course, from New York City to the southeast. No matter their reason for travel, as one corporate officer remembered, "an appreciable number of the despised race demanded transportation."[8]

In his 1883 memoir, the first president of the Boston and Providence Railroad claimed that the presence of black people on the railroads brought about "scenes of riot and violence." In turn, the president—Josiah Quincy Jr., a Boston politician and the brother of an abolitionist—sought to defuse the conflict by introducing the concept of the separate car. In so doing, Quincy became the father of what became known as the Jim Crow style of segregation, the "separate but equal" accommodations model. By 1838, to implement the separate car method, Quincy took advantage of the railroad's unique architecture to reserve a small stagecoach-style car for black passengers that was sometimes called the "short car." Often placed at the front of the train behind the engine, people who rode in the short car endured fumes and danger (see figures 3.2 and 3.3). Workers then attached this short car to the longer cars—cars with twenty-four seats and an aisle—that railroads reserved

FIGURE 3.3 Another portrait of a steam-powered train circa 1840s or 1850s, showing the boxcar in which conductors forced poor whites and colored travelers to ride. Courtesy, American Antiquarian Society.

for first-class passengers.[9] The separate car system proved effective enough that other railroad companies followed suit, especially those lines that hugged the New England coast, including the Eastern Rail Road (ERR), launched in 1838, and the New Bedford and Taunton Line (NB&T), an affiliate of the B&P that first carried passengers in 1840.[10]

Corporate officers claimed to implement the separate car in order to circumvent existing racial violence. In truth, there is no evidence of racial conflict on the railroads until 1838, after Quincy introduced the separate car.[11] David Ruggles's incident was the first such publicized case. Instead, there were other more pressing political and cultural reasons that encouraged the railroads to make the first-class car white only. Among these was the antiabolitionist ferment that was raging in Massachusetts. When the conductor called Ruggles a "[damned] abolitionist," it was profoundly meaningful.[12] By conjuring the abolitionist movement in their insult, railroad personnel belied the fact that they saw Ruggles as not just a person they imagined as a nigger trying to infiltrate public space but also as a political activist intent on dismantling the status quo. Also important to the practice of segregation was the experience of previous transportation operators. The proprietors of public conveyances in the North had a long history of excluding colored travelers. But most significantly, technology played a role in the creation of a formal practice of segregation, and whites conceptualized railroads and streetcars as symbols of progress.[13] As such, they envisioned the interiors of these machines as white-only spaces devoid of black people and their perceived back-wardness. Keeping colored travelers out signified the railroads' modernity.

The Jim Crow car was not only separate but was also profoundly un-equal to the accommodations reserved for middle-class whites. Black activists remembered the cars as a constant statement of their social ostracism. The cars were for cargo and luggage, and consequently were vile and unsanitary, stuffed with white travelers' pets and "almost all manner of dirty things—a buffalo skin filled with coal dust, and slippers, dirty rags &c."[14] One traveler called the separate compartment a "cage," another "a cold prison."[15] These were fitting descriptions given the way in which the separate car served to criminalize the mobility of the travelers within.

The separate car not only branded colored travelers as worthless, but for the poor, immigrant, or recalcitrant whites who could not afford first-class accommodations, the car also demonstrated the instability of whiteness in the antebellum North. Historian David Roediger argues that class and public behavior had the power to whiten or blacken a person's social identity, creating a sometimes flimsy racial divide between working-class whites and people of color.[16] Therefore, just as sitting in a first-class car advertised a traveler's respectability, crowding into the Jim Crow car signified one's social inadequacies. In 1841, the president of the Taunton and New Bedford Railroad exemplified this phenomenon when he admitted that his company used a segregated car to keep separate "the drunken, dirty, ragged and colored people from the others."[17] In his description, the railroad president conflated blackness with dis-order, but he also made it clear that white people who flouted notions of respectability—whether through their class or their behavior—would end up there too. Consider the case of two white sailors in October 1838, just two months after Ruggles confronted railroad workers on the B&P. A conductor on the Eastern Rail Road, a line that ran from Boston to Salem, Massachusetts, forced the sailors into "the 'refuse' or the 'Jim Crow' car." Although the men held first-class tickets, they were so drunk that they "disgusted and shocked the other passengers by their profanity, noise and abuse."[18] Skin color alone was not a guarantee of white status on the trains.

Colored travelers similarly recognized the role of social class in organ-izing seating on the railroads. When, in 1842, a ticketing agent banished Harriet Jacobs to the separate car, it was the act of being forced to ride among poor white folks and immigrants that made it clear to Jacobs that freedom in the North had its limits. Importantly, during the incident, Jacobs did not confront railroad personnel in the style of Ruggles. She was just days into her hard-fought freedom when, en route from Philadelphia to New York City, she found herself in the precarious position of riding unescorted in the Jim Crow car. Her unwillingness to deny the railroad's authority shows the gendered constraints of open protest. If she had done so, she would have spurned not only racial conventions but prevailing gender proscriptions as well. As historian Patricia Cline Cohen ascertains, the very act of traveling was dangerous for all women in the antebellum period.[19] Meeting unruly men in public posed a real hazard and even prompted one (unusual) conductor to place a black woman *into* first class, against the wishes of the railroad president, to protect her from a group of "drunken sailors" who had "annoyed" the woman.[20] Yet, under more normal conditions, a woman who stood up for herself and openly defied conductors placed herself at considerable physical and emotional risk, perhaps even worse than riding in the separate car alone. Therefore, Jacobs, like so many other black female travelers, did not assert herself on the railroad that day in 1842 but instead stayed within the confines of the short car, which was "crowded with people, apparently of all nations." Jacobs went on to describe the separate car by using language that highlighted her belief that she came from a higher social class than others in the car. According to her, the short car was akin to the most degraded urban spaces, with babies constantly crying, very few windows, and a space where "every other man had a cigar or pipe in his mouth, and jugs of whiskey were handed round freely." She was physically sickened by the bodies, smoke, and alcoholic fumes, and she was emotionally scarred by the "coarse jokes and ribald songs." She later admitted that the experience was "the first chill to my enthusiasm about the Free States."[21]

There is little doubt that riding in the separate car was demoralizing, but it also raised the stakes of segregation. Whereas separate seating on antebellum public vehicles had previously been a custom loosely practiced by individual proprietors, the railroads made it a de facto legal apparatus with a built-in process of discipline. Certainly, such formality grew out of the systems that criminalized black mobility, but importantly, on the railroads, the vigilantism was institutionalized. On some of the key New England lines, corporate representatives required workers to refuse black people equal access, what conductors called the "rules and regulations." When in May 1841 a conductor on the Eastern Rail Road denied black abolitionist Thomas Jinnings first-class seating, Jinnings refused to be cowed. He stood up to the conductor, but the railroad man insisted that racialized seating was a corporate mandate, arguing that "the Directors made all the rules regulating passengers' seats, and that their imperative orders to him were to permit no colored person whatever to ride in these cars." When he later reflected on this insult, Jinnings was astounded by the assault on his rights, but he was even more struck by the conductor's ability to enforce the rule. As with Ruggles and hundreds of other colored travelers who used public conveyances in the antebellum North, Jinnings's refusal to leave first class was met with the threat of violence. When he defied the conductor, Jinnings recalled, "in rushed baggage masters and brakemen," who were prepared to remove him bodily.[22] In fact, the railroad directors deputized conductors to impose segregation, encouraging all railroad workers to use physical means to police white space on the railroads. Thus, segregation on the railroads was not only the practice of separating white passengers from colored travelers but also included the mechanisms of enforcement. Black demands for equal access were read as so fundamentally criminal that several railroad companies gave their conductors carte blanche to refuse black entrée by any means necessary.

As a result, exclusion on the railroads was not only insulting to colored travelers but also dangerous, and the rigid style of segregation spread to other modes of transportation as well. Since the railroads provided only short-range routes, travelers relied on an infrastructure that included the combination of railroads, steamships, and stagecoaches to complete a journey.[23] Such was the case with the Stonington Line, a line that depended on multiple vehicles to get travelers from Boston to Providence and then to New York City. It was the line on which conductors assaulted David Ruggles in 1838. Remember that in Ruggles's case it was on the steamship, not on the railroad, that he first confronted the rigid enforcement of segregation. The fact that African Americans often worked as stewards or chambermaids on the steamship portion of the Stonington Line emphasized for whites the proper place on board for people of color. Of the steamship *Rhode Island*, Harriet Jacobs once remarked that the "boat employed colored hands, but I knew that colored passengers were not admitted to the cabin."[24] The exclusionary practice of the railroad companies penetrated the industry, negatively impacting the experiences of colored travelers no matter how they went.

If corporate directors such as Josiah Quincy Jr. hoped to curb black demands for equal access by institutionalizing strict rules and their enforcement, they were mistaken. In the late 1830s and early 1840s, black activists with the financial means increasingly countered such limitations by vocally and assertively insisting they ride in the seats for which they paid, despite conductor opposition. Thus, this early form of Jim Crow segregation became dialectal. Railroad personnel upped the ante, activists asserted themselves by confronting conductors, and, in response, corporate representatives initiated even stricter ordinances, making the rules and regulations official and public. In January 1840, the NB&T, which ran from New Bedford to Boston, began posting placards within the cars that advertised the policy. The next year, the ERR posted its version, on 2 September 1841. The signs read, "All passengers upon the road are required to take such seats in the cars, and in such cars as shall be designated by the respective conductors; and all tickets are sold subject to this rule."[25]

The Eastern Rail Road introduced its version of the seating rule during a summer of intense racial violence on the line, a summer in which black activists and their white allies confronted conductors almost daily and risked physical brutality in return. After the introduction of the public regulation, abolitionists such as Frederick Douglass "made it a rule" to sit in the first-class car to bait the conductor into confrontation.[26] On 8 September, Douglass and white abolitionist John Anderson "J. A." Collins left Boston and took first-class seats en route to an antislavery convention in New Hampshire when the conductor tried to "snake out the [damned] nigger." Frustrated by Douglass's defiance, the conductor ripped down the placard from the wall and waved it in the travelers' faces. When the two men remained seated, the conductor called in a mob of four or five "company minions." The group pounced on Douglass and thrust him into the short car. Collins was "considerably injured in the affray," and Douglass's clothes were torn. At the same time, another white abolitionist, out of solidarity, followed Douglass into the Jim Crow car but was immediately pushed out by the conductor, who argued that white men were not permitted to ride there.[27] Of course, as the travels of the two white sailors and Harriet Jacobs exemplified, this was not true. White folks were not only allowed in the Jim Crow car but were sometimes forced to ride in it. Whites who found themselves in the separate car were those who destabilized the parameters of white supremacy through their poverty, their foreignness, and/or their disorderly behavior.

At the same time, middle-class white reformers hoping to subvert the railroad's segregationist policies by voluntarily opting to sit in the Jim Crow car would not be allowed to choose where they sat. Colored travelers increasingly exposed the hypocrisy of the rules and regulations and, like Frederick Douglass, met segregation with a new style of protest: direct confrontation.

"DEMAND the treatment of FREEMEN"

What made Jim Crow segregation a contest rather than merely a top-down tenet of white supremacy was that, by inventing the separate car, the corporate directors of the railroad were reacting to the shifting strategies of black radicals. On 7 August 1838, when Ruggles openly confronted the conductor and faced down a mob on the Stonington Line, his response was not the result of a sudden, individual act. His fervent rebukes were part of ongoing conversations among black radicals that painted any acquiescence to exclusion as unmanly, and direct confrontation as not only respectable but an essential weapon to achieve citizenship.

It is important not to underestimate the transformation in strategy from moral improvement to direct confrontation that Ruggles undertook. As historian Stephen Kantrowitz argues about a later generation of black activists, "Free blacks openly promised defiance in part because they understood a critical dimension of American conceptions of liberty: it was earned in struggle." In the late 1830s, Ruggles bolder response echoed shifts among a new generation of black activists, many of whom, like Ruggles, called New York City home. As historian Leslie Alexander shows, these activists had become increasingly radicalized. One of the most telling examples of this change included the founding of the militant organization called the New York Committee on Vigilance.[28] Starting in 1835, this group of black abolitionists made it its mission to chase down slave catchers, expose New York City residents who illegally held slaves, and offer a beacon of hope to self-emancipated people throughout the city. This was groundbreaking work that placed human rights over property rights. The group challenged the 1793 Fugitive Slave Act, arguing that it was unlawful and immoral to hunt suspected runaways. The Committee on Vigilance was an organization so committed to using methods of direct confrontation that it was in pursuit of a notorious kidnapper that Ruggles was headed to Massachusetts when he ran into trouble on the Stonington Line in August 1838.[29] The group exemplified how black radicals throughout the North not only acknowledged slavery and its proponents as the most vicious enemies of black freedom but also recognized the necessity of actively assaulting the institution whenever possible.

In part, the move to radicalism allowed folks such as Ruggles to protect their enslaved brothers and sisters in the South. But northern activists also increasingly linked the fight for immediate abolition in the South to the fight for equality at home.[30] Their writings reflected the belief that "cruel prejudice" in the North—including the Jim Crow car on the railroads, the Negro pew that white congregations reserved for black people, and all-white schools—was a vicious tentacle of slavery. They argued that as long as the institution of slavery existed in the United States, equality and citizenship were impossibilities. In the late 1830s, just a few years after the 1827 abolition of slavery in New York and the 1832 introduction of the Jim Crow minstrel character, people of color found themselves accosted by racial insults throughout the North, especially by the slur nigger. The epithet, coupled with antiabolitionist violence, riots, and more formal modes of segregation, caused one black activist to assert that "prejudice binds the most galling chains" around the freeman.[31] Speaking before the Glasgow Emancipation Society in 1837, African American abolitionist and medical student James McCune Smith described how, in the United States, freedom was tainted because he was "an outcast in the land of the free . . . a victim of cruel prejudice."[32] In 1840, black abolitionist Charles Lenox Remond wrote that prejudice was "slavery's grand handmaid" in the North.[33] For these activists, prejudice was not a separate issue but one that was intractable from enslavement and the ideology of white supremacy. As one black writer announced, "the real battle ground between liberty and slavery is prejudice against color."[34] Therefore, when antebellum black activists dealt a blow to segregation, they were issuing a justifiable attack against slavery, in effect doing the work of abolitionism on the home front.

In the antebellum North, if prejudice was slavery's soldier-in-command, then the New England railroads were fast becoming its most prolific theater of war. Black activists recognized that the railroads were a combat zone. Moreover, they knew that exclusion from them threatened to obstruct the future of black mobility even as technology continued to progress. Yet, to launch the full-fledged battle for equality that they believed was necessary, colored travelers also had to jump one essential hurdle that might (and did) cause them to sacrifice their fragile social standing. Up until the late 1830s, black leaders espoused moral improvement as the basic philosophy to fight attacks against black citizenship. Respectability politics were the cornerstone of this belief.[35] The concept was so essential to the middle-class strivings of people of color that during the brief two-year run of the first black periodical, *Freedom's Journal*, from 1827 to 1829, the term "respectable" appeared more than 100 times as a descriptor of people of color, including "respectable men of Colour," "a respectable meeting," "respectable citizens of Colour," "respectable brethren," and "our most respectable and wealthy citizens."[36]

By the late 1830s, it was no longer as clear what respectability meant in the face of mounting antiblack hostilities. Did the kind of acquiescent propriety that white northerners expected contradict notions of true black respectability? Samuel Cornish, a frequent traveler and an early editor of the late 1830s black newspaper *The Colored American*, believed that it did. In an editorial, he asked if it was proper for "respectable colored citizens" to allow captains to shove them into ships' pantries and to banish them onto decks. Was it right for colored travelers to let themselves be treated like "slaughtered animals rather than free citizens?"[37] After returning from a brief trip in 1837, Cornish expressed his frustration that some colored travelers accepted segregation even as he, on the very same ship, demanded first-class accommodations and got them. He emphasized that passive behavior was not only not respectable but also disloyal, because it placed all travelers in jeopardy. Cornish was not alone in this thinking. When Harriet Jacobs was working as a nanny, an inn refused to serve her a meal at the same table as white servants. Jacobs stood up for her rights and was served as an equal. She concluded that "colored servants ought to be dissatisfied with *themselves*, for not having too much self-respect to submit to such treatment."[38]

In the late 1830s, Cornish joined a cohort of activists who began to construct notions of activist respectability that were closely linked to notions of class propriety. For example, Cornish believed that by choosing not to wear one's "Sunday clothes" while traveling, a colored traveler would be met with bad treatment. By way of example, he told the story of a reverend who while traveling wore "an old cloak, that would have disgraced a vagrant;—consequently he received the treatment of a brute."[39] Ironically, in an 1841 edition of a popular guidebook geared toward white "gentlemen," the author suggested exactly the opposite regarding proper attire. He advised, "In preparing for a journey, you should put on the shabbiest clothes you have, provided they are consistent with decency: none but very vulgar persons wear their best coat in a stage-coach."[40] Of course, middle-class white travelers had the luxury of wearing everyday clothing without threatening their class standing. Therefore, even as Cornish overlooked the reality that riding public vehicles was filthy business for all travelers, his central message remained that the way black people conducted themselves in public impacted how whites treated them. Still, this argument deviated from moral improvement, most critically in that a black sense of propriety was no longer genteel but instead included the fierce public defense of equal rights *during* the actual trip itself.

By telling colored travelers to dress well and to stand up for themselves, black leaders were asking their constituents to put their bodies in harm's way in the name of respectability. Importantly, writers such as Cornish presumed those bodies to be male—they did not expect women such as Harriet Jacobs or others to confront proprietors. But, for men, open defiance was not only appropriate but also a clear marker of black masculinity. Activists contended that in order to make their behavior legible to white northerners, black men had to boldly assert themselves in public ways that whites would read as manly. Antebellum white men understood their rights as both a necessary trait of citizenship and as a quality that black men, by virtue of their imagined dependence, implicitly lacked.[41] In 1837, Cornish encouraged black men to defend their equal right to travel by explicitly linking direct confrontation to masculinity and ultimately citizenship. He wrote, "Is not A MAN, A MAN, whatever be his complexion?" If so, then "Our brethren should DEMAND the treatment of FREEMEN, or cease traveling about the country."[42] Crucial to Cornish's complaint was the idea that colored travelers needed to demand equality or stay home. In so saying, Cornish anticipated the sentiments of Charles Ray, a future editor of *The Colored American*, who believed it was the duty of a black man to accept nothing less than equal treatment while traveling. On 30 June 1838, after he endured a particularly harrowing journey, Ray counseled, "Brethren, you are MEN—if you have not horses and vehicles of your own to travel with, stay at home, or travel on foot. Cease giving your money to men, who forbear not to degrade you beneath the dogs."[43] The messages of activists such as Cornish and Ray were not as much calls for boycott as they were reminders of the stakes involved. Activists contended that the acceptance of lesser accommodations was a public demonstration of weakness, a step backward that threatened black claims to respectability, masculinity, and ultimately citizenship. The time was nigh, they argued, for colored men to step up.

Gender proscriptions made it necessary for most black women to be less overt in their protest strategies but not necessarily less defiant. An incident in May 1839 on the *Massachusetts*, one of two steamships that completed the New York to Providence leg of the Stonington Line, demonstrates how middle-class black women navigated segregation. On 10 May, the steamship was filled with Boston abolitionists returning from the annual meeting of the American Anti-Slavery Society in New York. Before leaving, three black female activists returning from the Convention of American Women held in Philadelphia asked white abolitionist James Buffum to purchase first-class tickets on their behalf. Buffum, the editor of *The Lynn Record* (Massachusetts) and a person the women recognized from home, agreed to do so.[44]

It might be tempting to dismiss as passive the women's request to have a white man buy their tickets as a way to quietly circumvent the inevitability of segregation. However, by traveling this way, the women engaged in active defiance of racial proscription. They wanted to travel in the safety of first class, especially desiring the gendered protection of the ladies' cabin, and they were aware that they might not get tickets if they purchased them themselves. Deceiving the ship's crew was a calculated risk. In a testament to the power of white supremacy, however, it was a black chambermaid who noticed the three black women and reported them to the captain. The sources are silent as to how the maid discovered the women's identities or why she chose to expose them; in fact, none of the women involved ever published letters about the incident. Of the male observers who reported the case in the press—both pro-slavery and abolitionist—none acknowledged the women's activism. Nevertheless, by acquiring a surrogate to buy their tickets and by entering not only the first-class salon but also the ladies' cabin, the women engaged in a feminized version of respectable activism.[45]

Not all colored travelers opted to defy white authority. Instead, some believed radical tactics exacerbated racial tensions and caused segregationists to dig in their heels. The violence that inevitably ensued was particularly dangerous for black women, a fact that prompted at least one black male traveler to publicly voice his dissent over the strategy. Two months after Ruggles's 1838 altercation on the B&P, a young man from New Haven calling himself "Sinceritas" blamed radicals for the recent ousting of his mother and wife from a canal boat in New York. In a reversal of the philosophy espoused by black radicals, the young man reasoned that when an activist "kicks up a row and is perhaps 'lynched,'"—a reference to Ruggles, who in his 1838 letter described himself as being "most egregiously defrauded and lynched"[46]—"no colored man, decent or indecent, can be permitted to go in that boat." Complaints such as this aligned more closely with moral improvement than with the newly constructed activist respectability. "Sinceritas" contended that only by adopting a passive, humble attitude could colored travelers receive proper treatment. He wrote, "we never will gain any thing by an overbearing and haughty spirit; while, as an injured and submissive people, we will gain the love and esteem of all good men."[47] This was an old-guard philosophy similarly articulated in 1812 by colored traveler Paul Cuffe, who after one incident mused that "I believe if I am favoured to keep my place my Enemies Will Become friendly."[48]

Radicals openly acknowledged that the ongoing dialectic between colored travelers and railroad personnel led to more stringent segregationist policies. Charles Ray admitted that by publicizing "outrages against persons of color" on public conveyances, activists "seemed to aggravate the case." He believed, however, that by the summer of 1840 such publicity was "working well for our class."[49] Notwithstanding Ray's assessment, colored travelers designated the railroads the undeniable epicenter of racial protest. In fact, by 1840, the conflict between conductors and black activists had become so contentious and culturally significant that when the railroad's posse tossed people of color bodily into the so-called Jim Crow car, they unwittingly coined what was destined to become the most formidable nickname for segregation in the twentieth century.

Jumping Jim Crow

White railroad workers invented the term "the Jim Crow car." In doing so, they harnessed a vocabulary that highlighted the political and social value of their whiteness just as their specific job required them to provide services to railroad patrons, a population that sometimes included African Americans. Such work threatened social inversion when, in the idealized culture of the North, "none but negers are sarvants."[50] Of course, white workers did in fact perform domestic work and serve others, but to ask white workers to act as servants to colored travelers epitomized social flip-flopping. Thus, these workers gave birth to the phrase "the Jim Crow car," signifying how this specific style of segregation was a racial contest between black radicals and white supremacists.

Indeed, had free people of color not sought equal treatment, had they acquiesced on stagecoaches and steamships, had they made no demands for access, had they not organized against slavery, and had they not likened the free use of public space to liberty and citizenship, assigning the separate car a racialized moniker would have been unnecessary. All people of color would have ridden alongside poor whites in the "pauper" or "refuse" car, as poor blacks surely did. Instead, in a move that encapsulates the hostility over the prospect of black social and political mobility, when radicals demanded equal entrée, railroad personnel launched a decisive three-pronged retaliation. First, they refused colored travelers first-class service and cast them into the separate car. Next, they rigidly enforced the boundaries of the separate space, using violent means to police racial regulations on the trains. Finally, railroad workers gave this institutionalized style of segregation and surveillance a nickname that remains salient into the twenty-first century. Although scholars have speculated that "the origin of the term 'Jim Crow' as applied to Negroes [was] lost in obscurity" or that the harnessing of it "was a natural development," evidence suggests that this naming was not organic but was instead a concerted attack on a particular class of black activists, an attack coded in the racial and cultural politics of the antebellum North.[51]

The story of this process begins with the history of racial parody in the United States. By the 1830s, free people of color were the consistent targets of antiblack cultural productions, especially staged theatricals that starred white actors in blackface makeup. Called minstrelsy, these performances mocked black identity and were modern iterations of the literary blackface popularized in the early national period, as with the letters to "massa printer" from "Sambo" in the 1780s. Like their predecessors, audiences believed minstrel characterizations were authentic representations of black people. The most raucous and loyal fans of the performances came from the same ranks as those men who worked the railroads and also those who decimated New York City black communities in the July 1834 antiabolitionist riots—wage earners, shopkeepers, and small masters.[52] Throughout the North, mechanics halls were gathering spots for white workers and were the primary venue for these blackface theatricals.[53] Given its working-class appeal, it is no wonder that minstrelsy was the most popular performance art form of the nineteenth century.

After 1832, the reigning king of this antiblack feeling was the character of "Jim Crow." It was a white actor, Thomas Dartmouth Rice, who allegedly saw an enslaved man dance an unusual, flimsy-bodied jig and sing a self-referential song called "Jump Jim Crow" sometime in the late 1820s, somewhere in the South. Rice reenacted what he saw on the northern stage, and by the summer of 1832 he was headlining the show in cities across the North, particularly in New York City. Onstage, he put black cork on his face and dressed in a tattered top hat, vest, and coattails, clothes that ridiculed northern black prosperity.[54] Most dangerously, the Jim Crow caricature was a colored traveler, epitomizing the problems of unregulated black mobility. When the fictional Jim Crow traveled, he beat down other people of color, wrestled alligators, seduced multiple women, got drunk, espoused antibank sentiment, and was even unafraid to school President Andrew Jackson on how best to run the country.[55]

Ironically, even while the caricature mocked the prospect of black freedom and mobility, the ideas Jim Crow voiced were politically aligned with the white workers who cheered him on. As cultural theorist Eric Lott argues, working-class white men adored minstrel performances precisely because they represented their own voice, street smarts, and brazen masculinity. Lott contends that minstrelsy was "an oppositional, almost underground cultural form."[56] Above all else, Jim Crow flouted notions of respectability, a fact that empowered white workers and angered upper-class whites.[57] Clashes played out in the theaters themselves, a feature that was especially prevalent in Boston, with its tradition of wealthy white reformers. When Rice performed in 1833 at the Tremont Theater in that city, a "theatrical rumpus" took place. The argument pit white workers against highbrow theatergoers, with the workers' cries of "bravo" and "encore" overpowering the hissing of wealthier whites. A reviewer who was present complained that the show was "miserable stuff" designed for the masses.[58] In the end, working-class white men successfully defended their right to enjoy the performance that reified their racial worth and simultaneously subverted classed hierarchies.

How important was Jim Crow to working-class white masculine identity? The character was so venerated that fans carried him off the stage into the streets, especially sounding the oft-repeated chorus, "weel about and turn about and do jis so/Eb'ry time I weel about and jump Jim Crow."[59] By the mid-1830s, Jim Crow became an integral part of American vernacular, but at first the phrase was not exclusively deployed against black people, although it was fundamentally racial. Instead, whites used the term to ascribe disparaging qualities to their political enemies, espe-

FIGURE 3.4 "The Editorial Jim Crow," a caricature meant to castigate a prominent white editor for changing his views about the attack on Fort Sumter. From *Vanity Fair*, 27 April 1861. Mortimer Rare Book Room, Smith College.

THE EDITORIAL JIM CROW.
Wheel about, an' turn about,
An' do jis' so,
An' ebery time I turn my coat
I says I told you so.

cially ideological flip-flopping. This usage was both an allusion to the character's seemingly spineless dance and also a reflection of the belief that free black men were the political dupes of more powerful whites.[60] In 1834, the editor of the pro-labor periodical *The Workingman's Advocate* spoke out against the formation of a national bank, scathingly admonishing politicians who changed their position on the subject and "*jumped Jim Crow*, with great applause."[61] Other editors followed suit, often using the term to indict politicians who dismissed working-class concerns. They grumbled about the "'Jim Crow' Movements" of New York's Tammany Hall, of "jumping Jim Crow" in the Ohio House, "the Jim Crow financiers of Wall Street," and Martin Van Buren's "Jim Crowism" over the tariff.[62]

By the dawn of the Civil War, Americans so easily understood the blackened figure of Jim Crow as symbolizing a lack of political integrity that the image itself spoke volumes (see figure 3.4). In a biting cartoon from the April 1861 issue of *Vanity Fair*, published only two weeks after the attack on Fort Sumter, an Uncle Sam–looking "editorial Jim Crow" danced atop a directional weather vane that read "north, south, east and west." The image was meant to skewer the editor of the *New York Herald* for his changing position on the war.[63] The figure sang: "An' every time I turn my coat/ I says I told you so."[64] Comparing a politician to Jim Crow worked to blacken political indecisiveness, sharpening its sting.

Even as the term "Jim Crow" emerged as an antiblack invective, its attack against colored travelers on the Massachusetts railroads was not preordained. In the early 1830s and 1840s, whites tried to exclude black people from public spaces throughout the North but did not deploy the term to designate the separation anywhere else but in New England, and only on the railroads. In white churches, the separate pews were called "negro pews." In New York, New Jersey, and Pennsylvania, segregation existed, but conductors did not so nickname the separate cars.[65] Free people of color got roughed up on locomotives throughout the North, but in the late 1830s, Jim Crow remained a Massachusetts regional term.

Jim Crow became the symbol of racial segregation in Massachusetts because of space, geography, labor, and politics. The railroads themselves became contested terrain where railroad workers, radical white abolitionists, and colored travelers unintentionally converged. When, in 1838, New England conductors dubbed the space the Jim Crow car, it mattered that they were members of the white working class, men who felt marginalized by the middle- and upper-class abolitionists who detested the Jim Crow stage performance and increasingly used the railroads. The conflicts between abolitionists and white workers were political but also very personal, with class at their root. Meanwhile, some colored travelers also adopted classed attitudes toward white workers on the railroads. In 1842, Charles Remond confessed that he was "unwilling to *descend so low as to bandy words* with the superintendents, or contest [his] rights with conductors, or any others in the capacity of servants of any stage or steamboat company, or rail-road corporation."[66] Both black and white abolitionists flexed their moralistic muscles to position themselves as the social betters of the white men who worked the railroads.

Ultimately, the phrase "Jim Crow car" insisted that black economic and political strivings could never raise people of color above their tattered-clothes-wearing doppelganger, and more specifically not above white workers themselves. Moreover, it was a gendered denunciation of black respectability. The nickname alluded to a masculine figure even though conductors forced women of color to ride in them too. This was an implicit attack on the bodies of black women, dismissing as impossible those women's claims to domesticity, purity, and sexual vulnerability. In the tight spaces of the Massachusetts railroads, workers asserted their own sense of national belonging by brutally enforcing segregation. With a violence that demonstrated their own masculine virility, railroad workers forced colored travelers to jump Jim Crow from first class to the attached short car, staking their own claims to whiteness and citizenship. Therefore, when fighting Jim Crow, black radicals were battling spatial indignities, yes, but also a cultural foe that attacked black people's social identities. It explicitly decreed that free women of color were less than women and that free men of color were less than citizens.

Fighting the Railroads

The Jim Crow process of segregation added insult to injury, but more importantly it signified the birth of an increasingly legalized foreclosure on free black access to public space. Black activists very quickly recognized the stakes of this heightened surveillance of colored travelers; it was sometime during 1837 or early 1838 that Josiah Quincy Jr. instituted the separate car, and only a few months later that David Ruggles confronted the conductor on the Boston and Providence Railroad.[67] By so doing, Ruggles announced to the world that black radicals would not quietly accept banishment to the "Jim Crow car." Ruggles thus modeled a new incarnation of activist respectability that men such as Cornish and Ray had preached.

Not only did Ruggles make fighting back in public respectable; he also reframed the discourse and ultimately the strategy around exclusion from the railroads. Whereas previous colored travelers labeled segregation as rude, heartless, and ungentlemanly, Ruggles spoke of it in legal terms— as criminal. He painted the conductor's actions—both the vigilantism and the overcharging—as crimes. He described the conductor's insistence that Ruggles pay more to sit in lesser accommodations as "Highway Robbery," whereby criminals "commit larceny upon men's pockets and rights, and lynch them [enact vigilantism] with impunity."[68] By positing his actions as respectable and the conductors' as a violation of his rights, Ruggles laid the groundwork for future equal rights work, claiming freedom of mobility as a core and *legal* quality of U.S. citizenship.

From the moment that Ruggles stood up to the railroad workers in 1838, black activists used direct confrontation to test their rights against the Jim Crow car. The result was increasing brutality. By mid-September 1841, the battle became so heated that when a conductor tried to throw Frederick Douglass off the Eastern Rail Road, Douglass grabbed onto the seats so tightly that he pulled them up from the floor when the mob yanked him off the car.[69] On 30 September 1841, also on the ERR, the black female secretary of the Lynn Anti-Slavery Society, Mary Green, carried her infant and insisted on remaining in first class, despite the intervention of railroad personnel. Like Green, throughout the nineteenth century, some activist women did practice direct confrontation. In these cases, conductors reacted with the same physical aggression they used with black men.[70] In the case of Green, notwithstanding the baby in her arms, the conductor ordered three men to grab her by the head and the feet and to thrust her out of the car. When her husband tried to intervene, the mob pushed him back and bloodied his face. Meanwhile, Green's mother stepped in and smacked the face of one of the assailants, a reaction that was not the norm.[71] When black activists practiced open defiance and resisted removal between 1838 and 1843, it was more likely that conductors and their posses cut, kicked, carried, dragged, pushed, and demeaned them without recourse.

In response to the rising violence against them, black radicals took yet another profound leap in strategy: they began to appeal to the state for redress, bringing criminal charges against the culprits—conductors and their posses—in local courts. The small number of these cases brought by activists belies a greater shift in activist thinking. Bringing these episodes of violence to court demonstrated two things. First, it showed that free people of color believed they had the right to hold the state accountable to help protect their bodies. Next, it allowed activists to publicly insist that segregation was a defect in the law, not a quaint (and understandable) custom of society. This new version of direct confrontation was important even though activists are only known to have sought legal remedy five times during the height of the railroad battles. The first instance was in 1840, when a colored traveler from New Bedford, Massachusetts, became the first to file charges, and the last instance during this period was in 1842, when a group of interracial abolitionists demanded and got a hearing before the Massachusetts General Assembly. Although many violent incidents likely went unreported, those travelers who did file charges built their claims on David Ruggles's articulation of segregation and its enforcement as a crime. The first colored traveler to do so was a young man whose respectability was put center stage by the white press. Described by a reporter as "well-attired and well conducted," this first litigant was most likely Shadrach Howard, a grandson of wealthy sea captain Paul Cuffe.[72] Howard, a resident of New Bedford and an activist, refused to back down when a conductor and superintendent on the B&P tried to "forcibly remove" him to the Jim Crow car. In response, railroad personnel beat Howard, who later brought the matter to the New Bedford police court that was responsible for small-scale crime. The judge sided with the railroad.[73]

Despite Howard's loss, the turn to the courts marked an even broader understanding of activist respectability. In so doing, black activists insisted that the state make the railroad corporations—private entities that were chartered by state governments—respect their claims to citizenship. It was a bold move. Scholars such as Walter Johnson, Ariela Gross, and Edlie Wong have demonstrated that enslaved and free people sometimes sought redress from the antebellum U.S. courts to adjudicate so-called freedom suits.[74] Likewise, black laborers in the North relied on the courts to settle petty disputes, although judges and juries rarely decided in favor of African Americans.[75] Still, using courts was not commonplace.

Despite the likelihood that they would lose in court, black radicals used the courts to publicize their assaults and also to draw segregation and its enforcement as a violation of their citizenship rights. On 30 December 1840, a streetcar driver and agent in New York City told renowned restaurateur Thomas Downing, "no nigger should be in the car." The wealthy activist and owner of a famous oyster house had previously traveled the streetcar line—the Harlem Railroad—on equal terms with white passengers and therefore refused to budge.[76] In response, transportation workers pushed him out of the car, sliced his ear, bruised his face, and ripped his hat. Downing pressed charges but lost.[77] The judge instructed jurors to consider whether the rules benefitted "public convenience as well *as [the railroads'] own private benefit*." To prove this, the Harlem Railroad only needed to provide evidence that the regulation for separate seating was openly stated, that Downing and other colored travelers knew about it, and that the defendants "used no greater force than was necessary to carry the regulation into effect."[78] In an illustration of the extreme vulnerability facing black men and women in public space, the jury decided that because Downing did know the rule but protested anyway, the act of bloodying his body in the name of enforcement did not constitute undue force. That the courts condoned white violence against black bodies has obvious echoes in state-sanctioned violence against African Americans in the twenty-first century.

At the same time that the courts reinforced a conductor's right to violently maintain segregation, they also refused to recognize a colored traveler's right to defend himself. In early 1842, a conductor once again dragged Shadrach Howard and another colored traveler off the Taunton and New Bedford Railroad when the two men attempted to sit in first class. The conductor held Howard down while passengers cried "teach the nigger his place," and the conductor's posse kicked him, pulled his hair, struck his face, and tore his coat. This time, however, Howard came prepared. In self-defense, he pulled out a knife and cut the conductor. For doing so, the railroad had him arrested, and the judge charged him a $10 fine and expenses—a cost of more than $250, but the same court dismissed the charges against the conductor. Unable to pay the fees, Howard was jailed, signifying the dangers and sacrifice inherent when colored travelers asserted their rights to equal access, freedom of travel, and protection of their bodies from imminent harm.[79] No doubt, activist respectability came at a cost.

Ultimately, gender and class proved to be essential factors in swaying the courts to side with black plaintiffs, although throughout the nineteenth century it remained a rare occurrence for any black person to win their case against violent conductors and drivers. Still, middle-class black women had a better shot, and the first person of color to bring charges and win was a black female schoolteacher who a conductor violently ousted on her way to church.[80] In February 1855, a New York City court awarded Elizabeth Jennings $225 for damages caused by the Third Avenue railroad. Significantly, the perception that Jennings was a "respectable person" was paramount to her win. The judge argued, "*Colored persons, if sober, well behaved, and free from disease*, had the same rights as others; and could neither be excluded by *any rules of the Company, nor by force of violence*; and in case of such expulsion or exclusion, the Company was liable."[81] The jury agreed that Jennings was respectable, yet the judge's instructions illustrated the underlying assumption that most people of color were not. According to the judge, colored travelers could only gain access "*if*": if they dressed well, if they deported themselves well, and if they presented themselves as clean, black people could ride without racial proscription. Such assertions, even when made by well-meaning individuals such as the judge in Jennings's case, demonstrate how vital a strategy for black liberation activist respectability had become.

Throughout the nineteenth century, the ability to be considered a respectable person of color while utilizing public vehicles became so thoroughly understood as a notion that was gendered female that black men rarely won in cases against railroads and other carriers. In the wake of the *Jennings* decision, black activists quickly learned that the fight for equal access was not over. In May 1855, a few months after Jennings's court win, J. W. C. Pennington, a black minister from New York, tested the parameters of the verdict. He encouraged his congregants to demand first-class accommodations on the New York City streetcars. From his pulpit, he insisted that "nothing short of the utmost tameness and unjustifiable, indeed impious cowardice, would induce colored men and women, who valued their rights, to surrender" on the streetcars.[82] Despite Pennington's call to action, however, or perhaps because of it, when he and other male congregants took inside seats on the Sixth Avenue railway, the conductor assaulted them. The men took the company to court, but this time the courts had a different interpretation of justice. In one incident, a judge refused to even hear the case at all, and in another, Pennington lost. Moreover, indicating how rarely gender shielded African American women from violence, a driver's posse beat a pregnant woman on the Eighth Avenue streetcar, and her unborn child subsequently died.[83] The aftermath of the Jennings case proved that the state would refuse to recognize the rights of activists. It suggested that black men who rode with the intention of confronting white supremacy got what they deserved.

No Citizen Can Ride in the Cars

That the story of the Jim Crow car in Massachusetts is remembered as an oppressive custom imposed on colored travelers rather than as a fiercely fought contest between black radicals and their enemies is in large part, and surely unintentionally, because of white abolitionist intervention. Indeed, white abolitionists became vital supporters of colored travelers by the summer of 1841, and their involvement has often obscured the centrality of black activism in the historical record. No doubt, white activists suffered. In one instance, a conductor beat up white abolitionist Daniel Mann when he attempted to defend a colored traveler on the Eastern Rail Road. Mann, the chairman of the recently formed and interracial Boston Vigilance Committee, expressed outrage that the state empowered the railroads, a corporate entity, not only to attack people of color but also to force white men to "behave." He wrote, "No citizen can ride in the cars with any security for his person or rights, if he should happen to offend one of the menials of the establishment."[84] There is no question that white abolitionists fought in the trenches with black radicals, especially in the summer of 1841. Their activist work strong-armed the Massachusetts legislature into hearing testimony on the issue on 10 February 1842. Largely a call against the three most violent railroads—the ERR, the NB&T, and the B&P—the testimony was mediated through white abolitionists and their hand-picked representatives, even as black radicals moved for the hearing too.[85]

This is not to say that getting the matter of segregation before Massachusetts General Court was not significant. The opportunity to do so was an obvious result of the interracial pressure placed on the railroads through a variety of methods, including a series of petitions sent to the legislature over several years.[86] Moreover, it was also a radical break in tradition for the legislature to address an issue that most centrally concerned the rights of free people of color. Still, white abolitionists set the terms of the testimony, choosing revered white abolitionist Wendell Phillips to serve as the main spokesman for the issue. Although the railroads argued that they had fulfilled their obligations of "carrying" any person, Phillips asserted that the manner in which the railroads "carried" each citizen mattered. He reasoned that it was not enough to charge someone more money for lesser accommodations and call it equality.[87]

Notwithstanding Phillips's meaningful testimony, the most radical black activists did not appear before the Massachusetts General Court that February. The one person of color whom abolitionists in the Massachusetts legislature asked to speak illustrates the complicated relationship that even white radicals had with black folks who espoused the new activist respectability. It is unclear how Charles Lenox Remond, the free black abolitionist from Salem, was designated to tell his story before the court on 10 February 1842. On the one hand, Remond's freeborn status, his close relationship with William Lloyd Garrison, and his record of abolitionist lecturing made him a viable candidate. On the other hand, he was abroad from May 1840 to December 1841, during the occurrences of the most vigorous violence on the railroads. His absence from the controversy and his open opposition to the strategy of direct confrontation made him palatable.[88] Remond did not believe it was helpful or respectable to confront railroad personnel over the issue of segregation. In his words, it was "better to suffer wrong than do wrong."[89]

Despite Remond's moderate stance, his testimony still hinged on his identity as a respectable activist and relied on the intellectual legacy of black radicalism. Most centrally for this discussion, he defined himself as a respectable and transatlantic colored traveler. In 1840, Remond was a pioneer among transatlantic black abolitionists, joining a handful of black activists who pilgrimaged abroad. By 1860, more than 100 had made the same trip.[90] As one of the earliest colored travelers to make this journey, he raised his international perspective as his most salient evidence against the Jim Crow car. He boasted that during his protracted lecture tour in England, Scotland, and Ireland he was "received, treated and recognized, in public and private society, without any regard to complexion," never suffering an insult of any kind on "coaches, rail-roads, [or] steampackets."[91] Still, the moment he returned to Massachusetts, railroad personnel on the ERR made Remond ride in the Jim Crow car.[92] In response, Remond drew from the rhetoric developed by Ruggles, reminding lawmakers that "complexion can in no sense be construed into a crime." He also focused on his rights, arguing that on the grounds that people of color were citizens of the state of Massachusetts, they deserved the same rights and privileges guaranteed to all citizens of that state.[93] Lest the legislators might think that the brutality and insults he described were personal or periodic, he emphatically decried them as ubiquitous. He said, "The grievances of which we complain, be assured, sir, are not imaginary, but real—not local, but universal—not occasional, but continual—every day matter of fact things—and have become, to the disgrace of our common country, matter of history."[94]

ALTHOUGH THE SENATE COMMITTEE drafted a bill to regulate the railroads, instructing that the railroads make no "distinction or give a preference . . . on account of descent, sect, or color," the bill failed to pass in the Massachusetts House.[95] As a symbol of protest, William Lloyd Garrison, the white abolitionist editor of *The Liberator*, published a "Traveller's Directory," which offered commentary on each company's treatment of passengers. For example, the Eastern Rail Road was noted for "an odious distinction on account of color, and a bullying propensity to carry it out," and the Boston and Providence Rail Road for "a vile complexioned distinction, enforced by brutal assaults."[96]

In 1843, the Massachusetts railroads suddenly abandoned their commitment to segregate the railroads. Years later, in his 1855 autobiography, Frederick Douglass hailed this as a victory and credited pressure from the legislature for the result. Douglass and others celebrated too soon. Although it is true that after April 1843 there was no longer an official antiblack policy on the Massachusetts railroads, black folks continued to have run-ins with conductors. Charles Remond was one such person. He said he was relieved to abandon the "Jimmy," but even as the railroad companies tore down their placards and sat most passengers in the sections they could afford, in late April 1843 Remond found himself exiled from a railroad car, and as a result "in the station-house, disappointed in [his] feeling, and frustrated in [his] business engagements."[97] Even while tensions lifted in Massachusetts, the reality was that Jim Crow segregation remained a contest between radical men and women and those white people who reviled black freedom before, during, and after the Civil War. In New York, Philadelphia, Chicago, New Orleans, San Francisco, and Washington, D.C., streetcar and railroad conductors brutalized black passengers, who fought back.[98] By the 1860s, some states had already begun the formal process of legislating Jim Crow. As early as 1861, the state of Tennessee passed a bill that imposed a fine on any railroad president or conductor "who shall permit a free negro to travel on such road, unless under the control and care of a free white citizen of Tennessee."[99] Indeed, racial segregation on public conveyances remained a central weapon of white supremacy throughout the nineteenth century and for much of the twentieth. Consequently, public vehicles proved a site of renewed activism on which radicals mobilized for more than 100 years.

In the 1830s and 1840s, colored travelers launched this work. They made the fight against the Jim Crow car physical, not just rhetorical. They changed the vocabulary of exclusion, making segregation a crime, not just an insult. They brought their assaults to court and deemed the state accountable. Ultimately, black radicals made it clear for future generations that freedom of mobility and equal access were central tenets of U.S. citizenship. To them, equality and citizenship were qualities for which respectable activists could and should put their bodies on the line.

CHAPTER FOUR

Documenting Citizenship
Colored Travelers and the Passport

In 1849, black abolitionist William Wells Brown, a delegate to the Peace Congress in Paris, wrote a letter to Secretary of State John M. Clayton requesting an official U.S. passport for an upcoming trip to France. In his short note of 6 July, Brown explained that he was leaving from Boston for Liverpool via steamship in less than two weeks and hoped to acquire the passport by then. He then revealed the only details he believed mattered in issuing the document: proof that he was born in the United States and his physical description. He openly stated, "I am a native of the state of Kentucky, and I am a colored man."[1] But by the time he left for Liverpool on the transatlantic steamship *Canada* on 18 July 1849, the secretary of state had not replied, a tacit denial of Brown's application. Recognizing that by refusing him the document the Department of State was also denying his citizenship, Brown wryly observed "that none but an American slaveholder could have discovered that a man born in a country was not a citizen of it."[2]

When Brown applied for a U.S. passport, the question of black citizenship had not yet been settled in the United States. Brown's request predated by eight years the infamous decision of the Supreme Court in *Dred Scott v. Sandford*. In that 1857 case, the court decided, seven to two, that the question of black citizenship was not the intention of the founding fathers, nor was it a possibility under the slave regime.[3] There was some federal precedent for establishing a racialized prerequisite for citizenship. A 1790 edict on the naturalization of foreigners, for example, stated that applicants be "white persons."[4] Still, at the same time, the United States awarded citizenship based on birthright through the common-law practice of *jus soli*—literally, "of the soil."[5] Therefore, it was not far-fetched that an African American man such as Brown who had funds for a transatlantic voyage would apply for a passport. He believed that his birthright coupled with his freedom entitled him to the benefits of citizenship, including the acquisition of the document.

Brown and other African American applicants for U.S. passports catapulted conversations about black citizenship into the national spotlight.

Their travel forced the federal government to engage the question. Not many people of color applied for U.S. passports, because so few traveled abroad and even fewer went to destinations that required the document.[6] Still, some of the most elite abolitionists—Brown, Robert Purvis, and Sarah Parker Remond—did apply and, rather than acquiring the document, found themselves embroiled in ongoing debates about the citizenship status of free people of color living under a slave regime.[7]

In the 1840s, the Department of State—the executive office that was responsible for issuing the U.S. passport (also known as the State Department)—began the process of formalizing its procedures. Increasingly, the secretary of state, who was an appointed member of the president's cabinet and also the individual who headed the State Department, gained jurisdiction over the document, wresting control away from local and state governments, which had previously issued passports.[8] Importantly, the nineteenth-century version of the passport was much less formidable than it has become in the twenty-first century, and the passport procedure was still nascent. As the nineteenth century progressed, the Department of State issued to applicants a letter-sized piece of paper that identified the bearer as a "citizen of the United States." The passport not only referenced citizenship but also offered a traveler protections and security. The document asked foreign governments to permit the carrier to "safely and freely pass . . . and, in case of need, [be given] all lawful aid and protection."[9] American travelers did not need the document in order to leave or reenter the country until 1861, when war made it necessary. Nor did they need a passport to travel to Canada or the British Isles. But if a person traveled through continental Europe without the document, he or she risked police harassment and arrest.[10]

Despite the dangers of traveling abroad without a passport, the U.S. government almost always refused to knowingly issue the document to colored travelers. This refusal hinged on the fact that the document recognized the bearer as a U.S. citizen and simultaneously sanctioned international mobility, two ideals at odds with a system of slavery. As historian Linda Kerber argues, "No characteristic of slaves' statelessness had been more obvious than their lack of freedom to travel."[11] Moreover, if the federal government allowed black people to travel internationally, the sight of colored travelers could raise some potentially thorny issues for the United States. Would the categories of "free," "fugitive," or "slave" carry the same weight and meanings abroad as they held at home? How would black people be kept in their place if the place was no longer Charleston or New York City but rather London, Paris, or Berlin? The Department of State could not predict the answers, but it could avoid the question by rejecting black applicants and containing them within the confines of American borders. Colored travelers recognized the government snub as an assault on their citizenship and thus made passport rejections a matter of national import. Between the 1830s and the dawn of the Civil War, activists used the reformist press to express their outrage over race-based passport rejections by the Department of State. In so doing, colored travelers publicized their cases and forced the federal government to definitively address the issue of black citizenship.

I Am a Citizen of the United States

The idea that people might be born within a country but perceived as foreign was not a notion exclusive to the United States. The national passport was a formal identification document that amplified national boundaries and the surveillance of mobility. To navigate public space, travelers were required to show paper proof of national citizenship, a process that dated back to the French Revolution. Parisian officials used the document to tally visitors to the city in order to isolate threats to the government and promote ideas of national belonging.[12] As nation-states began to oversee the surveillance of individual movement, they also became more circumspect in their treatment of travelers, their purposes, and their destinations. A prevailing thought was that outsiders could be dangerous people who looked different and spoke different languages, but they could also be jobless, hungry, or transients from just beyond the city limits.[13] Hence, the modern concept of foreign emerged to identify not only a person who originated from far away but also someone homegrown who was actually or potentially threatening to the state.[14]

As the criminalization of black mobility attests, people of color who were born in the United States were cast as outsiders in the style of the French. This was true not only of enslaved people but also, and even more concertedly, of free people of color. In a case study of poor relief and the treatment of former slaves, legal historian Kunal Parker demonstrates that officials in Massachusetts actively diminished the birthright status of newly freed black people. As enslaved people became free, poor relief officials found themselves in bitter disputes with the commonwealth over the financial responsibility of those former slaves who had become public charges—the old, the poor, and the disabled. The disputes mounted when local officials recognized there was a glitch in the state law that might benefit the towns. If a person who sought poor relief was not locally born but was instead a foreigner, whether born in Virginia or across the Atlantic, the state would reimburse town officials for that individual's care. Knowing this loophole, poor relief officials in various towns manipulated the system to relieve themselves of the financial burden. They petitioned the state of Massachusetts to reimburse the local coffers by describing former slaves, even those who fought as patriots in the Revolutionary War and who were born locally, as people who were African-born. As a result, black people born in Massachusetts were not only imagined as foreign but were officially identified and legally understood as foreigners.[15] The notion that people of African descent were homegrown foreigners became endemic. As a result, the birthright status of African Americans continued to be legally precarious up until the passage of the Fourteenth Amendment to the U.S. Constitution, and as scholars of the Jim Crow South demonstrate, the citizenship rights of people of color remained elusive.[16] Thus, U.S. whites increasingly imagined free people of color as internal foreigners—born in the United States but also, as William Wells Brown astutely observed, not of it.

The perception of free people of color as internal foreigners was made even more pronounced when black people ventured outside U.S. borders. According to most whites, colored travelers proved how foreign they were simply by defying U.S. policy while abroad. The publicized arguments between black abolitionist Sarah Parker Remond and the Department of State over Remond's passport demonstrate this point. Remond was a freeborn woman, the much younger sister of Charles Lenox Remond from Salem, Massachusetts, and a fierce activist in her own right. She left the United States for Great Britain in 1858, armed with an official U.S. passport signed by Secretary of State Lewis Cass. In the British Isles, she toured and lectured for nearly a year before the U.S. Foreign Ministry in London refused to honor her passport. As Remond prepared to accompany her widowed sister Caroline Remond Putnam from London to Paris, she followed protocol and went to the American Embassy on 22 November 1859 to obtain a ministry signature or *visé* on her valid U.S. passport for travel to France. The assistant secretary to Minister George Mifflin Dallas rejected her application because, he said, as a "person of color" she was not a U.S. citizen and was therefore not entitled to hold a passport.[17]

Remond's first response was to appeal the decision, providing evidence of her national status. She wrote to the ministry and described herself as a person who was not only born in the United States but who was also a taxpaying citizen of Massachusetts. She also sent along a copy of her passport, signed by Secretary of State Cass. Importantly, she said, the document indicated "what is the fact—that I am a citizen of the United States."[18] The ministry, however, did not waver in its position. Countering Remond's claims, the ministry secretary asserted that she had been granted the document because of a clerical error. He argued, "the indispensable qualification for an American passport, that of 'United States citizenship,' does not exist— ... *indeed, it is manifestly an impossibility by law that it should exist.*"[19] According to the ministry, Remond was a free woman of color living under a complex economy of racialized slavery and therefore, because of her color, and despite her freedom, was not a citizen of the United States.

While the Department of State rejected Remond's visa application to curb the scope of her mobility, the negative British press generated by the incident stirred a public shaming of the United States. Remond protested the decision publicly and spoke of the trauma such a rejection had caused. She wrote, "no words can express the mental suffering we are obliged to bear because we happen to have a dark complexion. No language can give one an idea of the spirit of prejudice which exists in the States."[20] In response to her plea, the case became a momentary cause célèbre in January 1860. The details of her story—a respectable and free woman of color abroad and alone, denied recognition by her own government—encouraged British observers to publicly criticize the limitations of American democracy. British newspapers used the incident to chide the "miserably hollow" quality of liberty in the United States and decry "the boasted freedom and equality of every citizen."[21] A Liverpool newspaper simply acknowledged: "[People of color] were born in America, but America is not their country."[22] Meanwhile, some U.S. newspapers followed the story.[23] *The New York Times* tepidly admonished the Department of State, acknowledging that "the national dignity and the national reputation do require some such change in our passport regulations."[24]

At the Expense of Liberty

Even as some elite colored travelers hoped to acquire official U.S. passports, most white Americans who traveled to Europe considered the document nothing short of an attack on their liberty. The processes surrounding the passport system deeply challenged the sense of independence that undergirded notions of white American identity. As literary scholar John Cox asserts, "perhaps the central, even defining, freedom promised to citizens of the United States has been the freedom of movement."[25] By the late 1830s, technological advances in transportation allowed this sense of freedom to expand beyond U.S. borders, at least for middle-class whites, who increasingly sailed on the relatively inexpensive steamships that plied the Atlantic.[26] Despite new possibilities for international travel, however, those who wanted to go abroad had to adapt to the unavoidable system of passports employed by most European countries. The responses reveal how white travelers believed any kind of surveillance of their movement was unreasonable. When abolitionist author Harriet Beecher Stowe went from England to France in June 1853, she gently mocked her fellow Americans by announcing in her journal that "at Boulogne, came the long-feared and abhorred ordeal of passports and police. . . . It was nothing."[27] Although Stowe may have transcended the usual response of her countryfolk to passport inspections, her comment belied the anxiety U.S. whites had over the system. Unaccustomed to having their movement delimited, white travelers imagined the European passport system in dramatic terms. Even if, as one scholar suggests, comparing a foreign destination negatively to home was a "patriotic stratagem" for American travelers, U.S. whites voiced sincere displeasure with the passport system and congratulated their own country for not having one.[28] Even at its most unobtrusive, they grumbled, the passport was a nuisance. One American traveler described the system as "inexpressibly absurd" for the expense and the bother it caused.[29]

No doubt, passport procedures quashed the idea that European travel would be unencumbered. First, a traveler had to apply for the passport at home and then receive ministry endorsements on it while away. Next, he had to endure its constant inspection by foreign police as well as customhouse officials and even innkeepers. At certain destinations, the passport could be confiscated and held at a police station or an inn until departure. Upon leaving a city, the document had to be signed and inspected all over again. Waiting in long lines and paying large fees and gratuities ($2 or $3 for each signature) was part of the process.[30] Even the famed Murray's *Handbook for Travel* admitted that despite all the benefits of traveling in Europe, the passport system was a negative interruption to an otherwise pleasant experience. Yet, Murray discouraged griping and urged the American tourist to approach the problem with "good grace" in order to "spare himself a world of vexation and inconvenience in the end."[31]

For middle-class white travelers abroad, having to present a passport cut to the very heart of deeply held precepts about what it meant to be free and white. By virtue of requesting the document, travelers, unselfconsciously, accused foreign governments of launching a tyrannical assault on their personal freedom. One traveler who went to Rotterdam, Holland, in 1848 admitted that although the system kept the city safe, "the security of Government [was] being purchased at the expense of the liberty of the subject."[32] Another traveler to Naples, Italy, in 1839 complained that "such ceaseless interference of the government with the liberty of the governed tends to break the spirit of enterprise and cramps the mind."[33] Likewise, a visitor to Paris in 1839 wrote that the passport system was "an abridgement of liberty which accomplishes no good purpose." Freedom of mobility, a fundamentally racialized concept in the United States, was so crucial to this traveler's understanding of himself as an American that he bragged that at home "no one had a right to stop them, or ask them whence they had come, or whither they are going."[34]

Racialized Surveillance Documents

The irony, of course, was that white international travelers who denounced passport procedures were recoiling from the kind of treatment that African Americans had grown accustomed to in the United States. At home, police rarely challenged the comings and goings of middle-class white people. Yet, as people of color knew, the vigilante culture that criminalized black mobility made it commonplace for any white person to stop, interrogate, inspect, and detain a person of color in motion. Over time, the laws that dictated race and mobility produced a series of identity documents reserved for people of color. Unlike the U.S. passport, which denoted citizenship, however, these documents explicitly marked people of color in the United States as internal foreigners. In fact, the documents were designed not for identity but for surveillance, and they included slave passes, sailors' passports, and free papers. Each document signaled a person of color's proximity to slavery, no matter their temporal or psychological distance from the institution. Ultimately, the surveillance documents impeded black mobility.

The first of this style of documentation was the slave pass, a "certificate" that allowed for the close monitoring of enslaved people's movement, especially pervasive, although not exclusively so, in the antebellum South. The practice required that a slaveholder, a mistress, or another reputable white person sign the ticket, and that an enslaved person carry the document in order for her to move anywhere beyond the plantation or her proscribed workplace. Colonial legislators first legalized these documents in 1680 Virginia as part of an act to prevent slave insurrections. Similar laws passed in South Carolina in 1696, North Carolina in 1712, and Maryland in 1715. During the postrevolutionary period, even more such laws emerged in U.S. state constitutions.[35] These documents were so ubiquitous in the South that Carrie Davis, a former slave from Alabama, proclaimed "us couldn't leave de plantation widout a pass."[36] This sentiment was repeated again and again in the 1930s WPA interviews of former slaves. Another former slave from Georgia, Rias Body, noted that to go about without the document risked real violence. He said, "if the 'patarolers' caught a 'Nigger' without a pass, they whipped him and sent him home."[37]

Southern lawmakers did not reserve surveillance documents only for plantation workers. During the antebellum period, black sailors—both enslaved and free—found their movements under increasing scrutiny, a fact that eventually resulted in the issuance of black sailors' passports. Indeed, black seamen were an integral part of southern life and, in the name of their valued labor, were given considerable latitude to move freely, earn money, and avoid supervision.[38] They were such a common sight throughout the South that Harriet Jacobs donned the clothes of a sailor to facilitate her escape in 1835, and likewise Frederick Douglass made his 1838 escape from Baltimore disguised as a sailor.[39] Given their relative autonomy, whites feared black sailors. They could traverse the Atlantic, disseminate information, and establish economic stability, and therefore their presence was dangerous.[40]

The autonomy of black seafarers caused practical problems of surveillance that first resulted in the passage of a series of antimobility laws called the Negro Seamen Acts and ultimately led to legislation that required black sailors to carry a passport-like document. The antebellum assault against black sailors began in 1822, after whites in Charleston, South Carolina, thwarted a planned insurrection by a black religious leader named Denmark Vesey, and investigators determined that black sailors were Vesey's accomplices. Believing black sailors to be bad influences on local blacks, in the immediate aftermath of the failed revolt, South Carolina lawmakers sought to hermetically seal any further contact between local free people and black sailors. In an effort to do so, they passed the Negro Seamen Acts.[41] They made it a sea captain's responsibility to either quarantine black seamen on the boat while in port or pay to have the black sailor remanded to the local jail. Failure to comply resulted in large fines for the shipmaster—more than the price of a slave—and the auction block for the black sailor.[42] When, in 1829, African American militant and northerner David Walker used sailors to disseminate his antislavery *Appeal* throughout the South, southern lawmakers passed even more laws against black sailors. This was especially true when officials discovered the document in Savannah, Georgia. Although it was a white steward, not a black one, who distributed sixty copies of the abolitionist manifesto, legislators nevertheless quickly outlawed antislavery materials and also quarantined all ships that carried black sailors.[43] Demonstrating how southern lawmakers increasingly indicted black seamen for slave resistance, after the 1831 Virginia slave revolt, known popularly as Nat Turner's rebellion, where enslaved people murdered sixty white people in Southampton, Virginia, even more antisailor legislation passed throughout the South.[44]

As obsessed as southern lawmakers were with curtailing the movement of black sailors, however, the practice proved arduous. As historian Edlie Wong shows, it's likely that, under the Negro Seamen Acts, thousands of black sailors were arrested annually.[45] In fact, by the 1850s, southern officials arrested so many black sailors on the basis of this legislation that South Carolina and Louisiana each began requiring black seamen to carry locally issued passports when they arrived in port rather than face incarceration.[46] The decision to substitute this form of surveillance document for the arrest of black sailors was a practical move. Southern port jails often teemed with sailors who were victims of the Negro Seamen Acts. In light of this fact, the initial impetus for the law—to separate sailors from enslaved and local free people of color—was obscured when all three converged in these very jails.[47]

In addition to slave passes and sailors' passports, a third style of antiblack surveillance document was free papers. Although these documents ostensibly offered protection for free black laborers, in reality, they helped various states monitor their free black populations and to gain financially from what amounted to a free person's tax. In the South, free papers were usually issued by a county or city office and indeed verified that the carrier was not a slave. But, at the same time, state laws also required free people to officially register themselves and/or their papers. The states of Virginia, Georgia, Mississippi, and Arkansas all required free blacks to register.[48] In 1835, Missouri lawmakers passed an "Act Concerning Freed Negroes and Mulattoes" that required free people to carry licenses. When in 1843 Missouri legislators started to suspect that the system encouraged resourceful slaves to liberate themselves by using false papers, the General Assembly changed the law so that free people only carried the papers while traveling. Meanwhile, the same law dictated that the free papers of nontravelers be kept on file in the county court.[49] Frederick Douglass astutely surmised that southern governments perpetuated a type of financial fraud against African Americans through the free-papers scheme. He argued that, in Maryland, the system provided income to the state because free people had to renew the documents often and pay a fee to do so.[50] As with slave passes and sailors' passports, whites could demand to see these papers at any time.

Free papers were not only a system of regulation prevalent in the South. White people in the North also insisted on seeing the surveillance documents of people of color. First, in the spirit of anti-immigration legislation, state lawmakers from Massachusetts to California debated and sometimes passed laws that required people of color to carry free papers simply to cross the state's borders.[51] After the passage of the Fugitive Slave Law in 1850, free papers became crucial documentation for people of color in the North, who were presumed fugitive until proven otherwise.[52] The law was stacked against free people and relied on racial profiling to make the case. It required every American citizen to turn in a suspected runaway to a federal commissioner. Accused people could not testify on their own behalf, and the law had no statute of limitations. There was no jury and no appeals process. Moreover, the federal government offered economic incentives for commissioners to send suspects into slavery. The commissioner would be paid $10 if he deemed the accused a fugitive and only $5 if he determined the accused free.[53] Soon after the passage of the law, slaveholders and slave catchers peppered the North in search of "fugitives," but of course both self-liberated slaves and free people of color were vulnerable. It was as a result of the Fugitive Slave Law that Ellen and William Craft fled Boston and expatriated to England in December 1850.[54] In the first six years of the law, authorities accused

200 people of color of being fugitives, only 12 of whom secured their freedom. Nearly 20,000 self-liberated people and free blacks fled to Canada from 1850 to 1860 in an effort to escape the repressive legislation.[55] Free papers could only protect a person so far.

In this vein, free papers emerged as the unreliable "passport" for black people who moved from slavery to freedom but also from rural to urban or state to state. The necessity of carrying these surveillance documents enraged many free black northerners, some of whom had never been enslaved and therefore never had the need to possess free papers. In the 1850s, black radical Martin Delany bitterly argued that the need for these papers rendered formerly enslaved people more protected than free people because whereas the liberated slaves brought "their 'papers' with them . . . the Northern freeman knows no records; he despises 'papers.'"[56] In truth, these papers provided only moderate stability to the formerly enslaved. In 1834, kidnappers invaded the home of a free black family from Virginia, destroyed the family's free papers, and then brought the family to the town recorder, claiming they were slaves absconded from North Carolina. Without their free papers, the family had no recourse. They were sold into slavery as a result.[57]

In fact, any protection that free papers provided was decidedly precarious. One of the most dramatic examples of the instability of these papers comes from the story of free New Yorker Solomon Northup, who was kidnapped and enslaved in Louisiana for twelve years. His was a nightmare that began when he joined two white musicians and traveled with them from his home in Saratoga Springs to Washington, D.C., the city where his abduction took place. Northup admitted that the men built his trust by encouraging him to secure free papers before he left New York. These were documents that Northup, as a freeborn man, did not possess, so he went to the customhouse and paid six shillings for them. A few days later, when he awoke in a slave pen in Washington, however, he discovered that, in addition to his liberty, his "money and free papers were also gone."[58]

Although, on the one hand, the surveillance documents that black people carried offered (flimsy) protection from white reproach, on the other, the actual function of these papers, passes, and passports was to mark and identify people of color as foreigners who were outside the normal parameters of American identity. Indeed, these documents served as a constant reminder that freedom of mobility and citizenship were elusive rights. The laws required black people to hold these papers to ensure that their movement was legitimate but also to reinforce their status as a degraded class. The difference between the identification documents issued to U.S. whites and Europeans and the surveillance documents held by African Americans is that possession of a national passport denoted citizenship. The papers for people of color announced the very opposite, that black people were indeed *not* citizens of the United States. In fact, according to this system, people of color exercising independent mobility were imagined as fugitives and their movement as suspect.

His African Appearance Is Scarcely Perceptible

By traveling abroad and applying for U.S. passports, colored travelers cast off the mark of internal foreignness and demanded both freedom of mobility and recognition of their national citizenship. Free Philadelphian Robert Purvis was the first colored traveler to plant the seeds of the conversation over the meanings of black national citizenship when he traveled to England in 1834 to celebrate West Indian Emancipation. Purvis was just twenty-three years old when he applied for an official U.S. passport. Before he left for Great Britain, he requested the document, but the U.S. secretary of state under Andrew Jackson denied the application. In lieu of the passport, Purvis received "an informal ticket of leave sort of paper."[59] This was actually a document called a "certificate of protection," a letter requesting that foreign nations give the carrier "lawful aid and protection." It described Purvis not as a citizen but as a "free person of color."[60] Purvis believed that as a form of protection the paper was functionally worthless.[61] In fact, at the time, the Department of State only granted the certificate or "special passport" to people who were foreigners employed by the U.S. government or to U.S. citizens whom officials perceived as disabled.[62] In time, the State Department reserved the certificate only for free people of color, specifically those who were in service to white diplomats going abroad.[63]

Purvis dictated the terms of future debates by asserting his citizenship and therefore his right to acquire an official U.S. passport. He argued that in the past the federal government had issued documents denoting citizenship regardless of the race of the applicant. He cited a 1796 edict that allowed American sailors of all colors to receive "certificates of citizenship" in a move to protect seamen from British impressment.[64] In part, Purvis knew about this document because his own (white) father, Robert Sr., was a sailor who received one as a young man.[65]

The letter also claimed Purvis's birthright, contending that he was "a free born American." Purvis sent his appeal to Secretary of State John McLane through a well-connected white abolitionist, Roberts Vaux. Vaux relayed Purvis's message about citizenship but also added his own observations to the letter. He accentuated Purvis's wealth, education, and fair complexion. Vaux told Secretary McLane, "as to his African descent it is scarcely perceptible in his appearance, his hair is straight & many Southern complexions are as dark, in which not a drop of negro blood imparts the tinge." The issue of color convinced the Department of State that Purvis was worthy of the document, as evidenced by the fact that the federal government issued Purvis passport #3373 on 19 May 1834.[66]

It was not until 1849 that the Department of State openly admitted that color was the most important factor in the decision to issue Robert Purvis an official U.S. passport. At that time, the standing secretary of state, John Clayton, found himself entangled in another debacle over a black passport applicant, a case that will be illuminated in a moment. In attempting to prove that Purvis's acquisition of a passport did not set a precedent for all colored travelers, Clayton explained that although former secretary of state McLane had granted Purvis the official document, it was not "as a colored man."[67] In a move that historian Ariela Gross has provocatively called "the common sense of race," the Department of State determined that together Purvis's social and economic status and his color obscured his African heritage, ostensibly making his blackness null and void.[68] Using a rationale born out of the logics of racial slavery, the Department of State unwittingly proposed that people of color could lighten up, deracinate themselves, and thereby gain American citizenship. In this configuration, assimilation, the very idea most at odds with notions of white supremacy, was possible. As an activist and abolitionist, Purvis interpreted for himself what it meant to possess an official U.S. passport. He saw it as a decisive victory for himself and other people of color. Shortly after the 1857 *Dred Scott* decision, Purvis proudly declared before a large, black audience in Philadelphia that the passport he received in 1834 proved that he and they were citizens of the United States.[69]

Notwithstanding Purvis's win, the Department of State remained reluctant to grant colored travelers the coveted document and was haphazard about awarding it. There was precedent for this. The first African American to receive an official U.S. passport that denoted citizenship was likely Essex White in 1806 who was granted the document by then Secretary of State James Monroe. White only received the passport, however, because he was a slave to John Randolph of Roanoke, a U.S. Congressman.[70] As the century progressed, men of color were more often granted the special document originally offered to Purvis. In 1835, a man named John Browne is believed to be the first to receive a "certificate of protection."[71] Other times, the Department of State did issue the passport to colored travelers. In 1836, the Reverend Peter Williams, a black activist from New York, received an official U.S. passport. Perhaps the traveler's destination played a part in the Department of State's willingness to grant the document. Williams was headed to Liberia via London and therefore was not liable to embarrass the United States in Great Britain or Europe.[72]

Carrying the Badge of Slavery

Purvis settled the matter of his passport quietly between himself, his mediator, and the Department of State. In June 1849, however, two intersecting torrents in U.S. politics thrust the issue of black passport applications onto the national stage. The first was the activism of a colored traveler named Henry Hambleton about whom little is known, other than that he applied for a U.S. passport and was summarily rejected. Hambleton, a black Philadelphian, planned to go to England in the summer of 1849 and requested a passport in the customary way. He asked an attorney to write to the U.S. secretary of state on his behalf. This was a standard procedure because applicants needed a professional—a lawyer, judge, or politician—to vouch for their identity and character. He also sent along his birth certificate with his application letter. Rather than grant the request, however, Secretary of State John Clayton, the same politician who ignored the application of William Wells Brown, responded with a letter of rejection. Clayton said that Hambleton could not get a passport because he was black, claiming that passports were "not granted by this Department to persons of color" and, according to a long-standing precedent, never had been.[73] Instead, Clayton explained that sometimes the State Department awarded black applicants a "special passport"—the same certificate of protection offered to Purvis—but only if they were "in the service of diplomatic agents, &c., of the United States, going abroad."[74] Clayton made explicit what the State Department only hinted at in the case of Purvis. The U.S. government would not permit a free colored traveler to venture abroad of his own volition. At the same time, the Department of State would authorize the travels of a person in bondage or in service to whites. In so doing, the U.S. government implied what activists had long suspected: in the United States, an enslaved or servile person was entitled to a greater breadth of mobility than a person of color who was free.

When Clayton denied Hambleton a passport, the act belied a fundamental tactic of controlling free people's international mobility. All Americans were free to leave the United States without a passport in 1849, but problems arose once a traveler ventured beyond the British Isles, a fact the U.S. government recognized. In fact, lack of documentation proved such a problem for white travelers that in 1852 the Department of State warned that they would be asked to provide "authentic proof of their national character," and therefore it was essential to obtain a passport before leaving the country.[75] Passports were highly recommended for travel outside the United States, and therefore, when the Department of State denied Hambleton a passport, it knowingly forbade him the privilege of traveling internationally with safety.

Hambleton rightly interpreted the incident as a federal assault on his citizenship. This was different from a white person calling him nigger on the streets of Philadelphia or a conductor forcing him into the Jim Crow car in Boston. As pervasive as individual and even corporate attacks on black mobility were, in this scenario, it was the U.S. government itself that launched the assault. Hambleton thus employed a protest strategy designed to reach as many people as possible, a mainstay among black abolitionism in the North. He brought his rejection letter to a sympathetic editor and requested that he publish it. In turn, the reformist newspaper the *Pennsylvania Freeman* zealously circulated Clayton's rebuff.[76] When Hambleton marched into the local offices of the *Freeman* and offered up Clayton's letter, he waged war against the Department of State. The idea that the U.S. government placed barriers on black mobility by rendering a colored traveler stateless resounded in the subsequent critiques. The editor of the *Pennsylvania Freeman* was outraged that "the colored man is not only insulted and wronged at home . . . but if he would leave this cruel country he must go abroad as an outlaw."[77]

The story was picked up in abolitionist periodicals throughout the North and repeated the idea that the Department of State had criminalized black mobility, but now in a wholly new and international context. Perhaps understanding that black travelers would likely go abroad anyway, an editorial from the reformist paper *The Christian Citizen* called

Clayton's refusal letter "a villainous document" that forced international colored travelers to be "outcasts upon the face of the earth" without the aid or protection of the country of their birth.[78] A contributor to *The North Star* facetiously asked why Clayton singled out Hambleton for rejection. "Had he committed murder? Was he flying from justice? No! . . . his offence . . . he was—oh dreadful!—he was COLORED!!!"[79] The contributor observed that Hambleton's blackness made him ineligible for a passport, for American citizenship, and for a certifiable identity in an international context. As was the case for so many others, Hambleton's blackness coupled with his freedom relegated him to anticitizenship.

Hambleton was not the only man of color who faced off with the Department of State over passports and black citizenship in the summer of 1849. A few weeks after Clayton rejected Hambleton's application, he also refused to acknowledge the application of William Wells Brown. In return, Brown openly entered the brewing public debate over black citizenship. Brown, who was heading to France as a delegate for the Paris Peace Congress, went abroad without the passport in hand. Although his inability to get a passport was frustrating, it was Brown's discovery of the exception for slaves and servants of white diplomats that infuriated him most. He learned of the rule from a chance meeting with another free black man while crossing the Atlantic from Boston to Liverpool. On the Cunard ship *Canada*, Brown met a black servant of a newly appointed diplomat. Assuming that both he and the other man were non-passport-holding brothers-in-arms, Brown attempted to commiserate about their mutual problem of attempting to travel in continental Europe without a U.S. passport. To Brown's surprise, however, his companion did have a valid passport in his possession, signed by Secretary of State James Buchanan.[80]

Brown recognized that his very freedom as well as his status as a free person of color *not* in service to a white person prevented the United States from granting him the document, a point he made in a letter to white abolitionist Wendell Phillips. He protested, "wherever the colored man goes, he must carry with him the badge of slavery."[81] As Brown's voyage abroad indicated, he defied John Clayton's passport rejection by going to England and France without government sanction. When Brown arrived in France, the French made a kindly exception for him as well as all the Paris Peace Congress delegates, permitting them to enter the country without passports. Furthermore, when Brown went to London, he applied for and received an official passport from the U.S. foreign minister on 31 October 1849, denoting citizenship.[82] Brown assumed that Americans "dare not refuse us a passport when we apply for it in old England," but as Sarah Parker Remond's case proved in 1859, applying for a passport or a *visé* on British soil did not secure a person of color the rights of citizenship.[83]

To Maintain Slavery

Political antislavery (as opposed to immediate abolition) was the second current that propelled Hambleton's passport story and black citizenship into the national conversation. By orchestrating the publication of his story, Henry Hambleton forced the Department of State to enter into a conversation about black citizenship that it decidedly did not want to have. Indeed, President Zachary Taylor's secretary of state, John Clayton, who had been in office only since March 1849, could not have anticipated the raucous public response over Hambleton's case. In part, the reaction was precipitated by the controversy swirling in the U.S. Congress around new territories acquired as a result of the Mexican-American War. Congress was still reeling over the "Wilmot Proviso," which proposed eradicating slavery from all new territories on one side of the debate, and southern senator John C. Calhoun's state's rights platform, which buttressed slavery, on the other.[84] In 1849, northern politicians read the passport rejections as a political maneuver intricately tied to the economic interests of the southern slaveholders in Congress. In fact, Americans did not know what to expect when Taylor, a southern Whig, was inaugurated on 5 March 1849. They hoped the president would heal the nation and restore unity.[85] Hambleton's passport rejection offered an opportunity for Taylor's political enemies to accuse him of conspiring with slaveholders. For example, the abolitionist papers crystallized Clayton's actions as kowtowing to the whims of the proslavery cohort in Congress. *The Christian Citizen* sneered that by arbitrarily denying Hambleton a passport, Taylor "was not put in his present position to maintain the Constitution, but to maintain *slavery*."[86]

Given the political stakes, Hambleton's passport story caught fire.[87] The Free Soil and northern Democratic rivals of President Taylor uncharacteristically and vocally agreed with abolitionists that Clayton was motivated by proslavery leanings, but not because they valued black people or their rights. Rather, they argued that by suggesting that only servants and enslaved people could acquire a travel document from the Department of State, Clayton took a nuanced proslavery position that capitulated to southern interests in Congress. It was a political issue, not a moral one. A Wisconsin editor wrote, "Poor Clayton!" He has decided "that citizens of the Free States, if dark-skinned, have no rights, and can claim no protection unless they go abroad as slaves."[88] A New York editor agreed and argued that "the only objection" to black citizenship "will probably come from the slave holding portions of the Union."[89] Moreover, critics believed Clayton's reliance on the "established rule" proved that he and President Taylor were both proslavery. "Yes, the distinction of denying FREE CITIZENS of the United States the common right of a passport has been reserved for the administration of Zachary Taylor."[90] In response to the white northern outrage, one abolitionist periodical was quick to point out that it was laughable to hear the generally anti-black Free Soilers and northern Democrats so vehemently defend the equal rights of African Americans.[91]

At the same time, the Whig papers defended Clayton. Most steered the conversation away from citizenship and toward procedure. Yet, even more revealingly, some buttressed Clayton's decision to reject black citizenship and prevent black mobility. In one extreme case, a Massachusetts editor referred to Clayton detractors as "fanatical people" and indicted Hambleton for applying for the passport at all. The editor made it explicit that when people of color "imagine themselves men, and even citizens," the government is right to keep them in their place. He also focused particular criticism on the problem of black international travel. He asked, "What right has this man Hambleton to be travelling beyond the borders of the only country on the face of the earth where he can enjoy true liberty and equal privileges?" And in an attack on Hambleton's patriotism, the editor wondered if the United States was not good enough for Hambleton to stay within it. Then, getting to the heart of white fears over black international travelers, the editor asked, "Does [Hambleton] imagine we will consent to be disgraced in the eyes of all Europe and the greater part of Asia by having him exhibited as an American *citizen*?"[92] The disgrace, of course, was the possibility that Hambleton or any colored traveler, by virtue of their freedom and mobility, would expose as a sham the common excuses for slavery in the United States.

The Time Has Gone by for Colored People to Talk about Patriotism

Hambleton's protest, coupled with the brief but overwhelming response of white northerners, placed official U.S. passports squarely into black activist conversations about citizenship. Free people of color had long debated the question of their citizenship in the United States, including whether they could remain in the country to achieve it.[93] Despite the passage of the Fugitive Slave Law, and its attack on black freedoms, even in the mid-1850s, black activists still fought vehemently for suffrage and believed that the United States was their rightful home. Activists asserted their patriotism to make this point. In this light, in 1855, black Bostonian William Cooper Nell published a vast work titled *Colored Patriots of the American Revolution*, a nearly 400-page volume documenting the loyalty of enslaved and free people during and after the Revolutionary War. Implicit throughout the book was the subject of citizenship. In part, Nell made his case by documenting the passport acquisitions of "several distinguished colored Americans"—Robert Purvis, Peter Williams, William Wells Brown, and, most recently, in 1854, John Remond, father of abolitionists Charles and Sarah Remond.[94] Passport acquisitions proved such a vital measure of black national belonging and political status that even though there were only four known cases of black people who got one, Nell argued that having the document symbolized an individual's citizenship and, even more importantly, represented the same for all people of color as well.

While black intellectuals and scholars devised ways of reifying their citizenship, the Department of State was focusing its energy on undermining it. In an 1856 manual created for consular clerks—the first one to address passport procedures, U.S. citizenship emerged as the primary requisite for getting the document. In fact, citizenship proved of such paramount importance that consular agents faced penalties and jail time if they issued the document to noncitizens.[95] In turn, the Department of State finally linked the subject of color to the problem of citizenship. Rather than have its clerks face arrest, the office announced conclusively that people of color could not have the document because, as black people, they could not be citizens of the United States. This was a crucial transition because the federal government had not explicitly connected race and citizenship before.

Highlighting how the antiblack political climate of the late 1850s impacted people of color, the Department of State no longer minced words on the subject of black citizenship as it had when Taylor was president and Clayton secretary of state. This shift became apparent when, in the late fall of 1856, a large group of black performers went to Germany and hoped to get a passport to facilitate their travels. The troupe of eleven minstrel actors requested the documents from Secretary of State William L. Marcy. In response, the assistant secretary, J. A. Thomas, rejected the application. Thomas wrote on 4 November that none of the performers had provided "satisfactory evidence" that they were citizens. He coyly stated that the applicants were "represented in your letters as 'colored,' and described in the affidavits as 'black' from which statement it may be fairly inferred that they are negroes." As such, Thomas wrote, "there can be no doubt that they are not citizens of the United States."[96]

Foreshadowing the same arguments made by Roger Taney in his majority opinion for *Dred Scott* four months later, Assistant Secretary Thomas spent five paragraphs delineating why free people of color were not citizens. Like Taney, he relied on contemporary legal scholarship. He referred to the antiblack debates waged in Congress in 1821, citing U.S. Attorney General William Wirt's argument that sought to disqualify black men from commanding sea vessels because only citizens could do so. Next, Thomas related the 1833 case of Prudence Crandall, the white teacher who had attempted to teach black female students in her Connecticut school but was denied the right to do so. He also cited the precedent of *Tennessee v. Claiborne*, the case that prohibited free people of color from living in Tennessee.[97]

Even as Thomas launched into a thorough and well-informed diatribe against black citizenship, he exposed an underlying motivation to refuse the document: the need to control black mobility abroad. Making a contention particularly redolent of Taney, he asserted that according to the "construction of the constitution," free people "cannot be regarded, when beyond the jurisdiction of this government, as entitled to the full rights of citizens."[98] Fundamental to this argument was geography and place. At stake was the U.S. government's ability to regulate independent movement when people of color were abroad. When lack of power and proximity made it impossible for the federal government to control the movement of people of color, the Department of State opted to disavow black people who chose to travel outside the United States.

Black activists did not let the episode pass without comment and saw the incident as an assault on their rights. They were angry that Thomas disregarded the precedent of Purvis, Williams, Brown, and Remond. William Cooper Nell seethed that "American pro-slavery and colorphobia care nothing for precedent or rights; it substitutes caprice for the one, and might for the other."[99] Even more infuriating, although the secretary of state was not willing to offer the travelers a document endorsing their citizenship, he would offer a "certificate," but only if the secretary was "satisfied of the truth of the facts"; that is, that the travelers were actually born in the United States as they claimed. Still more insulting, Thomas demanded to know whether the travelers had a "legal and proper purpose" for being abroad. In so saying, the Department of State not only disputed black citizenship but also scrutinized the intentions of people of color leaving the country. No doubt, these antiblack regulations were designed to, and indeed did, foreclose on black mobility. However, Thomas did eventually permit the minstrel performers to go. Apparently, singing slave dirges and playing up antiblack comedy was a legal and proper reason for the troupe to travel. The secretary of state ultimately granted them the certificates of protection.[100]

It was the 1857 *Dred Scott* case and Taney's majority opinion that resolved once and for all the question of black citizenship, at least until the Civil War. Taney's writings reified the Department of State's racist interpretation of citizenship. And like that office, Taney indicted black allegiance and freedom of mobility. Taney's argument employed frustrating circular logic. He asserted that people of color were not citizens of the United States because they had never been treated as citizens in the United States.[101] As evidence, Taney gave a historical account of black exclusion, including a discussion of the antiblack surveillance documents issued to people of color. He reasoned that if people of color were citizens, they would be entitled to "go where they pleased at every hour of the day or night without molestation." They would be able to move about without surveillance documents.[102] However, this was not the case. Furthermore, Taney cited the recent decision of the Department of State that "refused to grant passports to [black people] as 'citizens of the United States.'"[103] The Department of State's practice of passport rejections helped build the foundation of *Dred Scott*.

The decision in *Dred Scott* caused black radicals, many of whom had long held their patriotism as a political stratagem, to openly disavow their allegiance to the United States. Instead, they heard Taney's fateful words—"no rights a white man is bound to respect"—as inspiration for radicalism.[104] One month after the decision, Robert Purvis, now an elder statesman, exclaimed that "no allegiance is due from any man to a Government founded and administered in iniquity."[105] Charles Lenox Remond, now also a veteran activist, was similarly furious that the federal government deigned to discredit his citizenship. He fumed that, "We owe no allegiance to a country which grinds us under its iron hoof and treats us like dogs. The time has gone by for colored people to talk of patriotism."[106] Two years later, abolitionist physician John Swett Rock provided context for Remond's message. He claimed that people of color *were* patriotic, that there were no black traitors, but the U.S. government had pushed people of color to the brink. "There must be an end to this persecution," and black people must take up arms to make that happen.[107] The federal government created among black intellectuals the very climate of disloyalty that it feared and attempted to control.

The Civil War forced the United States to change its stringent policies regarding the granting of passports to colored travelers, although the official question of black citizenship remained open until 1868 and the ratification of the Fourteenth Amendment. In 1861, Secretary of State William Seward required all Americans to carry their passport when leaving or entering the United States or when crossing Union lines.[108] The next year, the U.S. attorney general proclaimed that U.S. citizenship was "not dependent nor coexistent" with color, race, or with "the degradation of a people."[109] In other words, a personal history of slavery would not prevent a traveler from getting a passport. Months before Abraham Lincoln issued his Emancipation Proclamation in 1862, neither whiteness *nor* servitude was required for people of color to acquire the document.

Black activists considered the Department of State's shift in policy significant because the document confirmed what they already believed to be true: they were citizens of the country of their birth. In early 1862, people of color rejoiced when John Sella Martin, the antislavery minister and former slave, received a U.S. passport from the U.S. ambassador in London. The document described Martin as a "citizen of the United States," a claim the Department of State had refused to make just the year before, when Martin left for England.[110] By 1864, the "whites-only" policy regarding passports had come to an official close. *The Liberator* proudly published a letter from the passport clerk to an attorney from

New York who, before making an application for a passport on behalf of a person of color, wrote to the Department of State to discover if black people could be granted the document. In response to the inquiry, the passport clerk replied that as far as passports were concerned, "there is no distinction made in regard to color."[111]

In antebellum America, colored travelers forced the issue of the U.S. passport to make it of utmost importance, thus locating yet another site for waging war against white supremacy and containment. As they became free and gained wealth, they made the U.S. government painfully aware that their movement would not be restricted, at least not without a fight. The international travel of free people of color threatened the fabric of American identity that understood freedom of mobility as fundamentally raced. The vast apparatus of surveillance documents that monitored and controlled the movement of free and enslaved people alike made this plain. As black abolitionists exposed the inner workings of the plantation regime on foreign shores, it became impossible to regulate their rebelliousness while they were outside the boundaries of the United States. The Department of State determined that the best course of action was to prevent free people from international travel, at first because they were black and ultimately because they were not citizens. Black activists used these pronouncements to corner the U.S. government, making the State Department acknowledge its raced understandings of democracy. In so doing, colored travelers made debates over the passport a significant forum in which to fight for equal rights and citizenship before the Civil War.

CHAPTER FIVE

The Atlantic Voyage and Black Radicalism

In June 1845, Frederick Douglass published his memoir called *Narrative of the Life of Frederick Douglass: An American Slave*, a reflection on his life in slavery and his self-liberation.[1] The revelations in the book, including his fearless choice to expose the identities of violent enslavers, made Douglass a target for slave catchers. To avoid recapture, he sought refuge in the British Isles. On 16 August 1845, Douglass sailed from Boston to Liverpool on the Cunard steamship *Cambria*.[2] Although Cunard was a British-owned shipping line, the ticketing agent refused to sell Douglass any accommodations except in steerage, an open room with bunks in the bottom of the boat. Douglass agreed to the arrangement, including spending the fourteen-day journey isolated in the hull of the ship. But once the ship set sail, Douglass became something of a curiosity. He found that other passengers invited him to join them in the grand saloon and on the decks, hoping to learn more about the famous fugitive slave. Douglass became so popular, in fact, that on the last night of the voyage, the British captain, Charles Judkins, asked Douglass to give an antislavery lecture on the quarterdeck. When Douglass started to speak, however, proslavery Americans from both the North and the South spat out insults and threatened to throw the twenty-seven-year-old abolitionist overboard. After a heated exchange, and before Douglass even began in earnest, he returned to his room. Reflecting on the incident, Douglass disgustedly proclaimed, "They actually got up a MOB—a real American, republican, democratic, Christian mob,—and that, too, on the deck of a British steamer."[3]

Like other colored travelers who went abroad for a variety of reasons—whether to escape persecution, avoid recapture, lecture on slavery, preach about prejudice, attend university, or even for leisure—Douglass discovered that the experience of crossing the ocean on a steamship replicated the segregationist policies of the United States. White Americans on the *Cambria* behaved with much the same brutality as that of white railroad conductors and passengers on the northern railroads. Traveling as an elite and free person of color toward the promise of freedom in England, however, shifted the focus of Douglass's radicalism. The desire to be in a foreign land, to be free of slavery and U.S. racial barriers, outweighed the impulse to desegregate the ship. This fact was remarkable. Just four years earlier, Douglass had yanked the seats off the floor of a Massachusetts railroad car rather than allow a conductor to cast him off into lesser accommodations. Yet, when the ticketing agent forced Douglass to travel in steerage, he accepted his fate. When the white proslavery folks threatened him with violence, Douglass demurred. Transatlantic steamships that plied the Atlantic were alternative sites of racial contestation.

At the same time, the ships were new geographic locations that demanded responses to segregation different from those of public transportation back home. This was true in part because, for colored travelers in the mid-nineteenth century, transatlantic steamships were conduits to an unparalleled sense of freedom. Black activists endured segregation on the ship so they could eventually tour, speak, and socialize in the British Isles and in continental Europe. Getting abroad was a type of activist coming of age that enabled the most elite colored travelers to announce themselves to foreign publics as free, political, mobile, cultural, intellectual, and formidable. The very act of traveling abroad demonstrated to the world that free people of color were the equals of their white American counterparts. Freeborn people and former slaves defied the limits set on their mobility, eschewed passport regulations, and, like U.S. whites, came and went as they pleased.

Taking the trip was important for other reasons too. It allowed colored travelers to show each other, and especially the people of color back home, what true liberty looked like in an alternate space. At the same time, transatlantic steamships were unusual because they were psychologically and physically dangerous vessels in their own right. First and foremost, the symbolism of traveling on a ship as an unchained person of African descent in the opposite direction of the dreaded Middle Passage could not have been lost on radical black intellectuals, who were familiar with its infamous horrors.[4] Abolitionists had long made the connection between slave ships, torture, and black containment.[5] They certainly knew of the case of the slave ship *Amistad*, in which captured Africans who had suffered the Middle Passage overtook the ship before it ran aground. Colored travelers were also aware that, unlike on a stagecoach or a railroad, getting tossed off during a voyage was hardly an option. Meanwhile, as all transatlantic passengers faced extended confinement, tumultuous weather conditions, and the attendant seasickness, Douglass's story makes it plain that the threat of racial violence could, in the blink of an eye, lead to a watery death. All of these factors made the ship a unique and dangerous social space.

Recognizing the stakes of transatlantic travel, activists designated the voyage itself a significant and liminal stage between U.S. racism and what they perceived to be British egalitarianism. In their speeches, letters, and memoirs, they described the behavior of other white passengers not simply as criminal but rather as a visible extension of American racial ideologies and violence. Whether they confronted snubs, exclusion, or threats on a U.S.-owned ship or a British one, colored travelers vocally indicted white Americans for antiblack behavior on board. Colored travelers argued that the greater their geographic distance from the United States, the less likely they were to face racial exclusion. Despite the inevitability of segregation, they never refused to make the journey. Nor did they threaten to boycott transatlantic steamship lines. Instead, because the ultimate goal was to get abroad and to advocate for themselves and enslaved people in the United States, they endured, but seldom in silence. Colored travelers publicized the details of their experiences, highlighting how the Atlantic voyage and the rough treatment they faced symbolized the profundity and the power of American racism but also the hope that awaited them in a foreign land.

Too Pure an Air for Slaves to Breathe

Among colored travelers, England held a long-standing reputation as a place that offered freedom to enslaved African Americans. Although slavery existed throughout the British West Indian colonies until 1834, because of the famous case of an enslaved man named James Somerset, people of color in the antebellum United States wholeheartedly believed the adage, "That England was too pure an Air for Slaves to breathe in."[6] Somerset, the slave of a customs officer in colonial Virginia, accompanied the official to England in 1771. Once abroad, Somerset escaped his bonds in London and, with the support of famous British abolitionist Granville Sharp, demanded his freedom in the British courts. A judge granted Somerset his freedom in 1772.[7] The decision inspired subsequent people of color to seek liberty in England. One historian speculates that when the enslaved poet Phillis Wheatley traveled to England from Boston in 1773, she used the Somerset case as leverage to secure her own freedom.[8]

What is most important here is not that the Somerset case made England a bastion of freedom; it did not. But, in the nineteenth century, black intellectuals remembered it that way. In 1827, the black co-editors of *Freedom's Journal* reflected that "this trial established the following axiom, that, as soon as any slave sets his foot on English ground, he becomes free. A sentence to be engraved for ever on our hearts."[9] The British reputation was further bolstered by the Crown's refusal to extradite to the United States fugitive slaves who escaped to Canada or England after the passage of the first U.S. Fugitive Slave Law in 1793.[10] British antislavery politics of the early nineteenth century continued to strengthen England's reputation after the British Parliament passed the Slavery Abolition Act on 29 August 1833.[11] The act formally freed British slaves in the West Indies on 1 August 1834, a date that came to symbolize emancipation for black people in the United States.[12] African American abolitionists celebrated the act even before its passage. The freeborn Reverend Nathaniel Paul, who sailed from New York to Liverpool in December 1831, wrote expectantly from Bristol just months before the law passed that British slavery's "death warrant is sealed."[13] British abolitionism ramped up after West Indian emancipation, inspiring black abolitionists to travel to the British Isles. As historian R. J. M. Blackett argues, colored travelers hoped to use the trip to publicly shame the United States as morally corrupt and to expose internationally the horror of enslavement and prejudice.[14]

Despite the conviction of colored travelers, the end of West Indian slavery did not always translate into racial egalitarianism in England. Although British abolitionists advocated for black freedom, black people were rarely respected as equals by British reformers but were instead considered protégés at best and charges at worst. For many British abolitionists, the relationship between themselves and former slaves was fundamentally paternalistic.[15] As literary theorist Audrey Fisch argues, during the heyday of black abolitionism in Great Britain from the late 1840s to the 1860s, black activists appeared "in front of the English public as exotic spectacle."[16] Colored travelers were not only on display but, as historian Douglas Lorimer contends, there was an ideological shift during this same period from antislavery sentimentality toward a "new aggressively racist movement" that tired of the growing presence of black abolitionists abroad.[17] Notwithstanding the realities of British racial politics, the British Isles offered colored travelers an imagined space of liberation.

The Racial Alchemy of Transatlantic Travel

Going abroad held profound promise for black abolitionists, but getting there was trying. Transatlantic steamships (and, earlier, the sailing ships called "packets") were no easy mode of transportation for colored travelers. Although the steamers emerged as emblems of technological progress that blended speed and luxury, they also embodied the racial supremacies of modernity. The interior cabins and promenade decks were considered white-only space. Thus, colored travelers confronted the same old segregationist policies, even on British-owned ships plying the Atlantic. The most prolific steamship line—the British and North American Royal Mail Steam Packet Company (later, and more familiarly, the Cunard Steamship Company)—began its run out of Boston in 1840, during the height of antiblack violence on the Massachusetts railroads. Samuel Cunard, who started the line, partnered with members of the northern business elite to ensure its success.[18] His inaugural fleet of four ships—the *Britannia*, the *Columbia*, the *Acadia*, and the *Caledonia*—started delivering the British mail from Liverpool to Halifax bimonthly and eventually weekly (see figure 5.1).[19]

Cunard's ships cornered the market not only because of promised efficiency but also because travel on them was a luxurious experience that was decidedly raced and classed. The ships served chef-prepared meals and fine wines in the grand saloon, a room that was elaborately decorated with inlaid wood paneling, oak beams, and gilded moldings.[20] The boats were wooden, painted a simple black, 207 feet from bow to stern, and 34 feet across from starboard to port. Each Cunard ship had three dynamic sails and two paddles that churned the ocean, each positioned on the quarterdeck. Steam engines powered the paddles from below and expelled the exhaust through a single funnel on the deck that became Cunard's signature, famously painted red with one black stripe around the top.[21] The decks of a Cunard ship were a sailor's domain. But the underbelly of the ship was akin to the shop floor of a factory, with engines that needed constant feedings of coal by stokers who worked around the clock. Four separate boilers supplied the steam that propelled the paddles.[22] A transatlantic steamer, particularly one in Cunard's fleet, was a marvel of modern technology. These ships were able to do what no mode of transportation had done before: they shrank the Atlantic Ocean. Suddenly, England was just fourteen days away, often even less. Partaking of such luxury was reserved for middle-class whites and the elite.

THE "BRITANNIA" STEAM-SHIP LEAVING BOSTON, U.S.—(SEE PRECEDING PAGE.)

FIGURE 5.1 This sketch of the Cunard steamship *Britannia* as it set sail from Boston to Liverpool in 1847 illustrates the spectacle that Cunard ships made as they launched. Courtesy, Williams College.

Activists of color, strategically committed to defining racism as a U.S. pathology, at first refused to acknowledge that British-owned ships reified the segregationist policies of the antebellum North. Instead, they insisted such treatment was the purview of American ship owners. When, in 1840, a captain forced Charles Lenox Remond to sail on a packet ship for twenty-one days from New York to London on an outer deck, Remond attributed his plight to the American owner and southern captain of the packet ship.[23] Likewise, Remond reasoned that his better treatment on the return trip was dependent on the British ownership of his return vessel. Remond left Liverpool on 4 December 1841 on Cunard's *Columbia*, a ship under the command of Captain Judkins, the same British captain who was destined to invite Frederick Douglass to give an abolitionist lecture in 1845.[24] Remond could not afford a first-class berth but instead purchased a steerage fare. Nevertheless, once the ship plied the Atlantic, the second mate upgraded him from steerage to a berth in a second-class cabin. Remond gushed that "from that hour until my stepping on shore at Boston, every politeness was shown me by the officers, and every kindness and attention by the stewards."[25] To him, it was a testament to British liberalism.

Notwithstanding Remond's claims, in the 1840s and 1850s, colored travelers discovered that British ownership of a vessel did not necessitate equal treatment on board. Instead, the experience often mirrored travel in the United States. On the way home from his 1843 visit to the first Peace Congress in London, the Reverend J. W. C. Pennington sailed on the British steamship *The Great Western*—which in 1837 had been the first passenger steamship to cross the Atlantic—and was harassed by an American who "showed the strength of his prejudices" by demanding that Pennington not share the common table with white passengers.[26] Similarly, in 1844, on a voyage from Boston to Liverpool on the Cunard ship *Acadia*, a ticketing agent refused passage to a Haitian man. The captain, once again Charles Judkins, later accommodated the man on the boat, but only under the stipulation that he pay $50 more than a first-class fare, dine separately from other passengers, and not enter the saloon.[27] In this instance, the Cunard ticketing agent absolved the British ship owner of the responsibility of segregation. Instead, he said he had no personal problem with people of color, but "the reception of colored passengers . . . would not be permitted by the southern gentlemen."[28]

No doubt because of economic self-interest, British ship owners honored white American tastes. As such, the preferences of U.S. whites superseded any moral compunction ship owners may have had toward colored travelers on board. Black abolitionist Samuel Ringgold Ward was sailing on the Cunard steamer *Europa* in 1853 from Boston to Liverpool when a ship representative, Cunard's son Edward, prevented him from entering the first-class cabin. As in other cases of exclusion, Edward Cunard alleged that he had no personal problem with Ward's color but was obliged to attend to the "comfort of his passengers." Ward likened Edward's economic argument to that of northerners who benefited financially from slavery. He bemoaned, "here is an Englishman perverted . . . —like the Yankee, making the dollar come before right, law, or anything. He does not 'share' Yankee feeling—he only accommodates, panders to it, that is all, his passengers must be made comfortable, that is, if they be white."[29] Although such treatment angered colored travelers, they nevertheless identified U.S. whites as the true culprits. They argued, as did Frederick Douglass after his incident on the *Cambria* in 1845, that "American prejudice against color had triumphed . . . and erected a color test as a condition for crossing the sea in the cabin of a British vessel."[30]

Although economic interest drove ship owners such as Cunard to segregate colored travelers, there were other factors that rendered the transatlantic voyage a bastion of white supremacy. First and foremost, maintaining order on board was an important element of ocean travel. The fear was that the presence of black passengers threatened to introduce political and social controversy within the intimate spaces of the ship. This was a fact that Cunard officials openly acknowledged. In 1844, when the ticketing agent on the *Acadia* tried to keep the young Haitian gentleman from first-class passage, the agent claimed that southern passengers would recoil, but he also worried that "the reception of colored passengers would create great loss and confusion."[31] Unlike Josiah Quincy Jr., who rationalized his invention of the Jim Crow car to avoid similarly tense interactions, at sea, the threat of violent exchange posed serious and real dangers to all on board. Frederick Douglass's experience on the *Cambria* proves this.

Meanwhile, racial interaction and conflict was hardly the only source of social disorder on the ships. Cunard steamers had a multinational clientele.[32] After William Lloyd Garrison traveled abroad in 1846, he remarked, "we are all 'foreigners' on board—that is, we hail from the various quarters of the globe."[33] Of his 1845 voyage, Douglass noted that "our passengers were made up of nearly all sorts of people, from different countries, of the most opposite modes of thinking on all subjects."[34] With so many different views represented, heated debates were a natural occurrence. The last thing Cunard wanted was for his passengers to debate the already volatile subjects of slavery and abolition. When Edward Cunard explained his decision to segregate Samuel Ringgold Ward from the *Europa*, for instance, he suggested that for the passengers' sakes, the ship must not be "an arena for public discussion."[35] Cunard tried to create a regimen on his steamers to avoid the natural conflict that could arise between travelers of varying points of view by establishing set meal times, hours for lights out, and Anglican services on Sundays.[36]

Despite Cunard's best efforts to create a controlled social environment aboard his steamships however, order and disorder collided during the voyage from departure to return. For starters, the incredibly tight spaces of the ship upended order. Expecting an ample stateroom on the *Britannia* in 1842, British author Charles Dickens was astounded to find in its stead an "utterly impracticable, thoroughly hopeless and

FIGURE 5.2
A rendering
of Charles Dickens's
stateroom on the
Britannia in 1842
illustrates how
cramped the
luxurious
accommodations
could be. From *The
Bookman, An
Illustrated Magazine
of Literature and
Life*, 34 (February
1912), 577. Smith
College Libraries.

profoundly preposterous box" (see figure 5.2).[37] The "very small dimensions" of the staterooms disappointed another British traveler.[38] The sleeping cabins were modest rooms, with scant space to store a trunk, two bunk-bedded berths packed claustrophobically on top of each other, and a commode with a tight-fitting lid as a toilet.[39] Dickens was similarly shocked by the not-so-grandness of the grand saloon and described it as "a long narrow apartment like a gigantic hearse with windows in the sides."[40] In fact, the saloon consisted of two large tables for meals and entertainment, surrounded by sofas on one side and benches on the other. On board, there were also ladies' cabins, a smoking room for gentlemen, the captain's quarters, crew quarters, second-class cabins, a kitchen, a storage room, and other deckhouses.

As with the tight spaces of vehicles of transportation within the United States, ship captains and white passengers articulated their fears of sharing close quarters with colored travelers in sexualized terms. One of Frederick Douglass's later detractors picked up on the confinement of space when he editorialized about Douglass's segregation aboard the *Cambria*. The writer argued that Douglass's only complaint was that white Americans "refused to live cheek by jowl with their nigger brethren."[41]

These remarks reveal not only the author's obvious racism but the very intimacy, "cheek by jowl," of the transatlantic voyage and the danger this closeness posed to social order.

The length of the journey, from nine to fourteen days, resulted in bored passengers and thus further complicated social interactions. One British traveler in 1850 remarked that "the genius of Idleness presided over us all."[42] Another traveler observed that his 1845 voyage did "not afford much variety of incident . . . the first week was intensely dull."[43] Moreover, spending so much time in tight quarters with strangers was trying. To beat the monotony, some travelers drank, caroused, and gambled—playing shuffleboard or cards, or betting on the exact hour of the arrival of the ship.[44]

A great number of bodies came together in the tight spaces, too, adding to the forced intimacy of the close interior spaces. On Cunard's early vessels, in addition to the 100 first-class passengers, as many as 100 men labored at sea, including a highly proficient captain, his officers, and traditional sailors; the engine crew, who maintained the machinery below, including stokers who skillfully and continuously fueled the fire, trimmers who ushered the coal from storage, and of course engineers to monitor pumps and read valves; and the service crew to provide a luxury experience for the passengers, including gourmet and pastry chefs, cooks, stewards, a stewardess, waiters, and even a physician.[45] The cramped feeling was compounded by the filth, noise, and fierce odors. To feed its passengers well, the boat set sail with live animals that were kept in small houses near the ship's funnel. The funnel radiated heat but also emitted noxious smoke and fumes from the engines.[46] Despite the smell, passengers flocked to the smokestack. Harriet Beecher Stowe, who traveled on a Cunard steamship to Europe in 1853 in the glow of the success of *Uncle Tom's Cabin*, remembered the smokestack fondly. Stowe wrote that "our favourite resort is by the old red smoke-pipe of the steamer . . . in fact, the old smoke-pipe is the domestic hearth of the ship; there, with the double convenience of warmth and fresh air."[47] In addition to the odors of the smokestack, ships reeked of human vomit, evidence of seasickness, which seeped out into all areas of the ship. Stowe admitted that "ship life is not at all fragrant; there is a most mournful combination of grease, steam, onions, and dinners in general, either past, present, or to come upon you."[48]

Sometimes, the inevitability of seasickness disrupted gender dynamics on the ship. For one, the illness was gender neutral, a fact that amused some female passengers, who relished the fact that men got it. According to Stowe, there was an "inescapable-ness of the sea sicknesses" and "even those pompous men who try to say it's in the imagination get it."[49] And she was right. Men did get sea sickness too. Traveling in 1852, a male passenger complained that a rough sea had caused him a "death-like nausea." The travel experience was not only uncomfortable for him but also disembodying. He wrote that although the ocean inspired creativity and reflection, it was "an uncomfortable place for the *body* to inhabit."[50]

Race and Place on the Atlantic Voyage

In part, it was the unavoidable disorder of the transatlantic voyage that allowed colored travelers to shift their protest strategies. In 1834, black abolitionist Robert Purvis went to London to join British abolitionists in celebrating the emancipation of West Indian slaves.[51] Purvis was fair skinned—the son of a white cotton broker and an African woman—wealthy, and just twenty-three years old. Although he had been encouraged to go abroad by William Lloyd Garrison, the fledgling American Anti-Slavery Society could not fund his voyage, so he paid his own way for a pricey fare on a packet ship.[52]

Like Douglass, who made the trip ten years later, Purvis confronted segregationist practices when he sought to depart Philadelphia for Liverpool. A few weeks before his planned departure, the owners of the Cope shipping company refused to honor Purvis's ticket for a berth. It turned out that the demands of one white passenger, a wealthy Virginian named Bernard M. Carter, trumped Purvis's right to go. Carter had heard a rumor that a man of color (Purvis) was on the passenger list of the Cope ship and had threatened the captain that he would withdraw his business if that man was allowed to travel. Forced to relinquish his ticket, Purvis revised his travel plans, headed to New York City, and then sailed abroad on a different ship, which ultimately arrived in England before the Cope ship did.[53]

Although the situation resembled the exclusion of the Jim Crow car of the North, the unique setting of the ship allowed Purvis to quietly assert his activist respectability in a way unavailable at home. Understanding how he did so requires a close look at his return trip from London to New York, a journey that speaks to the kinds of revisions in black activism that the journey allowed. When Purvis originally arrived in London, he went to the dock where the Cope ship was scheduled to arrive and waited for passengers to disembark. It was then that he spied Bernard Carter in the flesh. After spending four months abroad, Purvis coincidentally returned to the United States on the same ship as Carter, who had never seen or learned Purvis's name back in Philadelphia.[54] The two joined others on the packet ship *Philadelphia* from London to New York City, a journey that likely lasted at least four weeks.[55] Carter assumed that Purvis was white. Purvis, who had always been free and wealthy, played up the possibility by acting like a young, white southern gentleman from South Carolina, the state in which he was born. The close quarters of the ship allowed Purvis to navigate the kinds of upper-class social circles to which he was accustomed without revealing his racial identity. Under the circumstances, Carter and Purvis became very friendly. The men spoke about their mutual love of horses and the South, and Purvis caught the attention of other white travelers as well. As reported by *The Anti-Slavery Record*, Purvis's plan went off without a hitch. He walked "arm and arm" with gentlemen on the decks, was "upbraided by fathers and mothers if he neglected to dance with their daughters," and was toasted by other passengers on the last night of the voyage.[56] After several weeks at sea, Purvis won the hearts and minds of his fellow passengers.

What made Purvis's behavior activist and not simply a story of racial passing was his big reveal, made shortly before the ship docked in Sag Harbor. Purvis's disclosure was made meaningful by the unique setting of the ship. Just hours before the *Philadelphia* arrived in New York, Purvis told a steward he was black and, as directed by Purvis, the steward shared the news with the other passengers on the ship.[57] Carter and others were furious, but a Scottish traveler thought the trick was hilarious.[58] If Purvis had kept quiet about his passing, his choice to do so would have simply been a crafty strategy for crossing the Atlantic without facing racial exclusion, a style of protest in the same vein as the black women who rode on stagecoaches in the 1820s and 1830s. But Purvis made sure that Carter was aware that he had just spent four weeks befriending a man of color, and he used the circumstances of the ship—confinement and intimacy among wealthy and surely racist whites, including, among others, the brother of the governor of South Carolina—to challenge excuses for racism that argued that whites could identify blackness not only by sight but by odor, lack of intelligence, and other telltale signs of racial difference.[59] In the end, Purvis's behavior should be described not as passing but instead as exposing. His was an act of defiance made possible by his fair skin but more importantly by the extended confinement of a long voyage.

The reason that a colored traveler chose a particular protest strategy on transatlantic packet and steamships is not often transparent. The truth is that African Americans did not circulate a lot of firsthand accounts of the Atlantic crossing, in part because so few made the trip between 1820 and 1860. There is, however, a farcical novel, published in 1840, that imagined a prominent presence of people of African descent, both enslaved and free, during the transatlantic voyage. The book is titled *Letter Bag of the Great Western or Life in a Steamer* and was named for an actual British-owned steamship that set sail for the first time in 1837, two years before Cunard's transatlantic shipping line launched.[60] Written by a white Canadian author, Thomas Chandler Haliburton, the novel was unapologetically xenophobic, anti-Semitic, classist, and racist. Frankly, the novel would verge on ridiculous if not for two important details. First, Haliburton, who was a friend of Samuel Cunard, was an actual passenger on *The Great Western* in 1839 at the same time as Cunard himself.[61] Furthermore, Haliburton's most emphatic gripe with the transatlantic steamship crossing was with the overwhelming presence of people of color on board—as stewards, as slaves, and, most provocatively, as free-roaming mulatto women—a topic he references multiple times in eleven of the novel's twenty-eight farcical letters.[62]

In the novel, Haliburton spends most of his time illustrating the slippages between racial and class hierarchies that he claims to witness during the voyage. Certainly, as far as the crew is concerned, scholars agree with Haliburton's assessment that from the colonial era onward, the Atlantic Ocean was a multicultural domain, teeming with male sailors from diverse nationalities and races.[63] African American sailors were a vital part of this sailor culture. Enslaved and free black men undertook servile positions on board ship, functioning as stewards, cooks, servants, and the like. Whereas these were underling positions on the ship, in black communities these jobs elevated men of color to, as historian W. Jeffrey Bolster argues, "every inch a man."[64] Because of the mobility it afforded men of color, life as a sailor epitomized freedom.

Haliburton's description of black workers on board became most scathing when he described the possible impact of interracial intimacy on the ship. This was an indictment that relied on the familiar trope that black bodies had a uniquely horrible odor.[65] Indeed, white commentators excused their vile treatment of people of color on Atlantic steamships by accusing African Americans of being rank. One editor blamed the incident on the *Cambria* on Douglass's purported stench, arguing that only when passengers' senses were altered so that "their noses [could] agreeably imbibe the odour of a negro" should ship captains allow colored travelers to sail as equals.[66] Haliburton similarly made the odor of black bodies a central theme of his fictional letters, although each time he did so, he belied an overall fear of physical intimacy between himself and people of color on the ship. For example, one of the faux letter-writers in the novel was reading past lights out when he was suddenly accosted by "that horrid perfume!" He quickly identified the source of the foul smell. "It is a negro—his shadow is now over me—I feel his very breath—my candle is rudely blown out."[67] Notwithstanding the author's racism, the interchange between the steward and the passenger reveals a homoerotic proximity between the two men, who, in the dark, were not only alone but also close enough to feel each other's breath and smell each other's bodies. The homoerotic overtones of Haliburton's writing here reflected how any interracial social exchange could quickly devolve into a discussion of the threat of interracial sexuality. It also demonstrated how, at least in Haliburton's mind, the unique spatial realities of the transatlantic voyage unwillingly thrust white passengers into forbidden social intimacies.

Thus, Haliburton's writing illuminated the kind of racially liminal space an Atlantic ship could be. This liminality was rooted in physical intimacy, which the author articulated as sexual desire, a fact made even more pronounced by the novel's description of free women of color on board. It is not clear why the women were on the ship to begin with, but Haliburton certainly imagined them not as workers but as colored travelers. According to the novelist, each of these mixed-race women had skin color only shades darker than that of white women. The novel suggests that the women were, perhaps, lovers of southern slaveholders on board. Was this just Haliburton's imagination? Or is it possible that there was at least one fair-skinned black woman on the ship? Whatever the case, Haliburton spends ample time playing with the idea of the sexual allure of the mixed-race women. In a passage from the novel, he described the happenings in the grand saloon after the ship confronted some rough seas. He wrote that after a tremendous gyration of the ocean, the rolling steamer righted itself, and everyone found their "*places* save a [white] lady immovably nailed to the wall by a mulatto girl in an unsuccessful attempt to pass in the narrow gangway."[68] The women are the only two people in first class who do not return to their rightful places following tumultuous seas. At this moment, the ship became a place not only for spatial passing but also for racial passing. But in Haliburton's imagination, the black woman did not successfully pass, even as her presence threatened to obscure the white woman's position in the social hierarchy of the ship. Again, the intimacy of the ship made the presence of free African American women, in particular, both sexually dangerous and very tantalizing to the white men on board.

In Haliburton's faux *Great Western*, white passengers are forced to confront and interact with women of color in ways that would have been entirely avoidable on land. Whether the woman was real or not, the idea of a beautiful black woman traveling on board made a lasting impression on the author. And we certainly know that the transatlantic journey was made by women of color, including Harriet Jacobs, who sailed abroad with her employer in 1845.[69] In extremely rare cases, African American women sailed as independent travelers. Abolitionists, fugitives, and performers such as Ellen Craft, Elizabeth Greenfield, Mary Webb, and Sarah Parker Remond and her sister Caroline Remond Putnam all traveled from the United States to England in the 1840s and 1850s. Each of these women faced varying degrees of segregation on board, and no doubt, their presence in first class disrupted white notions of place.[70]

Full of the Subject of Slavery

When Frederick Douglass agreed to sit in steerage on the *Cambria*, headed for Liverpool, his experience offered a topsy-turvy reality for a radical activist like Douglass, who was more concerned with being just ten days away from realizing the promise of freedom than with integrating a Cunard ship.[71] Although it was evident that Cunard steamships, in particular, mimicked U.S. customs, including segregation, activists did not see the boats as beating from the same heart as the nation they were trying to change. When, in August 1845, Frederick Douglass and his traveling companion, white abolitionist James Buffum, went to Cunard's East Boston Wharf to purchase tickets for Liverpool, each was seasoned and had fought on the front lines against the Jim Crow car.[72] That was why Buffum was outraged when the Cunard ticketing agent denied his request for a first-class cabin for the pair because, he was told, American passengers would not tolerate sharing the ship with Douglass.[73] Douglass, on the other hand, was unfazed. He recalled that "the insult was keenly felt by my white friends, but to me, such insults were so frequent and expected that it was of no great consequence whether I went in the cabin or in the steerage."[74] Douglass was not afraid to go toe to toe in episodes with Massachusetts conductors, but his response to segregation on the *Cambria* was remarkably blasé given his personal history of protest.

Then again, the voyage was just a means to an end. Charles Remond refused to travel in the "Jimmy" or "Jim Crow car" in Massachusetts and found alternative transportation from Salem to Boston, but when faced with the prospect of sleeping outside on the gangway of the packet ship *Columbus* all the way to Liverpool in 1840, he still chose to go.[75] Samuel Ringgold Ward, when Cunard refused him service in the grand saloon, protested in 1853 that "I *submit* [but] . . . I do not *consent*." Yet, Ward still went. Sarah Parker Remond, Charles's abolitionist sister, went abroad to lecture in 1858 and wrote in anticipation of the voyage that "no matter how I go" (meaning whether she took an American or British steamship), "I know the spirit of prejudice will meet me."[76] But Sarah still went. Submitting to the racism of the transatlantic voyage was just a bump in the road to freedom for colored travelers. While on the decks of an Atlantic-bound ship, they found themselves placed squarely between American racism and their perceptions of British egalitarianism. Douglass and others could temporarily relax their activism because they believed that in less than fourteen days they would be lifted out of a world consumed by racial proscriptions and transported to liberty on foreign shores. Of his segregation on the *Cambria*, Douglass said that "what gave [me] the greatest consolation was that every revolution of the ponderous wheels of their noble ship bore [me] farther from the land of those proscriptions which [I] had then escaped."[77]

Were such claims simply a rhetorical tool? Did black abolitionists designate the passage as an in-between stage of racial transition to strengthen their claims of difference between race relations in the United States and elsewhere? Historian Alasdair Pettinger contends that rather than depict racial conflict on board transatlantic steamships as the bleak moments of racism they were, black abolitionists framed their stories of discrimination during the passage "as simply signs of the intermediary character of the transatlantic voyage . . . so that unpleasantness might be seen as merely the residue of what has been left behind (if traveling east) or an anticipation of what is to come (if traveling west)."[78] In contrast, Cunard officials segregated colored travelers in response to the potential of real racial violence and the possibility of deadly consequences.

Douglass's episode on the *Cambria*, and the threats to throw him over-board, suggest as much.[79] But Pettinger's ultimate concern was the question of whether the Cunard Steamship Company was racist or righteous in its dealings with black travelers. In conclusion, he asserts that "it is easy to condemn Cunard captains for not making a more principled stand on the rights of speech and movement of black passengers . . . but it may have been a luxury they could ill afford."[80]

The concern here is less with what Cunard did or did not do than with the response of black radicals. These were folks who had spent years cultivating notions of activist respectability that promulgated a spectrum of protest strategies from outrage to direct confrontation. Yet, Douglass chose not to fight the *Cambria*'s ticketing agent and to submit to lesser accommodations during the voyage. These were the first signs that the docks, decks, and cabins of steamships were unique. The various elements of location and space—distance from the United States, British owner-ship of the vessel, confinement and intimacy during the voyage, and the promised freedom of the destination—made these behavioral shifts possible. The promise of freedom was more valuable to colored travelers than the integration of their current and temporary space.

Even as Douglass submitted to racial exclusion on the *Cambria*, how-ever, race relations on board were about to change. Abolitionist comrades Buffum and the famed Hutchinson Family Singers had circulated Douglass's *Narrative*—his recently published memoir of his life in en-slavement and his daring escape—among the ninety-five passengers.[81] Although Douglass was relegated to steerage, Buffum said he took Doug-lass through the ship "in his heart."[82] Buffum raised the topic of slavery with officers and passengers throughout the voyage, and thus Douglass became an instant celebrity.[83] First-class travelers came down to Doug-lass's "rude forecastle deck" to get a glimpse of him, and soon others, such as the Hutchinsons, invited him to visit them in first class. According to Douglass, within days, against the stated wishes of the land-based ticketing agent, the British captain, thirty-four-year-old Charles Judkins, allowed Douglass to traverse the ship freely.[84]

Douglass utilized his celebrity to his advantage to influence his visi-tors in the unusual space. Although it was likely that Douglass's fellow passengers sought out the young, handsome self-liberated traveler less as an equal than as a novelty, Douglass gave visitors more than what they bargained for when they dropped in on his steerage compartment. By insisting on engaging his guests on the topic of slavery, he turned these encounters into interactive meetings that he controlled. This was a fact made entirely possible by the liminality of the shipboard culture, and Douglass's prolonged physical proximity to white travelers. He saw himself as a messenger and remembered the experience fondly. "From the moment we first lost sight of the American shore, till we landed at Liverpool, our gallant steam-ship was full of the subject of slavery—commencing cool, but growing better every moment as it advanced.... If suppressed in the saloon, it broke out in the steerage; and if it ceased in the steerage, it was renewed in the saloon; and suppressed in both, it broke out with redoubled energy, high upon the saloon deck, in the open, refreshing air."[85] One of Douglass's detractors confirmed the ubiquity of slavery talk when he grumbled that "[Douglass] conversed in a very loud tone every day upon his favorite topic, slavery."[86] Clearly, not all passengers were pleased that Douglass had used the intimacy of the ship to proselytize about the plight of American slaves.

Douglass exploited his shipboard popularity and his ensuing conversations with white passengers to further the abolitionist cause, and, revealingly, other passengers engaged him in this debate. Regarding these interactions, Douglass claimed that "all color distinctions were flung to the wind."[87] Some scholars might read Douglass's response to his mobility on board as abolitionist hyperbole, especially considering the impending violent outburst of some of the passengers. But although it is hard not to read Douglass's optimistic pronouncement without cynicism, it is also important to remember that, for Douglass, being able to publicly debate slavery in an intimate setting with white travelers who were not abolitionists, without the fear of recapture and in an atmosphere that respected his authority, must certainly have felt remarkably egalitarian. Shipboard culture, with passengers' tedium and search for excitement, and its considerable distance from the racial expectations of home, rendered these encounters possible. Douglass wrote to Garrison that antislavery "delight[ed] in the sunshine of free discussion," and he sweetly confessed, "I was happy."[88]

Just as the ship rolled to and fro during the journey, so did the racial tenor of the ship shift once again. Captain Judkins, urged on by his passengers, invited Douglass to give an abolitionist lecture on board (see figure 5.3). Asa Hutchinson, a member of the famed Hutchinson Singers, also on board, verified that Douglass brought the subject of slavery

DECK OF THE CUNARD STEAMER ARABIA, AT SEA.

FIGURE 5.3 The deck of a Cunard ship, the *Arabia*, from 1859. Although this ship was larger than the *Cambria*, this illustration from *Ballou's Pictorial Drawing-Room Companion*, 26 February 1859, demonstrates the significance of Douglass being invited to give a speech on the deck, an obvious place of social interaction during the transatlantic voyage. Courtesy, American Antiquarian Society.

before fellow passengers as a heated point of discussion and that subsequently Captain Judkins invited Douglass to give a lecture. Asa confided that "Frederic [*sic*] had quite an exciting conversation with some of the passengers yesterday evening which caused some excitement."[89] And Asa's brother Judson confirmed that between bouts of seasickness, overeating, and spotting icebergs and whales, some of the passengers, a group of "gentlemen (and some ladies)," became more than mildly interested in Douglass's message.[90] Early in the voyage, the Hutchinsons befriended the *Cambria*'s Captain Judkins, singing songs and sharing stories with him well into the evenings of the voyage. John Hutchinson described Judkins as a "bluff old sterling Englishman," meaning he was a good man despite his reputation as a hard-boiled commander.[91] Perhaps the warm friendship that developed between Captain Judkins and the Hutchinsons encouraged the captain to invite Douglass to speak, despite the Cunard Steamship Company's policy of appeasing its British and American constituencies by not making waves.

On Wednesday 27 August, the last night of the voyage, Douglass awaited his introduction while a few first-class passengers made the traditional last-night-at-sea champagne toast honoring Judkins. To clear their heads of the alcohol, men and ladies promenaded on the quarterdeck. At half past five, Douglass ascended the deck, and Judkins ordered the steward to ring the bell to announce the speech. Murmurings of protest began instantly. Douglass remembered, "bloody threats were being made against me, if I attempted [the lecture]."[92] To quell the group, the Hutchinson Family Singers sang a hymn. Still, as soon as Douglass began to speak, the audience turned loud and dangerous.[93]

Douglass was undeterred by the pushback of his fellow travelers and therefore began his talk with his characteristic attacks on American democracy. Douglass would later defend his forcefulness, arguing that "enlightening the public mind—by exposing the character of slavery . . . is plainly my duty." At the same time, he was sure to explain that he had a "pressing invitation to do so."[94] Douglass felt that upsetting white Americans was an occupational hazard if he hoped to spread the truth about enslavement. A man from Connecticut was his first heckler.[95] The heckler's regional identity is significant because Douglass told Garrison his attackers were "mobocrat Americans." This was a specific reference to the "gentlemen of property and standing" that historian Leonard Richards describes as the leaders of the antiabolitionist mobs, who were a northern phenomenon throughout the 1830s and 1840s.[96] The man from Connecticut interrupted Douglass and shouted several times at him, "You are a liar!" Douglass was unwilling to be labeled a liar on the topic of slavery. So, rather than rely on his own authority, he whipped out a book of slave codes and began to read from them directly to his audience.[97] In response, a mob formed, Douglass spat out insults at the mob, and the mob roared back.

Unlike in confrontations between abolitionists and antiabolitionists in the antebellum North, on the Atlantic, the captain was the ultimate authority. Judkins intervened, making it clear that he was a reformed British slaveholder who would not tolerate antiabolitionist violence on his ship. When both Douglass and his enemies began swearing oaths at each other, Captain Judkins stepped in again, sided with Douglass, and tried to break up the skirmish. Once he got the crowd's attention, Judkins told them a tale of abolitionist conversion. He confessed that his family had once owned more than 200 slaves, was rendered penniless by the abolition of British slavery in 1834, and he was therefore obliged to "follow the sea." The end of slavery in the West Indies changed the course of the young man's life. Nevertheless, Judkins argued, "[his slaves] were liberated, *and it was right*."[98] He then told his passengers that there had been ample time for all political sides to be heard, and now it was Frederick Douglass's turn to speak.

Douglass tried to get his message out for a third time, but now three slaveholding passengers, one each from Georgia, New Orleans, and Cuba, threatened to throw Douglass overboard. Douglass asserted that these men were "under the influence of slavery and brandy," and another traveler concurred that at least the New Orleans man was drunk the entire voyage.[99] One of the enslavers was a small man who tried to push Douglass in the chest. The captain stepped in, pushed the man back, and the smaller man fell to the floor.[100] Realizing that the scene would not stop unless he imposed extreme measures, Judkins promised to put the culprits in irons if they failed to back off, and he actually called for the steward to get the implements. Rather than see the conflict through to the end, as he surely would have done in Boston, Douglass descended into steerage, never having given his speech. He was resigned to make it to foreign soil, where his voice could (and would) truly be heard. On the deck and in the grand saloon, spirited debates and condemnations continued until the steward blew out the last candle at eleven.[101]

At first glance, this episode contradicts the possibility that shipboard culture allowed Douglass and other black travelers to disrupt racial customs during the voyage. Douglass never made his speech, and the men he called "mobocrats" prevailed. The rioters behaved precisely as they would (and did) on land by silencing a vocal black radical and, more precisely, shutting down the topic of abolition. In fact, Douglass's abolitionist message caused even more outrage than his blackness among white passengers, whose greatest complaints were against Americans who "attempt to vilify our country as these wandering abolition lectures do." Writing under the unoriginal pseudonym "Traveller," one passenger was particularly angry that Douglass compared the United States negatively to what he called "philanthropic England."[102] Another American traveler unleashed a vitriolic attack against Douglass that he was "permitted to vomit his foul stuff."[103] Others griped that Douglass "abused America and the Americans," and even "the ladies were much alarmed."[104] In other words, by abusing America and disturbing white women, Douglass had conducted himself exactly as the antiabolitionists back home predicted free men of color would. In the minds of these proslavery Americans, the reactions of the Connecticut man were patriotic and chivalrous. Who else but a white man could protect the "alarmed" white ladies, given the abolitionist and anti-American message and the sexual subtext that Frederick Douglass espoused, all in the intimacy of a transatlantic steamer?

So the real question is, why had the mob not attacked Douglass sooner? The answer lies with location, the culture of the steamship, and racialized authority. Although the mob was influenced by American antiblack tastes, they behaved with reserve because in this new location—the decks of a British-owned steamship—their authority was in question. The practice of Anglo-American superiority looked different on the *Cambria* than it did on land. The mob experienced shifts in its racialized behavior too. And location was paramount to this transformation. Even when the mob formed and readied for attack, it was unwilling to handle Douglass on the *Cambria* the way it would on land. One of the enslavers threatened, "I wish I had you [Douglass] in Cuba!" Then another replied, "I wish I had him in Savannah! We would use him up!"[105] The enslavers wanted to move Douglass from their current location—the *Cambria*—to another because they did not feel able to mete out the justice they hoped to on the British ship. Even in the midst of their anger over this black abolitionist insulting them, their country, and their favored institution, they were unwilling to behave on an Atlantic steamship as they would in the United States. The ship, under the captain's watchful eye, in the middle of the Atlantic, was not the place.

The events on the steamship *Cambria* in August 1845 demonstrate that the processes of travel allowed racial interactions to shift, marking the ship itself as a liminal territory. By the time Douglass and others arrived in Great Britain, they had undergone a transformation, the seeds of which had begun to germinate at sea. Geography was everything. The Atlantic emerged as a psychological, transitional space between America's racism and Europe's relative egalitarianism. The peculiar nature of the transatlantic voyage—a hundred passengers living close together for up to two weeks under somewhat grueling circumstances—allowed for a relaxing of racial proscriptions and interactions. For Robert Purvis, this meant he was emboldened to reveal his imposture while posing as a white South Carolinian on his 1834 voyage. For Frederick Douglass, this meant quelling the demands for first-class accommodations he would have made at home. And it meant using his repression on the *Cambria* as a rhetorical stratagem to launch his tour of the British Isles. The racial shift at sea even meant that white travelers could reorder their racist attacks to fit this new locale, the Atlantic Ocean, where their strategies for silencing an African American protester were reconfigured. While the fear of black freedom that haunted many Americans may have driven the mob into action, the unique circumstances of travel and mobility transformed the nature of their reaction. Most importantly, the decks and cabins of ocean vessels allowed colored travelers such as Frederick Douglass to begin their own transformations toward free personhood.

Publicity over Frederick Douglass's violent confrontation did not end the Cunard Steamship Company's unofficial policy of segregating black passengers. In fact, it may have entrenched it. On Douglass's return trip in April 1847, also on the *Cambria*, the company made sure that it relegated Douglass to steerage for the duration of the trip to allay, it said, "scenes of confusion."[106] Even though Douglass expressed anger and disappointment with Cunard officials for segregating him during his return, he once again saw the real culprit as U.S. whites. He wrote, aside from "the numerous perils of the deep, I had the cruel, and almost omnipotent and omnipresent spirit of American slavery with which to contend." In this case, Douglass indicted not only American passengers but the very direction in which the ship traveled. He raged, "and while yet three thousand miles" from U.S. shores, "at the first step, I am smitten with the pestilential breath of her slave system!"[107] The shipping line blamed Douglass for the fight that broke out on the *Cambria* in August 1845. For Douglass, the possibilities for a liminal experience had been foreclosed on as he headed toward the complicated land that he called home. And, as his mobility and freedom seemed entirely insecure and uncertain, he was sure to fight mightily for his right to travel equally. He did not win his battle with *Cunard* in 1847, but once in the United States he nevertheless resumed the style of radical activist respectability that he had put on hold and revised while at sea.

Epilogue
Abroad: Sensing Freedom

In late 1851, William and Ellen Craft arrived in England, and something visceral happened. They reflected, "It was not until we stepped upon the shore at Liverpool that we were free from every slavish fear."[1] When he traveled from New York to England in 1850, black abolitionist William Powell noticed a change so "sudden and unexpected" that he could "hardly believe [his] senses."[2] Frederick Douglass claimed to undergo an immediate transformation when he went to the British Isles in 1845. When he spied the shores of Ireland from the deck of the transatlantic steamship, he wrote, "I breathe, and lo! The chattel becomes a man."[3] The trip abroad changed William Wells Brown, too. In 1855, he noted that, "In the so-called Free States, I had been treated as one born to occupy an inferior position,—in steamers, compelled to take my fare on the deck; in hotels, to take my meals in the kitchen; in coaches, to ride on the outside; in railways, to ride in the 'negro car'; and in churches, to sit in the 'negro pew.' But no sooner was I on British soil, than I was recognized as a man, and an equal."[4]

The Crafts, Powell, Douglass, Brown, and others equated citizenship with the right to travel freely in and through public space. Yet, as they made their way to the British Isles and Europe during the first half of the nineteenth century, the most elite colored travelers discovered something remarkable about the freedom of mobility they found there. Freedom, they learned, was not only a legal status but also a sensory and emotional state. Indeed, walking the streets or riding public conveyances without confronting stress, anxiety, and fear impacted colored travelers profoundly. The letters, lectures, and sermons of transatlantic abolitionists were often exuberant precisely because travelers basked in the ability to move about unimpeded. It is tempting to read their accounts as rhetorical or hyperbolic, but to do so is to dismiss the fact that every time they stepped out of their homes, people of color were under siege no matter where they traveled in the country of their birth. Writing and speaking about the experience of moving through space without facing segregation and white vigilantism allowed colored travelers to highlight the emotional toll of traveling in the United States and also describe freedom from it as transformative.

IT IS FITTING TO CLOSE a discussion of black travel in the United States with the writings of colored travelers who went abroad. Between 1833 and the 1860s, fewer than one hundred black activists went to the British Isles or elsewhere in Europe. Yet historians recognize the significant impact these activists had on the transatlantic abolitionist movement.[5] What scholars explore less is how these early activists used the trip abroad to construct their definitions of freedom. Indeed, by describing their experiences abroad in emotional and sensory terms, colored travelers made visible the fact that freedom of mobility was more than just a political right. International travel afforded people of color the opportunity to exercise their ideas about citizenship, centered on unobstructed mobility, and, by extension, the ability to feel, breathe, hear, see, and assert that freedom in practice. Only by landing on foreign shores where the constant barrage of racism was absent, where shouts of nigger did not chase them through city streets, could activists embody the full scope of what equality and citizenship could mean for themselves and for other people of color back home.

Gendered Freedom

Colored travelers described the freedom they encountered abroad as an emotional phenomenon that allowed them, for the first time in their lives, to feel the full breadth of their gendered humanity. Indeed, these travelers deeply believed that part of the horror of surveillance and segregation in the United States was in how consistently it emasculated black men and defeminized black women. At forty-four years old, Powell felt "for once in my life though under a foreign flag—a man, indeed." William Wells Brown went so far as to claim that when he arrived in Liverpool, "The very dogs in the streets appeared conscious of my manhood."[6] At first glance, Brown's statement seems metaphorical, and in part, it likely was. Yet his choice of imagery—dogs in the streets—demonstrates how racial violence consumed the consciousness of black people who moved through public space in the United States. In antebellum slave states in particular, slave catchers used ferocious dogs to hunt down so-called fugitives.[7] Brown had firsthand knowledge of this practice. In 1826 or 1827 in St. Louis, a slaveholder set the bloodhounds on Brown when

The author caught by the bloodhounds. (See p. 21.)

FIGURE 6.1 When William Wells Brown was a young, self-liberated man living in St. Louis, a slave catcher used dogs to hunt and find Brown. It was such an important experience that the scene was illustrated in the London publication of Brown's narrative. See Brown, *William W. Brown, An American Slave*, 1849. Rare Book Collection, Wilson Special Collections Library, The University of North Carolina–Chapel Hill.

he made his first attempt at self-liberation, a memory so impactful that Brown included an illustration of the scene in the 1849 London publication of his narrative (see figure 6.1).[8] Dogs were not only a southern problem. If, as Connecticut minister Hosea Easton described, white northerners instructed their young children to despise people of color, it is not far-fetched to assume that some whites trained their dogs to similarly growl and attack at the sight of a black person. The notion that even British dogs could recognize black masculinity was an idea also articulated by Douglass. In a farewell speech for a London audience in March 1847, he told Londoners that "the Americans do not know that I am a man. They talk of me as a box of goods; they speak of me in connexion with sheep, horses and cattle. But here, how different! Why, sir, the very dogs of old England know that I am a man! [Cheers.]"[9] The universal recognition of black manhood was a powerful sensation. Freedom thus emerged as something observable, a state unencumbered by constant surveillance and anxiety. Ultimately, the proclamations of Brown and Douglass suggest that freedom was so visceral that, in its midst, the hounds cowered before black men, not the other way around.

Even when male travelers did not claim that manhood suddenly materialized on foreign shores, they nevertheless argued that U.S. racism was most harmful precisely because it assaulted black masculinity. After traveling to England in 1853, black abolitionist Samuel Ringgold Ward revealed that it was his strong sense of himself as a man that made the attacks on his mobility most galling. He wrote, "I did not feel as some blacks say they felt, upon landing [in Liverpool]—that I was, for the first time in my life, a man. No, I always felt that; however wronged, maltreated, outraged—still, a man. Indeed, the very bitterness of what I had suffered at home consisted chiefly in the consciousness I always carried with me of being an equal man to any of those who trampled upon me."[10] Although Ward maintained that his personhood was not transformed by going abroad, he nevertheless described the travel experience as emotionally liberating and significant, particularly because Britons interacted with him as an equal.

Far fewer women of color traveled abroad, and even fewer of these wrote extensively about the experience. Nevertheless, like black men, they deemed freedom of mobility as a sensory phenomenon that was transformative in explicitly gendered ways. In England since late 1851, Ellen Craft, a woman reticent about appearing publicly, was so passionate about one particular assault to her freedom that she used the press to defend it.[11] In late 1852, the Georgia enslaver who claimed ownership of her circulated a rumor that she was unhappy being free. He said that Ellen Craft had asked an American man to bring her home from England and return her to the safety of slavery in Georgia. These spurious allegations prompted her, uncharacteristically, to publish a very public letter.[12] She refuted the claim that she would be "so false to liberty as to prefer slavery in its stead," and she argued that only outside the United States was freedom possible. Writing to the editor of London's *Anti-Slavery Advocate*, she emphatically stated that even if she were destitute, which she was not, "I had much rather starve in England, a free woman, than be a slave for the best man that ever breathed upon the American continent."[13] Craft highlighted the enormity of her transformation now that she resided on British shores, and she did so in gendered terms. She made explicit how in the United States she occupied the status of the gender-neutral "slave," subjugated by white masculine authority but not recognized for her feminine humanity. In England, she said she was a "free woman" and thus capable of navigating the social category of womanhood, an elusive status for both enslaved and free black women in the United States. Travel abroad offered Craft the mobility not only to enact freedom the way she envisioned it, but also the ability to embody a free and respectable femininity.

The ability to perform a raced, gendered, and classed freedom while abroad was a sentiment reflected in the writings of another colored traveler, Eliza Potter. Potter was a nanny and a hairdresser from New York, who in the early 1840s traveled to France and England in her capacity as a servant to several white families. She published a memoir of her life—*A Hairdresser's Experience in High Life*—in 1859. Although her travels abroad preceded those of the most celebrated black abolitionists, she nevertheless made the same comparisons between the United States and Great Britain. Potter's observations illustrate how being abroad allowed her to practice a feminized respectability that would not have played well for a black woman in the United States. In one story, she tells of arriving in London from Paris in 1842 on the day of a citywide celebration. Caught up in the frenzy, she lost her way and could not remember the name of her hotel. Noticing her apparent distress, several British men and women took the time to help her find her way. She realized that her rescue was a scenario that would never have been replicated back home. "I cried with a joy I never felt before, and wondered what rich or grand person in America would have done so charitable an act."[14] For Potter, this was a moment where she got to perform the tropes of damsel in distress and lost waif, both social identities that would have been illegible to U.S. whites on her black body. Even for free black women such as Potter, the opportunity to enact a self-consciously gendered self was one of the freedoms that foreign travel allowed.

Losing Sight of Color

Colored travelers experienced a gendered sense of freedom on foreign shores, but there were still times when they did confront racism abroad. When this happened, U.S. whites were usually at the center of the conflict. William Craft, Ellen's husband, wrote about the "evil & wicked influence" of Americans who while traveling in the British Isles slandered black people, poisoning public opinion against them.[15] In an 1859 incident in Paris that made British headlines, two white Americans demanded that the waiters in the restaurant in the Hotel de Louvre expel two "gentlemen of colour." When the waiters and the hotelier refused, the Americans, in their own words, physically kicked "the 'niggers' out of the hotel."[16]

Incidents such as these were not particularly shocking to colored travelers. Charles Remond, Frederick Douglass, Sarah Parker Remond, and others had openly acknowledged that U.S. whites carried their racism with them abroad. What did surprise colored travelers, however, was how easily Americans could give up their antiblack stance as long as doing so served their objectives. It is true that a kind gesture from a previously aggressive white American provided certifiable evidence that even white people recognized how racism was arbitrary and opportunistic rather than natural and biological. The impact of such incidents on colored travelers was profound. They were overwhelmed by the newfound ability to move through space without racial proscription and by the possibility that white racial behavior could transform in a foreign locale. It also meant that American racial practices could be transformed, not only away, but at home.

When U.S. whites shifted their racial behavior, colored travelers were exuberant and took the time to write about the change. In one instance, two days after Douglass arrived in England in 1845, he visited a famous British landmark and saw a few white American passengers there who had sailed with him on the *Cambria*. When the Americans realized Douglass would be admitted into the building as an equal, "They looked as sour as vinegar, and bitter as gall." But, significantly, Douglass wrote, neither they nor the servants of the place came out to say, "we don't allow niggers in here."[17] Even more pronounced was an interaction that William Wells Brown had with a white American at the Paris Peace Congress of 1849. During Brown's voyage to Liverpool, a white passenger called him, among other insults, a nigger. In Paris, Brown coincidentally encountered the same American at the Peace Congress in August. The attitude of this particular individual had changed markedly, however, once in Paris. This transformation was in no small part because some of the most important members of the Congress treated Brown with high esteem, including novelist Victor Hugo, the presiding officer of the Congress, and a British Member of Parliament Richard Cobden. The previously rude American wanted to meet these dignitaries and, in an astounding change in behavior, sought out Brown to conduct the introductions. Brown was furious and remarked that he had no doubt the man would have refused to shake his hand in New York or Boston, not even "with a pair of tongs ten feet long." But when the man wanted an introduction to Cobden, this man, who earlier had no qualms about attacking Brown with racial epithets, approached Brown, hat in hand, demonstrating "how easily Americans can lay aside their prejudices when they reach this country."[18] Brown remembered the exchange like this:

> RUDE AMERICAN: (hat in one hand, other hand extended) "How do you do, Mr. Brown? I hope I find you well, Sir."
> BROWN: "Why, Sir, you have the advantage of me—I do not know you."
> RUDE AMERICAN: "Why, Sir, . . . don't you know me? I was a fellow-passenger with you from America. I wish you would introduce me to Mr. Cobden."

Brown was "so indignant at the downright impudence" of the man's approach—calling him a "fellow-passenger" as if he had been equally cordial at sea—that he walked away without comment.[19] By reporting the incident, Brown could demonstrate his own gentlemanliness and respectability.[20] On the other hand, Brown's story exposed the fact that U.S. racial proscription was expedient rather than innate. Being abroad taught Brown that such behaviors were malleable.

Some colored travelers wrote that while abroad they were so emotionally overwhelmed by their freedom of mobility that they underwent a type of racial amnesia. When in 1845 Harriet Jacobs traveled to England for ten months as a servant to a white family, she said that she "never saw the slightest symptom of prejudice against color"; in fact, while abroad, she "entirely forgot it, till the time came for us to return to America."[21] Charles Remond, who traveled in 1840, declared that in the British Isles he nearly lost "sight entirely of [his] own color."[22] These confessions of forgetting were not just rhetorical. On foreign soil, colored travelers negotiated public space without hearing nigger or confronting seething white passengers, segregationist captains, or railroad workers who enforced segregation. They traveled without being afraid. By writing of the unencumbered ways in which they moved through British and European cities, towns, and streets, colored travelers highlighted that there existed an elusive and emotional component to freedom. They suggested that freedom was contingent on the right to travel and to come and go as one pleased, but at the same time the absence of racism and fear just as powerfully informed their freedom of mobility as did their physical movement.

My Country, My Country

Despite celebrating their freedom in the British Isles and in continental Europe, in the end, few black activists permanently emigrated from the United States. Instead, activists returned home, even when they did not relish doing so. Jacobs expressed sorrow upon returning to New York after her time in England. She wrote, "it is a sad feeling to be afraid of one's native country."[23] Still, many more expressed their need to return in emotional terms, as a yearning to transport and reconstruct the freedom they discovered abroad within the United States. In an 1840 letter, Charles Remond mused, "I long to tread again the country of my birth, again to raise my feeble voice in behalf of the suffering."[24] In 1843, J. W. C. Pennington explained to a London audience, "though I have a country that has never done me justice, yet I must return to it."[25] Black activist Alexander Crummell revealed that he did not want to get too attached "to the freedom of English life and society" because if he did he would be "ultimately unwilling to return to the U.S."[26] In 1851, William Powell, with patriotic anguish, pronounced, "Oh! My country, my country, with all thy faults I love thee none the less."[27]

Still, other colored travelers, namely William Wells Brown and Frederick Douglass, were even more deeply conflicted about returning home, in part because they believed citizenship would remain forever elusive. Brown told a London audience that he longed to defend his country because he "loved America" as much as the lovers of slavery. But he was not able to do so. "How can I! America has disfranchised me, driven me off, and declared that I am not a citizen, and never shall be, upon the soil of the United States."[28] He nevertheless returned in 1854. Douglass, who returned home in 1847 after nineteen months abroad, conceded that he had family and friends in the United States and would probably die there, but he had no "respect for that country . . . the entire network of American society, is one great falsehood." In March 1847, Douglass told an audience that, from the beginning, the founding fathers had constructed the American constitution to protect the lie of slavery. Therefore, Douglass returned to the United States not to love it but "to unmask her pretension to Republicanism."[29] The move to return home was a quest that imagined citizenship as its most pressing objective.

Conclusion

Douglass had been back in the United States for just a few months in 1847 when an Albany newspaper editor publicly attacked him for traveling on a Hudson River steamship with a white woman. The headline of *The Switch* read "NIGGERS AND NASTINESS: The offence is rank—it smells to Heaven." The editor was careful not to cast aspersions on the unnamed white woman, but he emphasized that as for Douglass, "he should be kicked into his *proper place, and kept there.*"[30] Packing a familiar discursive punch, the scathing article accused Douglass of being a nigger, of smelling badly, of sexual amalgamation, and finally of stepping out of black geographies and into white ones. Douglass admitted to accompanying the white woman from Albany to New York City and back again, albeit in separate berths. He explained that he asked his white friend to purchase his tickets because he did not want to travel by deck overnight. Furthermore, he denied the allegations of sexual impropriety. Douglass characterized the editor's vitriol as an assault on his freedom of mobility, one born out of an impulse "so daringly wicked" that "none but one over whom the sway of the devil is complete, could have invented and penned them."[31] Of course, Douglass surely knew that the verbal assault against him was not the invention of a supernatural evil or even a particularly original enemy. Instead, by 1847, such antiblack discourse was a well-developed trope meant to characterize black mobility as suspicious, unnatural, illegal, dirty, and dangerous to U.S. society at large. Douglass's reaction demonstrated a bitter loss of the sense of exhilaration that characterized his travels in the British Isles. His passionate refutation illustrated that oppression was also an emotional phenomenon, one that was just as visceral as freedom had been.

The fight for equality in the antebellum United States was emotionally taxing for activists such as Douglass. But then, so were the assertions they made to the right of mobility that were crucial to developing a full-fledged sense of U.S. citizenship. Indeed, state and federal law along with popular culture profoundly circumscribed all elements of travel for people of color. Walking down the northern streets, a man or woman of color could expect that little children and young adults would chase them down, shouting nigger as they ran. The criminalization of any kind of black mobility—whether enslaved or free—encouraged antiblack surveillance as well as other forms of white vigilantism. Depending on where in the country a person of color lived, white observers and patrollers could demand to see slave passes, free papers, and even a black sailor's passport. Several of the constitutional conventions of northern states outlawed free black immigration, and most states, including the venerated abolitionist stronghold of Massachusetts, debated the issue. At the same time, black international travel was also under federal surveillance, because the U.S. Department of State, in all but four recorded cases, refused to grant colored travelers an official U.S. passport because it denoted citizenship. Meanwhile, in northern cities, colored travelers could anticipate insult, segregation, or exile when they sought entrée into public conveyances. Perhaps just as gallingly, depending on the mood or beliefs of a particular transportation proprietor, a colored traveler could make the trip without confronting segregation at all. Yet, rather than allay black fears, the arbitrariness of this racism only served to solidify white supremacy and increase black anxiety. By the time railroads developed in the mid-1830s, colored travelers were ready to fight against the institutionalization of segregation that made railroad cars the sites of mounting violence and established "Jim Crow" as the dominant nickname for racial separatism in the United States. Despite the emotional and physical stakes, colored travelers fought vehemently for their right to travel because they recognized freedom of mobility as the most fundamental element of American citizenship.

It is impossible to understand the story of black activism in the United States without making it plain that African American radicals intentionally shaped the battle for equality as a fight over unobstructed movement, with the hope that one day they could not only walk the streets or ride the cars as equals but also be free of anxiety while doing it. This was citizenship. No doubt, the freedom of mobility that colored travelers sought before the Civil War was contingent on the financial ability to afford the fare and the leisure time to make the trip. Activists with economic resources wanted full access to public space and the emotional freedom to occasionally forget, if not their race, then at least racism. As a result of their protests, they laid the groundwork for a century of black activism that placed mobility and the vehicles of transportation at the epicenter of a movement. By the latter part of the nineteenth and throughout the twentieth centuries, access to public conveyances became increasingly democratized and also racially contentious. From Ida B. Wells's 1884 fight against a railroad company in Tennessee, to Homer Plessy's 1892 protest against the Separate Car Act of Louisiana, to Rosa Parks and other black female workers in 1955, who spent more than a year boycotting the buses in Montgomery, Alabama, all activists who defied transportation restrictions were the descendants of a protest tradition born on northeastern stagecoaches and steamships and on the Massachusetts railroads. Whether they knew it or not, future activists learned from folks such as Cornish, Ray, Paul, Douglass, Brown, Jacobs, Jennings, and Pennington that the vehicles themselves were the front lines for the battle over equal rights. Moreover, these activists changed the parameters of respectability by encouraging black people to fight segregation and white vigilantism by putting their own bodies in harm's way. Colored travelers refused to capitulate to white supremacy because the struggle over public space and freedom of mobility was worth the fight. It still is.

Notes

Introduction

1. *Frederick Douglass' Paper*, 13 May 1852.
2. Woodward, *The Strange Career of Jim Crow*, 22–65; Litwack, *Trouble in Mind*, 229–246; Kelley, *Right to Ride*, 38–40, 66–67, 79–85.
3. *Frederick Douglass' Paper*, 13 May 1852.
4. White activists may have been the first to use "colored traveler" to describe free black travelers, but at least as far back as 1837, when Hosea Easton, a black minister from Hartford, Connecticut, used the phrase, African Americans had also adopted the term. See *The Liberator*, 13 August 1831; *The Philadelphia National Enquirer*, 31 August 1836; Easton, *A Treatise on the Intellectual Character*, 40–41.
5. Although both white and black people commonly used the phrase "people of color," it had a complicated racial history that indicated caste differences, even within black communities. See Rael, *Black Identity and Black Protest*, 102–104; Alexander, *African or American*, 82–83.
6. Walker, *Appeal*, title page.
7. Alexander, *African or American*, 78–83. Rael demonstrates that, between the 1830s and 1850s, "colored" was the most common descriptor in the titles of black conventions in the North, even though it was not universally adopted. See Rael, *Black Identity and Black Protest*, 102–107.
8. Rael, *Black Identity and Black Protest*, 102–104.
9. Easton, *A Treatise on the Intellectual Character*, 40–41.
10. Among the many examples of free people of color who described their run-ins with transportation proprietors and/or white passengers on public vehicles, see Wiggins, ed., *Captain Paul Cuffe's Logs and Letters*, 213; *Freedom's Journal*, 23 March 1827; "Unhandsome Treatment," *The Liberator*, 10 December 1831; Nathaniel Paul to William Lloyd Garrison, *The Liberator*, 22 June 1833; "Disgraceful," *The Liberator*, 3 August 1833; Susan Paul to William Lloyd Garrison, *The Liberator*, 5 April 1834; "Feelings of Colored Men," *The New York Evangelist*, 9 July 1836; Charles Ray to Samuel Cornish, *The Colored American*, 16 September 1837; *The Colored American*, 6 October 1838; *The Liberator*, 11 October 1839; Charles Lenox Remond to Charles Ray, 30 June 1840; *The Colored American*, 3 October 1840; Jabez P. Campbell to William Lloyd Garrison, *The Liberator*, 28 April 1843; Frederick Douglass to William Lloyd Garrison, "Colorphobia," *The Liberator*, 3 October 1845; *The Liberator*, 30 January 1846; "Colorphobia in New York," *The North Star*, 25 May 1849; "Speech by William G. Allen Delivered at the Stock Exchange, Leeds, England, 1 December 1853," in Ripley, ed., *The Black Abolitionist Papers*, 372–378; *The Provincial Freeman*, 22 September 1855;

"Brooklyn Correspondence," *The Christian Recorder*, 23 May 1863; "Colored Persons in the City Passenger Cars," *The Liberator*, 17 February 1865.

11. Kelley, *Right to Ride*; Welke, "Rights of Passage," 73–93; Zylstra, "Whiteness, Freedom, and Technology," 678–702; Giesberg, *Army at Home*, 92–118; Biddle and Dubin, *Tasting Freedom*, 323–354; Masur, *An Example for All the Land*, 107–112; Kahan, "Pedestrian Matters," 34–82.

12. Kelley, *Race Rebels*, 56. On black performance and the theater of public transportation, see also Fleetwood, "'Busing It' in the City: Black Youth, Performance and Public Transit," 33–48.

13. Merrill Perlman, "'Scare' Tactics: Quotes around Single Words," *Columbia Journalism Review* 28 (Jan. 2013), http://www.cjr.org/language_corner/scare_tactics .php, accessed 20 December 2015.

14. On the "transportation revolution," see Taylor, *The Transportation Revolution*.

15. At least 12,000 African Americans emigrated to Liberia between 1820 and the Civil War. See Wiley, ed., *Slaves No More*, 1. On people of color traveling to other parts of the world, see Power-Greene, *Against Wind and Tide*; Dorr, *A Colored Man round the World*, 114–133, 163–188; Miller, *The Search for a Black Nationality*.

16. Monica Davey and Mitch Smith, "Justice Dept. to Investigate Chicago Police after Laquan McDonald Case," NYTimes.com, 6 December 2015, accessed 7 December 2015; Peter Hermann and Victoria St. Martin, "Detention of Black Teens by Police Outside D.C. Bank Sparks Protests," Washingtonpost.com, 14 October 2015, accessed 7 December 2015; "The Events Leading to the Shooting of Trayvon Martin," NYTimes.com, 21 June 2012, accessed 7 December 2015; Nick Wing, "A Grand Jury Did Indict One Person Involved in Eric Garner's Killing—The Man Who Filmed It," Huffingtonpost.com, 3 December 2014, accessed 7 December 2015; Frederick Kunkle, "'Walking while Black' Can Be Dangerous too, Study Finds," Washingtonpost.com, 26 October 2015, accessed 7 December 2015.

Chapter One

1. Easton, *A Treatise on the Intellectual Character*, 40–41.

2. "Remarks of Dr. Blake. On Proposing for Adoption of the Following Resolution in the Young Men's Convention Last Week," *The Colored American*, 16 September 1837 (emphasis in original). Regarding the early education of white children in the act of taunting African Americans with the use of the word nigger, see also "Cora, Moral: The Story of Poor Jack," *The Liberator*, 11 April 1835; William Drown to William Lloyd Garrison, "Communications: Colored People of Rhode Island," *The Liberator*, 18 October 1839.

3. Zilversmit, *The First Emancipation*. On Connecticut's gradual abolition laws, see Menschel, "Abolition without Deliverance," 183–222. On New York's, see Harris, *In the Shadow of Slavery*, 50–95; Alexander, *African or American*, 2–4. On Pennsylvania's, see Nash and Soderlund, *Freedom by Degrees*, 76–80. Dunbar, *A*

Fragile Freedom, 28–43. On New Jersey's, see Finkelman, "Chief Justice Horn-blower of New Jersey," 113–120.

4. Sweet, *Bodies Politic*, 354–355.

5. Harris, *In the Shadow of Slavery*, 8.

6. The work of cultural theorist Raymond Williams informs my thinking about how to define a word as controversial as nigger. Williams argues that people make "explicit and implicit connections" that inform meanings and that the definitions are more often than not "inextricably bound up with the problems [the word] was being used to discuss." In the U.S. context, nigger was profoundly tied to ideas about slavery, race, labor, gender, and class. Speaking about the word without considering these factors obscures its real meanings. See Williams, *Keywords*, 15. When thinking about how African Americans used the word nigger among themselves, I am inspired by Ed Baptist's discussion of the "vernacular history" of African Americans in the WPA ex-slave narratives. Baptist writes, "by *vernacular history*, I mean a narrative about the past constructed by laypeople in their every-day tongue." I see nigger as an example of this vernacular history. Baptist, "'Stol' and Fetched Here': Enslaved Migration, Ex-slave Narratives, and Vernacular History," in *New Studies in the History of American Slavery*, 245.

Moreover, the examination of the word nigger that I undertake in this chapter would not be possible without the scholarly and often personal reflections of several scholars. These works include Chideya, *The Color of Our Future*, 7–9; Kennedy, "Who Can Say 'Nigger'?" 86–96; Kennedy, *Nigger*; Rael, *Black Identity and Black Protest*, 91–102; Bernard, "Teaching the N-Word," 46–59; Asim, *The N Word*.

7. Walker, *Walker's Appeal . . . to the Colored Citizens of the World*, 61 (emphasis in original).

8. Walker, *Walker's Appeal*, 11.

9. Stuckey, *Slave Culture*, 125–126.

10. Walker, *Walker's Appeal*, 33.

11. Ibid., 59.

12. Ibid., 35.

13. Harris, *In the Shadow of Slavery*, 5.

14. Kennedy, *Nigger*, 10–11; Asim, *The N Word*, 9–43; Rael, *Black Identity and Black Protest*, 91–102; Roediger, *The Wages of Whiteness*, 19–36.

15. Johnson, "On Agency," 113–124.

16. Kemble, *Journal of a Residence on a Georgian Plantation*, 281; Lieber, *The Stranger in America*, 90.

17. Litwack, *North of Slavery*, 185–186; Stuckey, "Through the Prism of Folk-lore," 427, 427n30; Asim, *The N Word*, 42–43.

18. Stuckey, "Through the Prism of Folklore," 427n30.

19. Asim, *The N Word*, 43. In his thoughtful 2003 essay, historian Walter John-son raises a problem that exists among historians of enslavement. He argues that scholars have preferred to pursue histories of enslaved peoples when those people's actions can be read as resistance. He suggests that such thinking, such as when Asim contends that African Americans played into the hands of those who

oppressed them, is "a mis-posed question: African-American slaves: agents of their own destiny or not?" See Johnson, "On Agency," 113–124, esp. 113–116.

20. Smith, *The Generall Historie of Virginia by Captain John Smith*, 337. The word nigger had several spellings and incarnations, including "negar," "neger," "negur," "negor," and "niger." For a discussion of the fluidity of the word's spellings, see Rael, *Black Identity and Black Protest*, 91–93. Linguist Geoffrey D. Needler dates the modern variant of nigger in the North American colonies to 1689. Although spelled as "niggor," he located the term in an advertisement for the inventory of an estate sale in Brooklyn, New York, listing among other items "one niggor boy." See Needler, "An Antedating of 'Nigger,'" 159–160.

21. Although Massachusetts, Vermont, and New Hampshire each underwent some form of immediate emancipation, scholars continue to debate what exactly that meant for African Americans living in those states and whether individual slaveholders upheld the laws. Joanne Pope Melish notes that, in 1870, the chief clerk of the U.S. census bureau, a Vermonter, revised the census record of Vermont to list as free sixteen people previously recorded as enslaved. There were also still 157 enslaved people counted in New Hampshire in the 1790 census. Melish ultimately contends that the "immediate freedom" thesis put forth by New Englanders relied more on historical memory than reality. Furthermore, Margot Minardi argues that a legal dispute over black freedom decided in 1783 and later known as the Quok Walker case did not in fact free all blacks in Massachusetts as some historians assert. See Melish, *Disowning Slavery*, 64n31; Minardi, *Making Slavery History*, 16–20. For statistics on the free black and enslaved population in New England, see U.S. Department of Commerce, *Negro Population*, 57.

22. Melish, *Disowning Slavery*, 88–89.

23. Zilversmit, *The First Emancipation*, 121–122, 123–124, 128–129, 180–182, 193–194, 202.

24. Mars, *Life of James Mars*.

25. Easton, *A Treatise on the Intellectual Character*, 40.

26. Wood, *Black Majority*, 170–171. The word nigger was part of a transatlantic lexicon rooted in slavery and the blending of African, European, and North American cultures and derived from the Latin, Spanish, or Dutch words for "black." On the linguistic etymology of nigger, see Kennedy, "Who Can Say 'Nigger'?" 86.

27. Thornton, *Africa and Africans in the Making of the Atlantic World*, 212–217.

28. Gomez, *Exchanging Our Country Marks*, 167–173, quotations at 171.

29. White, *Somewhat More Independent*, 187–192, quotation at 187.

30. For example, Herbert Gutman demonstrated that enslaved people had surnames that they kept hidden from whites who insisted that enslaved people did not use surnames. Gutman, *The Black Family in Slavery and Freedom*, 230–237.

31. Scott, *Domination and the Arts of Resistance*, 24–34; Hine, *Hine Sight*, 37–47.

32. Camp, *Closer to Freedom*, 7.

33. An early incarnation of these letters appeared in 1747 in *The New York Gazette*, which reprinted a supposedly authentic letter sent to a London-based slaveholder from an enslaved man he owned in Herring Bay, Maryland, named "Toby." Writing in "broken" English, "Toby" told the enslaver that all was well

except that Sue, presumably an enslaved woman on the plantation, and an old horse were dead. "Toby" signed the letter "from yure oal Negur." "From *The Maryland Gazette*, 7 July 1747," reprinted in *The New York Gazette*, 27 July 1747.

34. On broken English, see Rael, *Black Identity and Black Protest*, 91–102; Melish, *Disowning Slavery*, 169–171; Gomez, *Exchanging our Country Marks*, 167–173.

35. Melish, *Disowning Slavery*, 169–171; White, *Somewhat More Independent*, 56–75, 187–194; Mahar, "Black English in Early Blackface Minstrelsy," 260–285.

36. *The Massachusetts Spy*, 11 December 1788.

37. Norton, *Liberty's Daughters*, 117.

38. *The Independent Gazetteer*, 4 July 1789, reprinted in *The Norwich Packet*, 17 July 1789.

39. White, "Afterword," to *Our Nig*, ed. Harriet Wilson, *vii–x*.

40. This was a path to indentured servitude that befell other African American children as well, including female preachers Jarena Lee, born in New Jersey in the 1780s, and Zilpha Elaw, born in Pennsylvania in the 1790s. See Lee, *The Life and Religious Experience of Jarena Lee*, 27; Elaw, *Memoirs*, 53. Ruth Wallis Herndon and John E. Murray call these contracts "pauper apprenticeships." They were often official indentured relationships that impacted the care and work of destitute and/or orphaned children such as Wilson, Lee, and Elaw. See Herndon and Murray, "'A Proper and Instructive Education,'" 4–8. As men were more likely than women to acquire positions in manual labor or at sea, more girls than boys served out the contracts. On the gendered nature of black indentured servitude, see Dunbar, *A Fragile Freedom*, 28.

41. Wilson, *Our Nig*, 9–11, quotation on 10.

42. On African American interviewers in the Virginia WPAs, see Perdue and Barden, eds., *Weevils in the Wheat*, xvii–xxvi, 357–359; Stewart, *Long Past Slavery*, 5, 120–228.

43. Liza Brown interview; Perdue and Barden, *Weevils in the Wheat*, 63.

44. Cornelia Carney interview; Perdue and Barden, *Weevils in the Wheat*, 67.

45. Interview with Mrs. Virginia Hayes Shepherd; Perdue and Barden, *Weevils in the Wheat*, 255.

46. Interview with Charles Grandy; Perdue and Barden, *Weevils in the Wheat*, 117.

47. Levine, *Black Culture and Black Consciousness*, 112–121.

48. Each song is quoted in Brown, "Negro Folk Expression," 51. Other slave songs and rhymes confirm that African Americans used the word nigger in this context. For just one example, see Northup, *Twelve Years a Slave*, 219–220.

49. Interview of Charles Crawley, in Perdue and Barden, eds., *Weevils in the Wheat*, 79.

50. Levine, *Black Culture and Black Consciousness*, 103–104.

51. Quoted in Cohen, "In Search of Carolus Africanus Rex," 157; and in Washington, *Sojourner Truth's America*, 39. According to Mrs. Fannie Berry of the WPA interviews, this song was also sung in the South. Interview of Mrs. Fannie Berry, in Perdue and Barden, eds., *Weevils in the Wheat*, 38.

52. Roediger, *The Wages of Whiteness*, 19–36; Jacobson, *Whiteness of a Different Color*, 28–31; Glenn, *Unequal Freedom*, 27–36.

53. Roediger, *The Wages of Whiteness*, 43–92.

54. Harris, *In the Shadow of Slavery*, 49.

55. Roediger, *The Wages of Whiteness*, 55–57.

56. It is possible that the oyster-house owner in question was Thomas Downing, who went on to become one of the wealthiest black New Yorkers of the period. Downing owned an establishment in the vicinity during the period. See Hewitt, "Mr. Downing and His Oyster House," 233–235.

57. *The Nantucket Inquirer*, 3 May 1824. The story likely originated from Mordecai Noah's *The National Advocate*, 14 April 1824, and was then recirculated in several other newspapers in the region, including *The New York Spectator*, 16 April 1824; *The American Sentinel* (Middletown, CT), 21 April 1824; and *The Salem Gazette*, 23 April 1824.

58. Moon-Ho Jung uses this phrase in his thoughtful definition of the term "coolies" used to describe nineteenth-century Asian immigrants to the United States. See Jung, *Coolies and Cane*, 5.

59. Cockrell, *Demons of Disorder*; Lott, *Love and Theft*.

60. For a discussion of Edward Clay, see Rael, *Black Identity and Black Protest*, 161–173; Jones, *All Bound Up Together*, 18.

61. On black women and domestic work, see Dunbar, *A Fragile Freedom*, 43–47; Jones, *All Bound Up Together*, 23–27; Harris, *In the Shadow of Slavery*, 98–100.

62. Merchants erected similar retail spaces in Boston (Quincy Market) in 1825 and in New York City in 1829. See Blumin, *The Emergence of the Middle Class*, 93.

63. Jones, *All Bound Up Together*, 18–20.

64. E. W. Clay, "Life in Philadelphia": *What you tink of my new poke bonnet*, aquatint cartoon, 1830, Library Company of Philadelphia.

65. Easton, *A Treatise on the Intellectual Character*, 42.

66. Richards, *Gentlemen of Property and Standing*, 10–19.

67. McDaniel, *The Problem of Democracy in the Age of Slavery*, 53–56; Moulton, "Closing the 'Floodgate to Impurity,'" 3–4. For just one contemporary example of the violence, see "Another Mob," *The Liberator*, 23 July 1841.

68. Roediger, *The Wages of Whiteness*, 121. On *Oh Hush*, see "The Celebrated Opera of—Oh, Hush," *The New York Mirror*, 5 October 1833.

69. Lhamon, *Jump Jim Crow*, 96–98.

70. Quoted in Rael, *Black Identity and Black Protest*, 91–102 at 98.

71. *The Pennsylvania Freeman*, 17 December 1838; *The National Aegis*, 3 April 1848.

72. Rogers in *The Herald of Freedom* and *The Liberator*, 5 July 1839. Rogers had been the editor of *The Herald of Freedom* since 1835.

73. *The Liberator*, 5 July 1839.

74. Sancho, *Letters of the Late Ignatius Sancho*, 70.

75. Kantrowitz, *More Than Freedom*, 28–40.

76. Alexander, *African or American*, 1–2.

77. *The Colored American*, 29 April 1837 (emphasis in original).

78. Brown, *Clotel, or, the President's Daughter*, 70, 130–136. It is important to note that black writers who wrote black dialogue are not immune from criticism, al-

though one theorist argues that they often did so as a gimmick to attract white abolitionists. See Gilmore, "'De Genewine Artekil,'" 743–780.

79. Jacobs, *Incidents in the Life of a Slave Girl*, 103 (emphasis in original).

80. Ibid., 131.

81. *Freedom's Journal*, 20 July 1827.

82. Delany, *The Condition, Elevation, Emigration, and Destiny of the Colored People*, 43.

83. In her book on black New Yorkers, Leslie Harris discovered that although some activists continued to assert that menial labor was inappropriate for a quest to citizenship, others "defended these occupations, claiming dignity for all labor and pride in their own work." See Harris, *In the Shadow of Slavery*, 218–219.

84. *Freedom's Journal*, 9 January 1829.

85. Walker, *Appeal*, 30.

86. "Speech by J. W. C. Pennington Delivered at Freemasons' Hall, London, England, 14 June, 1843," in Ripley, ed., *The Black Abolitionist Papers*, 104–128, quotation at 106. A similar antiblack rhyme was documented a decade earlier in *The Liberator*, 8 September 1832.

87. I borrow the term "white face" from Marvin McAllister, who likens it to a type of "racial cross dressing." See McAllister, *Whiting Up*, 9.

88. A thorough search through *Freedom's Journal* for nigger and all its spelling variants turned up no evidence that these early activists wanted to incorporate the word into their antiracism strategies. Similarly, it was not until 1834 that an African American male was quoted as using the white version of nigger in his speech. See *The Liberator*, 28 June 1834.

89. Frederick Douglass to Francis Jackson, 29 January 1846, quoted in McFeely, *Frederick Douglass*, 131, 398n.

90. Douglass, *Narrative of the Life of Frederick Douglass*, 37.

91. Frederick Douglass to William Lloyd Garrison, *The Liberator*, 30 January 1846 (italics in original).

92. Wilson, *Our Nig*, 81.

Chapter Two

1. Remond's trip to England, including his fare, accommodations, and eighteen-month extended stay, was sponsored by three New England women's groups: The Bangor Female Anti-Slavery Society, the Newport Young Ladies Juvenile Antislavery Society, and the Portland Sewing Circle. See Usrey, "Charles Lenox Remond, Garrison's Ebony Echo," 113–114.

2. Charles Lenox Remond to Charles Ray, London, 30 June 1840, published in *The Colored American*, 3 October 1840.

3. Nathaniel Peabody (N. P.) Rogers to Charles Ray, London, n.d., published in *The Colored American*, 3 October 1840, 3. Rogers was an Anglo-American abolitionist, and Ray was the editor of the African American newspaper *The Colored American*.

4. Welke, *Recasting American Liberty*; Mackintosh, "'Ticketed Through,'" 61–89. Taylor, *The Transportation Revolution*. More specifically, on infrastructure, see Minicucci, "Internal Improvements and the Union," 160–185. On steamships and the Mississippi River, see Johnson, *River of Dark Dreams*. On canal boats, see Sheriff, *The Artificial River*. On railroads, see Majewski, *A House Dividing*.

5. Welke, "Rights of Passage," 77.

6. Kelley, *Race Rebels*, 55–58.

7. In a provocative blog post on the racially motivated murder of unarmed African American teenager Trayvon Martin, historian Stephanie Jones-Rogers also grapples with the idea of the criminalization of black mobility. Arguing that Martin's murder was part of a long history of violence against the mobility of people of color, Jones-Rogers wrote, "British settlers decided to implement a system of racial slavery in North America, and they very quickly developed bodies of laws which restricted and criminalized black mobility and autonomy." Jones-Rogers, "If Only Trayvon Had Freedom Papers," 16 July 2013, http://historynewsnetwork .org/article/152622, accessed 15 April 2016.

8. McKittrick, *Demonic Grounds*, x–xii.

9. Camp, *Closer to Freedom*, 12.

10. Hadden, *Slave Patrols*, 14–40.

11. Ibid. On the slave pass system and patrollers, see Goodell, *The American Slave Code in Theory and Practice*; Martin, *The Office and Authority of a Justice of the Peace*; Camp, *Closer to Freedom*, 12–34.

12. Robert Rohmer and Joanne Melish helpfully guided me toward the Connecticut statute on slave surveillance. The law is reprinted in Williams, *History of the Negro Race*, 257, 264 (emphasis mine).

13. "Article IV," *The Articles of Confederation*, in Brown, *The Declaration of Independence*, 14.

14. Jacobson, *Whiteness of a Different Color*, 1–31, esp. 22–31; Glenn, *Unequal Freedom*, 18–40.

15. "Article IV," *The Articles of Confederation*, in Brown, *The Declaration of Independence*, 14. Also see Parker, "U.S. Citizenship and Immigration Law (1800–1924)," 172.

16. "Article IV, Section 2, Clause 3," *The Constitution of the United States*, in Brown, *The Declaration of Independence*, 40.

17. "An Act respecting fugitives from justice, and persons escaping from the service of their masters," 12 February 1793, in *A Century of Lawmaking for a New Nation*, 1414–1415.

18. Euan Hague discusses how U.S. Supreme Court justices have long imagined the right to domestic travel as contingent on whiteness. See Hague, "'The Right to Enter Every Other State,'" 333–336.

19. Neuman, "The Lost Century of American Immigration Law," 1865–1867.

20. Branagan, *Serious Remonstrances*, 68; Turner, *The Negro in Pennsylvania*, 151–154. On Thomas Branagan, see Nash, *Forging Freedom*, 177–181.

21. *Niles' Weekly Register*, 14 July 1821; Massachusetts House of Representatives, "Free Negroes and Mulattoes," 16 January 1822.

22. Gridley, "A Case under an Illinois Black Law," 403; Litwack, *North of Slavery*.

23. Finkelman, "Chief Justice Hornblower of New Jersey," 115.

24. *The Colored American*, 8 April 1837.

25. Miles, *Ties That Bind*, 149–161.

26. Power-Greene, *Against Wind and Tide*, 17–19; Alexander, *African or American*, 69–71; Davis, *The Problem of Slavery*, 105–125.

27. Clay, "An Address: Delivered to the Colonization Society of Kentucky, 17 December 1829," 13.

28. Hietala, *Manifest Design*, 10–54.

29. Horton and Horton, "A Federal Assault," 1179–1181; Blackett, *The Underground Railroad*, 32–67.

30. Sweet, *Bodies Politic*, 353–356.

31. "High Life below Stairs," *The Pennsylvania Gazette and Democratic Press*, 29 February 1828, reprinted in *Freedom's Journal*, 14 March 1828.

32. For example, *The Boston News-Letter* published runaway slave advertisements. See the issues of 4 November 1704, 3 December 1705, and 9 April 1711.

33. Cole, *Suspect Identities*, 10–11. Regarding the medieval context, historian Steven Epstein wrote that "slaves, when sold, taxed, or pursued by the law, were among the best-described people" in the past. See Epstein, *Speaking of Slavery*, 103. The same was true of enslaved people in the United States. On the prose of slave advertisements, see Woodson, "Eighteenth Century Slaves," 163–216; Hodges and Brown, *"Pretends to Be Free,"* xxi–xxxv; Windley, *Runaway Slave Advertisements*. A search through the digital archive *America's Historical Newspapers* (http:/ /infoweb.newsbank.com/) makes plain the frequency with which these advertisements appeared in the American press.

34. Even before the image of the runaway slave appeared in the specimen books of metal foundries in the 1830s, printers standardized it in various newspapers throughout the South. See *The City Gazette* (South Carolina), 3 January 1815, 4 January 1815, 10 January 1815, 11 January 1815. For just a few examples from the 1830s in slave and free states, see *National Banner and Nashville Whig*, 2 January 1835; *Indiana Democrat*, 9 January 1835. On runaway slave advertisements as a distinctive early American art form, see Ewen and Ewen, *Typecasting*; Lacey, "Visual Images of Blacks," 143–145; Wood, *Blind Memory*, 78–142; Blackwood, "Fugitive Obscura," 99–110.

35. Saidiya Hartman writes about the "fungibility" of the "captive body" in her analysis of how abolitionist empathy rendered the sufferings of enslaved people invisible. See Hartman, *Scenes of Subjection*, 21.

36. Kaye, *Joining Places*, 77–78.

37. Douglass, *Narrative of the Life of Frederick Douglass*, 69–73.

38. *The Mississippi Herald and Natchez Gazette*, 21 September 1804 (emphasis mine).

39. Bibb, *The Narratives of the Life and Adventures of Henry Bibb, an American Slave*, 167–168.

40. Kaye, *Joining Places*, 38.

41. Camp, *Closer to Freedom*, 36–40.

42. Jacobs, *Incidents in the Life of a Slave Girl*, 111–112. I owe a thank you to Katy Morris, who was an undergraduate at Smith College in the spring of 2010, for her observation about the gender-bending significance of Jacobs walking through the streets of Edenton.

43. Johnson, "The Slave Trader"; Gross, *What Blood Won't Tell*, 1–72.

44. Craft and Craft, *Running a Thousand Miles*; Still, *The Underground Railroad*, 265–271.

45. Still, *The Underground Railroad*, 123–133. William Still also describes the story of another woman, in addition to Ellen Craft and Maria Weems, who liberated herself dressed as a man. Clarissa Davis escaped in 1854 and arrived in male attire. See Still, *The Underground Railroad*, 33.

46. Welke, *Recasting American Liberty*, ix–xv.

47. Mackintosh, "'Ticketed Through,'" 61–89.

48. In 1794, such a trip involved six days, or sixty hours of continuous travel, on a "snail-paced" stagecoach, and by 1824, it took just three days via stagecoach and steamship. The time it took to make these trips is gleaned from travel timetables in *The Columbian Centinel*, 20 August 1794; *The Evening Post*, 13 December 1824; *The Newark Daily Advertiser*, 19 May 1838; *Saturday Morning Transcript*, 12 May 1838; *The Colored American*, 6 June 1838; Weed, *A Chapter from the Autobiography of Mr. Thurlow Weed*, 4.

49. Historian Barbara Welke contends that by the 1830s "railroads and streetcars made possible the physical mobility at the heart of American liberty." See Welke, *Recasting American Liberty*, x. More darkly, Walter Johnson recently described Mississippi steamships and the type of capital they produced as "a sort of alibi for imperialism and dispossession." See Johnson, *River of Dark Dreams*, 76.

50. Welke, "Rights of Passage," 76.

51. "Advertisement," *The Federal Gazette and Baltimore Daily Advertiser*, 31 May 1800, 4. For wages in Baltimore, see Rockman, *Scraping By*, 72.

52. Stansell, *City of Women*, 92–93.

53. Cohen, "Women at Large," 45.

54. Higginbotham, "African-American Women's History," 261.

55. Anonymous, *The Laws of Etiquette* (1836), 106–107. While the 1836 edition argued that working women should not be offered a seat, the 1841 reprint of the same book interestingly omitted a reference to treating women differently according to class. See Anonymous, *The Laws of Etiquette* (1841), 191–192.

56. Johnson, *Soul by Soul*.

57. Wiggins, ed., *Captain Paul Cuffe's Logs and Letters*, 213.

58. Schor, *Henry Highland Garnet*, 12–13.

59. Henry Drayton and Henry Johnson to William Lloyd Garrison, 28 June 1832, published in *The Liberator*, 7 July 1832.

60. *The Colored American*, 4 September 1841.

61. Black travelers repeatedly complained that proprietors forced them to pay full price to accept lesser accommodations. For just a few examples, see *The Liberator*, 10 December 1831, 3 August 1833, and 11 March 1837. As historian Barbara Welke argues in regards to transportation companies in the 1860s, "The level of

informality reflected the sense of right and power" on the part of corporations. Welke, "Rights of Passage," 77.

62. Nightingale, *Segregation*, 13.

63. Jacobs, *Incidents in the Life of a Slave Girl*, 176.

64. Kelley, *Right to Ride*, 42, 105.

65. Thomas Van Renselaer to Reverend Joshua Leavitt, 26 October 1838, *The Herald of Freedom*, 8 December 1838.

66. Cohen, "Women at Large," 45.

67. Karsten, *Heart versus Head*, 268; Garrison, William Lloyd Garrison to Alonzo Lewis, 13 September 1832, published in *The Liberator*, 13 October 1832.

68. "A Take Up," *The Antheneum; or Spirit of the English Magazines*, 1 September 1825.

69. Harris, "From Abolitionist Amalgamators to 'Rulers of the Five Points,'" 191–198.

70. *The Liberator*, 13 July 1838.

71. Wiggins, ed., *Captain Paul Cuffe's Logs and Letters*, 213.

72. Garrison, *The Liberator*, 10 December 1831, 1.

73. *The Liberator*, 3 August 1833 (emphasis in original); *The New York Evangelist*, 11 March 1837.

74. Douglass, *The North Star*, 13 June 1850 (emphasis in original).

75. "Have They Got a 'Jim Crow Car'?" *Boston Daily Bee*, published in *The Liberator*, 1 August 1845.

76. Sander Gilman asserts that odor was historically a method of ascribing difference to the "Other," particularly Africans and Jews. See Gilman, *Difference and Pathology*, 145. See also Wesley, "The Concept of Negro Inferiority," 545. Constance Classen argues that there is "a certain empirical basis" for different odors in different cultures, and people tend only to smell the scent of others and not themselves and their own group. With that said, odor emerges as a scapegoat for racial and cultural attacks, and African Americans have specifically suffered from this. Classen quotes from John Dollard's *Caste and Class in a Southern Town* (1957): "Among beliefs which profess to show that Negro and white people cannot intimately participate in the same civilization is the perennial one that Negroes have 'a smell extremely disagreeable to white people.' . . . White people generally regard this argument as a crushing final proof of the impossibility of close association between the races." See Classen, "The Odor of the Other," 134–135.

77. Smith, *How Race Is Made*, 20–27; Smith, *Sensing the Past*, 65–68. Others who demonstrate that deregulation of colored bodies led to more complaints about black odor include Chiang, "The Nose Knows"; Ferranti, "An Odor of Racism."

78. *The Colored American*, 5 August 1837.

79. Quoted in *The Liberator*, 13 August 1831. William Lloyd Garrison entered the discussion and noted that white Americans took "the blacks into our houses and carriages, and feel no sensations of disgust . . . if they are servants or slaves; but if they are free and independent, our republican sensibilities are dreadfully annoyed." Garrison, *The Liberator*, 10 December 1831.

80. *The Liberator*, 5 November 1841; *The Liberator*, 12 November 1841.

81. Frederick Douglass, "Prejudice against Color," *The North Star*, 13 June 1850.

82. Zylstra, "Whiteness, Freedom, and Technology," 683.

83. Jennings quoted in Hewitt, "The Search for Elizabeth Jennings," 391.

84. *The Provincial Freeman*, 17 March 1855.

85. *Freedom's Journal*, 20 July 1827.

86. *The Liberator*, 10 December 1831.

87. Ibid.

88. *The New York Evangelist*, 4 November 1837; *The Emancipator*, 26 October 1837; Freeman, "The Free Negro in New York City," 103; Walker, *The Afro-American in New York City*, 18–19; Swift, *Black Prophets of Justice*, 101.

89. *The Liberator*, 10 December 1831.

90. *The Liberator*, 5 April 1834.

91. *The Colored American*, 30 June 1838.

92. Child, *An Appeal*, 203.

93. Gross, *What Blood Won't Tell*, 36.

94. Weed, *A Chapter from the Autobiography of Mr. Thurlow Weed*, 8–9.

Chapter Three

1. From a letter from David Ruggles to *The Providence Courier*, 9 August 1838, reprinted and editorialized in *The Colored American*, 25 August 1838.

2. Melish, *Disowning Slavery*, 166–206; Lhamon, *Jump Jim Crow*, 95–116.

3. Woodward, *The Strange Career of Jim Crow*, 7n; Ruchames, "Jim Crow Railroads," 62.

4. Mackintosh, "'Ticketed Through,'" 62; Bradlee, *The Eastern Railroad*, 12; Directors of the Boston and Providence Railroad Corporation, "Fourth Annual Report, 1836," 23–25.

5. *Annual Reports of the Railroads in the State of Massachusetts*, 4.

6. Mackintosh, "'Ticketed Through.'"

7. Laurie, *Beyond Garrison*, 23; Yee, *Black Women Abolitionists*, 82–83.

8. Quincy, *Figures of the Past*, 341.

9. Ibid., 340–341; Carter, *When Railroads Were New*, 29–31; Cohen, "Women at Large," 47; Zylstra, "Whiteness, Freedom, and Technology," 682; Grant, *The Railroad*, 28; John Anderson "J. A." Collins to William Lloyd Garrison, 4 October 1841, published in *The Liberator*, 15 October 1841.

10. Quincy, *Figures of the Past*, 340–341; Directors of the Taunton Branch Railroad Corporation, "First Annual Report, 1836," 39–41; Directors of the Taunton Branch Railroad Corporation, "Second Annual Report, 1837," 61–62.

11. Boston and Providence Railroad Corporation, "Sixth Annual Report, 1838," 17–20.

12. Ibid.

13. Zylstra, "Whiteness, Freedom, and Technology," 678–702.

14. *The Liberator*, 20 September 1839; "Rail Road Incident," *The Emancipator and Republican*, 4 April 1842.

15. *The Liberator*, 14 January 1842; *The Colored American*, 30 January 1841.

16. Roediger, *The Wages of Whiteness*, 43–92.

17. "Testimony of Joseph Grinnel," *The Liberator*, 6 August 1841.

18. "Obstructions on the Railroad," *Salem Gazette*, 12 October 1838.

19. Cohen, "Women at Large," 44–50.

20. "Testimony of Joseph Grinnel," *The Liberator*, 6 August 1841.

21. Jacobs, *Incidents in the Life of a Slave Girl*, 162.

22. *The Liberator*, 11 June 1841.

23. Gassan, *The Birth of American Tourism*, 38.

24. Jacobs, *Incidents in the Life of a Slave Girl*, 181. For black workers on the ship, see also *The Columbian Centinel*, 18 May 1839; "'Unparalleled Outrage!' in *The Herald of Freedom*," published in *The Liberator*, 31 May 1839; William Lloyd Garrison, "Scene on Board of a Steam-Boat," Letter to the Editor of *The Boston Courier*, *The Liberator*, 24 May 1839.

25. "From *The Lynn Record*," *The Liberator*, 1 October 1841; "A Letter of David Ruggles, 24 July 1841," *The Liberator*, 6 August 1841.

26. Douglass, *My Bondage and My Freedom*, 393–394.

27. Anderson "J. A." Collins to William Lloyd Garrison, 4 October 1841, printed in *The Liberator*, 15 October 1841.

28. Alexander, *African or American*, 82–86; Kantrowitz, *More than Freedom*, 177.

29. Hodges, *David Ruggles*, 131.

30. Alexander, *African or American*, 122, 131–134.

31. *The Weekly Advocate*, 14 January 1837.

32. "Remarks by James McCune Smith Delivered at a Meeting of the Glasgow Emancipation Society, 15 March 1837," in Ripley, ed., *The Black Abolitionist Papers*, 65–67, quotation at 66.

33. *The Weekly Advocate*, 14 January 1837.

34. *The Colored American*, 9 June 1838.

35. On black radicalism and respectability politics, see, for example, Rael, *Black Identity and Black Protest*, 202–206; Mitchell, *Righteous Propagation*, 84–85; Jones, *All Bound Up Together*.

36. See *Freedom's Journal*, 1 June 1827, 30 July 1827, 22 February 1828, 25 April 1828, 11 July 1828, 25 July 1828.

37. Samuel Cornish to Thomas L. Jennings, Ransom F. Ware, Zachariah Barbary, and Charles B. Ray, Esqrs., 20 November 1838, *The Colored American*, 25 November 1838.

38. Jacobs, *Incidents in the Life of a Slave Girl*, 177 (emphasis in original).

39. Ibid.

40. Anonymous, *The Laws of Etiquette* (1841), 192.

41. Bederman, *Manliness and Civilization*, 20.

42. *The Colored American*, 25 November 1838.

43. *The Colored American*, 30 June 1838.

44. Garrison, "Scene on Board of a Steam-Boat," Letter to the Editor of *The Boston Courier*, *The Liberator*, 24 May 1839.

45. *The Columbian Centinel*, 18 May 1839; "'Unparalleled Outrage!' in *The Herald of Freedom*," *The Liberator*, 31 May 1839; Garrison, "Scene on Board of a Steam-Boat," Letter to the Editor of *The Boston Courier*, *The Liberator*, 24 May 1839.

46. *The Colored American*, 25 August 1838. It is important to pause here to sort out exactly what Ruggles meant when he decried the incident a lynching. Later in the nineteenth century, the crime became an undeniably racialized and classed event in which mobs of white marauders hung, mutilated, and murdered black men and women for perceived and fabricated transgressions. In 1838, lynching was a violent act that stepped outside of legal channels to deploy vigilante justice, but it did not necessarily translate to murder. And although the act was not strictly racialized and, as such, it did not yet conjure images of white violence on blacks, it should not be discounted that Ruggles harnessed the term precisely at a moment when northern emancipation threatened to destabilize white supremacy in the antebellum North.

47. Letter from Sinceritas, New Haven, 29 September 1838 to the editor, *The Colored American*, 13 October 1838.

48. Wiggins, ed., *Captain Paul Cuffe's Logs and Letters*, 213.

49. *The Colored American*, 27 June 1840.

50. Janson, *The Stranger in America* (1807), 88, quoted in Roediger, *The Wages of Whiteness*, 47.

51. Woodward, *The Strange Career of Jim Crow*, 7n; Ruchames, "Jim Crow Railroads," 62.

52. Wilentz, *Chants Democratic*, 269.

53. Roediger, *The Wages of Whiteness*, 115.

54. Melish, *Disowning Slavery*, 166–209.

55. Lhamon, *Jump Jim Crow*, 95–116.

56. Lott, *Love and Theft*, 52.

57. Cockrell, *Demons of Disorder*, 63–64, 72.

58. *The Workingman's Advocate*, 13 April 1833; *The Boston Commercial Gazette*, 15 April 1833.

59. Cockrell, *Demons of Disorder*, 71; Lhamon, *Jump Jim Crow*, 96–106.

60. Kerber, "Abolitionists and Amalgamators," 28–39; Richards, *"Gentlemen of Property and Standing"*; Harris, "From Abolitionist Amalgamators to 'Rulers of the Five Points,'" 191–212.

61. *The Workingman's Advocate*, 4 October 1834, 19 April 1834.

62. *The Daily Herald and Gazette*, 28 July 1837; *The Daily Ohio Statesman*, 8 March 1838; *The Morning Herald*, 21 April 1838; *The Raleigh Register and North Carolina Gazette*, 23 April 1838.

63. Crouthamel and Jackson, "James Gordon Bennett, the *New York Herald*," 294–316.

64. *Vanity Fair*, 27 April 1861.

65. See *The Newark Daily Advertiser*, 2 January 1836; *The Public Ledger*, 8 March 1838.

66. *The Liberator*, 25 February 1842 (emphasis mine).

67. Directors of the Taunton Branch Railroad Corporation, "First Annual Report, 1836," 39–41; Directors of the Taunton Branch Railroad Corporation, "Second Annual Report, 1837," 61–62.

68. *The Colored American*, 25 August 1838.

69. Douglass, *My Bondage and My Freedom*, 393–394.

70. Welke, "Rights of Passage," 73–93; Giesberg, *Army at Home*, 92–118; Giddings, *When and Where I Enter*, 22–23; Kelley, *Right to Ride*.

71. Anderson "J. A." Collins to William Lloyd Garrison, 4 October 1841, published in *The Liberator*, 15 October 1841.

72. Although Howard is not mentioned by name in the original discussion of the case, in July 1841, Ruggles mentioned Howard when he brought charges against the NB&T for assault and lost belongings. When he lost his case, Ruggles argued that New Bedford judges had a tradition of protecting the "minions" of the railroads, as evidenced by "a similar outrage inflicted upon the person of Shadrach Howard, of New Bedford." Howard was the only activist in the region before mid-1841 to take the railroads to court. The original case is referenced in *The Liberator*, 15 January 1841; Ruggles references that Howard was the victim in *The Liberator*, 6 August 1841. On Howard's family tree, see Grover, *The Fugitive's Gibraltar*, 87–88, 121, 126, 139.

73. *The Liberator*, 6 August 1841.

74. Johnson, "The Slave Trader," 13–38; Gross, *What Blood Won't Tell*, 1–110; Wong, *Neither Fugitive nor Free*, 1–6 and 19–76.

75. Litwack, *North of Slavery*, 93–95.

76. *The Liberator*, 15 January 1841.

77. *The New York Spectator*, 2 January 1841; *The Liberator*, 15 January 1841, 26 February 1841; Alexander, *African or American*, 110–112; Hewitt, "Mr. Downing and His Oyster House," 229–252.

78. *The Liberator*, 26 February 1841.

79. *The New Bedford Register*, 20 March 1842; *The Liberator*, 22 April 1842.

80. On black women and the struggle against public transportation providers before emancipation, see Kelley, *Right to Ride*, 16–32; Welke, "Rights of Passage," 73–93.

81. *Frederick Douglass' Paper*, 2 March 1855; *The Newark Daily Advertiser*, 24 February 1855 (emphasis in original).

82. *Frederick Douglass' Paper*, 18 May 1855.

83. Alexander, *African or American*, 128.

84. Daniel Mann to 'The Public,' *The Liberator*, 12 November 1841; *The Liberator*, 11 June 1841, 8 October 1841, 5 November 1841.

85. Daniel Mann to 'The Public,' *The Liberator*, 12 November 1841; *The Liberator*, 11 June 1841, 8 October 1841; Ruchames, "Jim Crow Railroads," 61–75.

86. See petitions, Massachusetts State Senate Unpassed Legislation. 1842 session, Docket 11057. SC1/series 231 and Massachusetts State Senate Unpassed Legislation. 1841 session, Docket 10903. SC1/series 231. On petitioning in Massachusetts, see Moulton, "Closing the 'Floodgate of Impurity,'" 2–34.

87. *The Liberator*, 18 February 1842.

88. *The Liberator*, 22 April 1842.

89. *The Liberator*, 25 February 1842.

90. Ripley, ed., *The Black Abolitionist Papers*, 571–573; Blackett, *Building an Anti-slavery Wall*.

91. Charles Lenox Remond, "Testimony before the Massachusetts General Court," *The Liberator*, 25 February 1842.

92. "The Joint Special Committee," 7–8.

93. *The Liberator*, 25 February 1842.

94. Remond, "Testimony before the Massachusetts General Court," *The Liberator*, 25 February 1842.

95. "The Joint Special Committee," 4, 7.

96. The example of Garrison's chiding is taken from *The Liberator*, 22 April 1842, but Garrison launched this column on 8 April 1842 and ran the column nearly weekly for a year until he abruptly ended the column on 24 March 1843.

97. *The Liberator*, 28 April 1843.

98. Kelley, *Right to Ride*; Welke, "Rights of Passage," 73–93; Zylstra, "Whiteness, Freedom, and Technology," 678–702; Giesberg, *Army at Home*, 92–118; Biddle and Dubin, *Tasting Freedom*, 323–354; Masur, *An Example for All the Land*, 107–112; Kahan, "Pedestrian Matters," 34–82.

99. American Anti-Slavery Society, *The Anti-Slavery History of the John-Brown Year*, 215.

Chapter Four

1. See "William Wells Brown Passport Application," U.S. Passport Applications, 1795–1905 (M1372), 1795–1855, Roll 030, 9 June 1849–29 September 1849, at Ancestry.com.

2. "Williams Wells Brown to Wendell Phillips, Esq.," *The Liberator*, 30 November 1849.

3. From the Majority Opinion of Chief Justice Roger Taney, *Dred Scott v. Sandford*, 13.

4. Jacobson, *Whiteness of a Different Color*, 22.

5. Smith, *Civic Ideals*, 176.

6. On colored travelers abroad, see Ripley, ed., *The Black Abolitionist Papers*; Blackett, *Building an Antislavery Wall* and *Beating against the Barriers*; *The Liberator*, 2 November 1849; Stovall, *Paris Noir*, xiv; Dorr, *A Colored Man round the World*; Stowe, *Going Abroad*, 62–73.

7. There is not much scholarship on passport rejections of African Americans, yet these works are formative. Leon Litwack, first in a 1958 article and then in his seminal 1961 book about free people, *North of Slavery*, demonstrated how the federal government sought to limit citizenship rights for African Americans through a series of antiblack decisions and opinions before the Civil War. Litwack's discussion of the passport is invaluable because he broadly describes the passport denials of African Americans from 1834 to 1858 and explains the federal rationale for such rejections. Craig Robertson's 2004 dissertation and 2010 book each argue

that the institution of passport bureaucracy helped to articulate definitions of citizenship in the nineteenth-century United States. Edlie Wong's important 2009 book on African American mobility uses the passport rejections of colored travelers to illustrate the "fictions of free travel." See Litwack, "The Federal Government and the Free Negro," 271–273 and *North of Slavery*, 54–57; Robertson, "'Passport Please,'" 121–129 and *The Passport in America*, 125–159; Wong, *Neither Fugitive nor Free*, 240–262.

8. Hunt, *The American Passport*, 43.

9. Ibid., 79.

10. Ibid., 50–51.

11. Kerber, "Toward a History of Statelessness," 733.

12. Torpey, *The Invention of the Passport*, 4, 20–24; Salter, *The Passport*, 43–44; Robertson, "'Passport Please,'" 8–34.

13. Salter, *The Passport*, 43–44.

14. Torpey, *The Invention of the Passport*, 4, 20–24.

15. Parker, "Making Blacks Foreigners," 98, 115–119.

16. On black political and social citizenship in the South before the civil rights movement, see Litwack, *Trouble in Mind*.

17. *The Liberator*, 17 February 1860 (emphasis mine); Moran, *The Journal of Benjamin Moran*, 608; Hunt, *The American Passport*, 4.

18. *The Liberator*, 17 February 1860; *The Scottish Press* (Edinburgh), 20 December 1859; *The Liberator*, 20 January 1860; "Letter to the Editor of the *Liverpool Morning Star*," *The Liberator*, 6 January 1860.

19. *The Liberator*, 17 February 1860 (emphasis mine).

20. *The Liberator*, 20 January 1860.

21. *The Leeds Mercury*, 10 January 1860; *The Derby Mercury*, 11 January 1860.

22. "The Aristocracy of Colour," *The Liverpool Mercury*, 10 January 1860.

23. *The Liberator*, 20 January 1860; *The Commercial Advertiser*, 22 January 1860; *The Evening Post*, 23 January 1860; *The New York Times*, 24 January 1860; *The New York Herald*, 24 January 1860; *The New York Tribune*, 27 January 1860; *The Constitution*, 27 January 1860; *The Ohio State Journal*, 31 January 1860; *The Milwaukee Sentinel and Gazette*, 1 February 1860.

24. *The New York Times*, 25 January 1860, 4.

25. Cox, *Traveling South*, 2, 64–66. Cox goes on to contend that slavery prevented slaves from "acting or moving in their own interests."

26. In 1839, Canadian shipbuilder Samuel Cunard promised to harness the technology that would allow steam-powered vessels to ply the Atlantic at such astounding speeds that a fleet of four ships—the *Britannia*, the *Columbia*, the *Acadia*, and the *Caledonia*—would start delivering the British mail from Liverpool to Halifax bimonthly, and eventually weekly. See Fox, *Transatlantic*, 7; *Albion: A Journal of News, Politics and Literature*, 29 April 1839; "Samuel Cunard to Messrs. Dana, Fenno and Henshaw," *Christian Register and Boston Observer*, 27 April 1839.

27. Stowe, *Sunny Memories*, 143.

28. Mulvey, *Transatlantic Manners*, 6.

29. "Foreign Passports," *The Massachusetts Ploughman and New England Journal of Agriculture*, 11 October 1845. Here are a few other examples from contemporary newspapers. On travel to Antwerp, Brussels, and the Citadel: "Break up the Union and the Potomac will bristle with citadels like this, and passports and all such nuisances will follow in their train," *The New Yorker*, 17 December 1836. On travel in Le Havre, France: "the intolerable nuisance of the custom house and passport office," *The Christian Advocate and Journal*, 4 August 1837.

30. Robertson, "'Passport Please,'" 10.

31. Murray, *Murray's Handbook*, vi–vii.

32. "Boppart to the Editor of *The National Era*," *The National Era*, 6 April 1848.

33. "J. M. to the Editor of *The Episcopal Recorder*," *The Episcopal Recorder*, 27 July 1839.

34. *The Christian Watchman*, 19 April 1836.

35. Camp, *Closer to Freedom*, 12–16; Goodell, *The American Slave Code in Theory and Practice*, 226–227.

36. Davis, formerly enslaved, interviewed by Preston Klein in Alabama, 24 July 1937, 106. Rawick, ed., *The American Slave*, Volume 6, 106.

37. Body, formerly enslaved, interviewed by J. R. Jones in Georgia, 28 July 1937, 86. Rawick, ed., *The American Slave*, Volume 12, 86. The quotation marks bracketing the words "patarolers" and "nigger" are original to the text of the WPA interview.

38. Bolster, *Black Jacks*, 135–138.

39. Douglass, *Narrative of the Life of Frederick Douglass*, 70; Jacobs, *Incidents in the Life of a Slave Girl*, 111–112.

40. Bolster, *Black Jacks*, 158–189.

41. Wong, *Neither Slave nor Free*, 183–239; Egerton, *He Shall Go Out Free*, 217; Neuman, "The Lost Century of American Immigration Law," 1873–1877.

42. See South Carolina judge William Johnson's opinion regarding the (state) constitutionality of the Negro Seamen Acts, printed in *Niles' Weekly Register*, 6 September 1823; Hamer, "Great Britain, the United States, and the Negro Seamen Acts," 3–4; Bolster, *Black Jacks*, 202.

43. Walker, *Appeal*; Crockett, "The Incendiary Pamphlet," 310–311.

44. North Carolina passed antisailor legislation in 1831. After the slave revolt known familiarly as Nat Turner's Rebellion in 1831 in Southampton, Virginia, several more southern states attempted to curb the mobility of black sailors in port, including Florida in 1832, Alabama in 1839, and Louisiana in 1842. See Hamer, "Great Britain, the United States, and the Negro Seamen Acts," 12, 16, 18; Bolster, *Black Jacks*, 198–199.

45. Wong, *Neither Fugitive nor Free*, 189.

46. *The New York Observer and Chronicle*, 13 March 1851; *The Liberator*, 14 May 1852.

47. Bolster, *Black Jacks*, 202; *The New York Evangelist*, 8 January 1857.

48. Neuman, "The Lost Century of American Immigration Law," 1871n248; Wolf, *Almost Free*, 46–47; Bullard, "Deconstructing a Manumission Document," 287.

49. Frazier, *Runaway and Freed Missouri Slaves*, 91.

50. Douglass, *Life and Times*, 643.

51. Litwack, *North of Slavery*, 70.

52. Douglass, *Life and Times*, 643.

53. Litwack, *North of Slavery*, 248–249.

54. Craft and Craft, *Running a Thousand Miles*.

55. Litwack, *North of Slavery*, 249.

56. Delany, *The Condition, Elevation, Emigration and Destiny of the Colored People*, 155–156.

57. *The American Anti-Slavery Reporter*, February 1834.

58. Northup, *Twelve Years a Slave*, 32–38.

59. *The Liberator*, 10 April 1857.

60. Hunt, *The American Passport*, 15.

61. *The Liberator*, 10 April 1857; Roberts Vaux to Secretary of State John McLane, 16 May 1834, United States Passport Applications, 1795–1925 (M1372), Roll 002, 13 May 1833–31 December 1834, Ancestry.com.

62. Hunt, *The American Passport*, 18–19.

63. *The Emancipator and Republican*, 26 July 1849; *The Liberator*, 10 August 1849; *The North Star*, 24 August 1849.

64. Newman, "Reading the Bodies," 150–152.

65. U.S. Seamen's Protection Certificate, 29 October 1807, M1880 Roll 08, Ancestry.com.

66. Roberts Vaux to Secretary of State John McLane, 16 May 1834, *United States Passport Applications, 1795–1925* (M1372), Roll 002, 13 May 1833–31 December 1834, Ancestry.com.

67. "The Essex County Freeman," *The Emancipator and Republican*, 16 August 1849.

68. Gross, *What Blood Won't Tell*, 16–72.

69. *The Liberator*, 10 April 1857.

70. American Anti-Slavery Society, *The Anti-Slavery History of the John-Brown Year*, 221.

71. Hunt, *The American Passport*, 15.

72. *The New York Evangelist*, 11 March 1837; "The Essex County Freeman," *The Emancipator and Republican*, 16 August 1849; Alexander, *African or American*, 46.

73. *The Liberator*, 10 August 1849. Edlie Wong's study of the contradictions surrounding the antebellum "law of passports" and specifically the Clayton passport denial of Henry Hambleton, have informed my thinking here. Wong, *Neither Fugitive nor Free*, 243–262.

74. *The Liberator*, 10 August 1849; *The Emancipator and Republican*, 26 July 1849; *The North Star*, 20 July 1849.

75. "From Department of State Circular," *New York Daily Times*, 25 December 1852.

76. *The Pennsylvania Freeman*, n.d., reprinted in *The National Era*, 5 July 1849; *The Pennsylvania Freeman*, n.d., reprinted in *The National Era*, 27 September 1849. *The Annual Report of the Massachusetts Anti-Slavery Society* also gives credit to *The Freeman* and the *National Anti-Slavery Standard* for breaking the story. See *Eighteenth Annual Report*, 23 January 1850, compiled in *Annual Report, Massachusetts Anti-Slavery Society*, Volumes 18–24, 44.

77. "Official Injustice," *The National Era*, 5 July 1849.

78. *The Christian Citizen*, published in *The Liberator*, 10 August 1849.

79. *The North Star*, 20 July 1849.

80. *The Liberator*, 2 November 1849; Brown, *The American Fugitive in Europe*, 95.

81. Williams Wells Brown to Wendell Phillips, Esq., 22 November 1849, published in *The Liberator*, 30 November 1849.

82. Nell, *Colored Patriots of the American Revolution*, 323. Ironically, William Wells Brown received this passport on the day after the new U.S. foreign minister received his credentials and two months after the previous minister had left office. In other words, it is possible that he received the passport not because the English shamed the Americans into making the U.S. government do the right thing but rather because he approached the embassy while it was in transition and thus his application slipped through the cracks.

83. *The Liberator*, 30 November 1849.

84. Baptist, *The Half Has Never Been Told*, 326–342.

85. Perkins, "A Neglected Phase of the Movement for Southern Unity," 154–159.

86. *The Christian Citizen*, published in *The Liberator*, 10 August 1849 (emphasis in original).

87. Northern newspapers carried the story throughout July and August 1849. For example, see *The Wisconsin Democrat*, 25 July 1849; *The Milwaukee Sentinel and Gazette*, 26 July 1849; *The Evening Post*, 10 August 1849; *The New-Bedford Mercury*, 3 August 1849; *The New York Spectator*, 9 August 1849; *The New Hampshire Patriot and State Gazette*, 16 August 1849; *The Farmer's Cabinet*, 23 August 1849; *The Watchman*, 23 August 1849; *The Pennsylvania Freeman*, 23 August 1849; *The Oshkosh True Democrat*, 24 August 1849.

88. *The Wisconsin Democrat*, 25 July 1849.

89. *The New York Spectator*, 9 August 1849.

90. *The Norfolk Democrat*, 17 August 1849.

91. *The Pennsylvania Freeman*, 23 August 1849; Baptist, *The Half Has Never Been Told*, 326–342.

92. *The New-Bedford Mercury*, 3 August 1849.

93. Alexander, *African or American*.

94. Nell, *Colored Patriots of the American Revolution*, 320–327.

95. U.S. Department of State, *The United States Consular System*, 165.

96. "Assistant Secretary of State J. A. Thomas to Superior Court Clerk of New York City H. H. Rice," *New York Observer and Chronicle*, 20 November 1856.

97. Ibid.

98. Ibid.

99. *The Liberator*, 21 November 1856.

100. "Thomas Lockwood Certificate of Protection," *The Liberator*, 28 November 1856; Hunt, *The American Passport*, 49. In 1857, the Department of State took up the idea of a loyalty pledge for all American passport applicants. An applicant

had to sign the pledge before a notary public, who asked them to disclose their precise destination abroad, divulge their status as a naturalized or native citizen, and vow that they were a "loyal citizen of the United States."

101. United States Supreme Court, *The Case of Dred Scott in the United States Supreme Court*, 7.

102. Ibid., 15.

103. Ibid., 18.

104. For just a few examples, see "Spirited Meeting of the Colored Citizens of Philadelphia," *The Liberator*, 10 April 1857; William Cooper Nell, "Our Proscribed Colored Citizens," *The Liberator*, 8 May 1857. In each of these speeches and editorials, and in many others in the abolitionist weekly *The Liberator* between 1857 and 1865, the phrase "bound to respect" in reference to Taney's opinion is used to alert, rally, and even egg on people of color to take action against the infamous decision.

105. *The Liberator*, 10 April 1857.

106. Ibid.

107. "Speech of Dr. John S. Rock," *The Liberator*, 30 January 1860.

108. Hunt, *The American Passport*, 50–51.

109. Litwack, "The Federal Government and the Free Negro," 275.

110. *The Liberator*, 28 February 1862.

111. *The Liberator*, 30 December 1864.

Chapter Five

1. McFeely, *Frederick Douglass*, 116.

2. *The Liberator*, 22 August 1845.

3. "Letters from Frederick Douglass and James N. Buffum," *The Liberator*, 26 September 1845.

4. On the Middle Passage and the physical as well as spiritual agony of the journey for captured Africans, see Smallwood, *Saltwater Slavery*.

5. Black and abolitionist periodicals often described the "horrors of the Middle Passage." See *Freedom's Journal*, 14 March 1828, 25 April 1828; *The Liberator*, 5 May 1832, 6 October 1832.

6. Quoted in Fryer, *Staying Power*, 122.

7. Waldstreicher, *Slavery's Constitution*, 39–42; Fryer, *Staying Power*, 120–126, 203; Wise, *Though the Heavens May Fall*, esp. 111–119; Walvin, *Black and White*, 117–129. Another factor that fortified the British reputation as a destination for social equality was Lord Dunmore's Proclamation of 1775. Dunmore was Virginia's royal governor, who promised liberty to slaves who fought for the British in the American Revolution. Although enslaved soldiers were treated badly by the British, tens of thousands of African American men chose to fight as loyalists anyway. In 1784, hundreds, maybe even thousands, of adult male loyalists held Dunmore to his promise and descended on London as free men. See Fryer, *Staying Power*, 191.

8. Minardi, *Making Slavery History*, 100–101.

9. *The Colored American* published an excerpt from Prince Hoare's 1820 memoir of Sharp, *Memoirs of Granville Sharp, ESQ*. See *The Colored American*, 30 November 1827.

10. Riddell, "The Fugitive Slave," 343–345.

11. Gough, "Raising the Moral Conscience," 16.

12. Kerr-Ritchie, *Rites of August First*.

13. *The Liberator*, 14 January 1832; quotation from Reverend Nathaniel Paul to William Lloyd Garrison, Bristol, England, 10 April 1833, published in *The Liberator*, 22 June 1833.

14. Blackett, *Building an Antislavery Wall*, 6–13.

15. Lorimer, *Colour, Class and the Victorians*, 12.

16. Fisch, *American Slaves in Victorian England*, 70.

17. Lorimer, *Colour, Class and the Victorians*, 12–13.

18. *The Christian Register and Boston Observer*, 27 April 1839.

19. *Albion: A Journal of News, Politics and Literature*, 29 April 1839; Fox, *Transatlantic*, 42, 47, 88–94.

20. *The Niles National Register* (Baltimore), 12 July 1848; "The Cambria Steamship," *Albion: A Journal of News, Politics and Literature*, 21 December 1844.

21. Fox, *Transatlantic*, 93–98.

22. *Albion: A Journal of News, Politics and Literature*, 21 December 1844.

23. "Anti-Slavery Breakfast in Scotland," *Scottish Pilot*, published in *The Liberator*, 21 August 1840.

24. *The Morning Chronicle* (London), 6 December 1841; *The Liberator*, 10 December 1841.

25. *The Liberator*, 25 February 1842.

26. *The Leeds Mercury*, 16 September 1843.

27. "The Cunard Steam Packets—Prejudice against Color," *The Liberator*, 16 August 1844.

28. *The Liberator*, 15 November 1844.

29. Ward, *Autobiography of a Fugitive Negro*, 229.

30. Douglass, *Life and Times*, 677–678.

31. *The Liberator*, 16 August 1844.

32. Fox, *Transatlantic*, 201.

33. *The Liberator*, 7 August 1846.

34. "Letters from Frederick Douglass and James Buffum," *The Liberator*, 26 September 1845.

35. *The Liberator*, 16 August 1844.

36. See Lockwood, *Passionate Pilgrims*, 161–163; Fox, *Transatlantic*, 200–201; *The Wesleyan-Methodist Magazine*, September 1845.

37. Dickens, *American Notes*, 4.

38. Bird, *The Englishwoman*, 6.

39. Johnson, *The Cunard Story*, 14–15.

40. Dickens, *American Notes*, 5.

41. "Gossip of the Month," *The U.S. Democratic Review* (New York), January 1848.

42. Bird, *The Englishwoman*, 8.

43. Warburton, *Hochelaga*, 354.

44. "Letters from Mr. Garrison—No. 1," *The Liberator*, 7 August 1846; Bird, *The Englishwoman*, 11.

45. *Harper's Monthly Magazine*, June 1852; Fox, *Transatlantic*, 211–219.

46. *The Niles National Register*, 12 July 1848.

47. Stowe, *Sunny Memories*, 8.

48. Ibid., 5.

49. Ibid.

50. *Harper's Monthly Magazine*, June 1852.

51. Bacon, *But One Race*, 43; Borome, "Robert Purvis," 9.

52. Fox, *Transatlantic*, 7.

53. *Friend, a Religious and Literary Journal* (Philadelphia), 12 April 1834; Bacon, *But One Race*, 44; Borome, "Robert Purvis," 9. Also see Robert Purvis to William Lloyd Garrison, 13 July 1834, published in *The Liberator*, 23 August 1834, 1 March 1834. For more on Cope, see "Thomas P. Cope Obituary," *The New York Times*, 28 November 1854.

54. Bacon, *But One Race*, 44.

55. Lockwood, *Passionate Pilgrims*, 32.

56. *The Anti-Slavery Record* (New York), December 1835.

57. Although Purvis makes no mention of it in his retelling, it is likely that the steward was also a person of color, because most stewards on early packet ships were men of color. See Fox, *Transatlantic*, 7.

58. Bacon, *But One Race*, 47.

59. *The Workingman's Advocate* (New York), 8 November 1834; Smith, *How Race Is Made*, 13–16, 18, 27; Gross, *What Blood Won't Tell*, 32–41.

60. Haliburton, *Letter Bag*.

61. Machar and Marquis, *Builders of Canada*, 222–224; Brinnin, *The Sway of the Grand Saloon*, 106.

62. Haliburton, *Letter Bag*, 13–31, 43–49, 68–69, 77–84, 91–99, 153–158.

63. Rediker, "Liberty beneath the Jolly Roger"; Dugaw, "Female Sailors Bold"; Springer, "The Captain's Wife"; Bolster, "'Every Inch a Man,'" 4, 34, 92, 138; Fox, *Transatlantic*, 7.

64. Bolster, "'Every Inch a Man,'" 138; Fox, *Transatlantic*, 7.

65. On race and complaints of odor, see Classen, "The Odor of the Other," 134–135.

66. Burrop, *The Times* (London), 13 April 1847. Samuel Cunard later refuted the authenticity of Burrop's letter. See "Samuel Cunard to the editor of the *Times* (London)," *The Times* (London), 14 April 1847.

67. Haliburton, *Letter Bag*, 29; Brinnin, *The Sway of the Grand Saloon*, 137.

68. Haliburton, *Letter Bag*, 23 (emphasis added).

69. Jacobs, *Incidents in the Life of a Slave Girl*, 183; Beers, *Nathaniel Parker Willis*, 284–285.

70. Several of these female travelers ran into problems on Cunard steamships. A representative from the Cunard Company tried to prevent Ellen Craft and her

husband, William, from sailing on a Cunard steamship from Halifax to Liverpool in November 1850. Actress Mary Webb and her husband, Frank, were refused service by Cunard in 1856, and Caroline Remond Putnam and her son, niece, and nephew were all cordoned by Cunard in November 1859. On the Crafts' exclusion, see Craft and Craft, *Running a Thousand Miles*, 107. On the Webbs' exclusion, see *The Liberator*, 15 August 1856. On Caroline Remond Putnam's exclusion, see Caroline Putnam to Samuel Cunard, 29 November 1859, and Edward Cunard and J. G. Bates to Caroline Putnam, 27 October 1859, published in *Lloyd's Weekly Newspaper* (London), 8 July 1860.

71. To tell the story of the violence Douglass confronted at sea, I have layered Douglass's own description of events—including those in his second (1855) and third (1882) memoirs, the letters he wrote home, and the speeches he gave in Ireland in 1845 and 1846—with other passengers' reports of events. These come from two British army officers on the *Cambria*, neither of them fans of Douglass, who were traveling home after touring America. Another set of descriptions comes from members of the Hutchinson Family Singers, a famous American protest group, who were headed for Europe on the same ship, were friends of Douglass, and recorded events individually: brother Asa in a travel journal written during the voyage, brother Judson in letters sent home from abroad, and brother John in a memoir written years later. Other reports come from letters sent anonymously to the editor of the antiblack *New York Herald* by travelers who claimed to have been on the ship with Douglass. See *The Liberator*, 26 September 1845, 3 October 1845, 10 October 1845, 16 January 1846, 13 February 1846; *The New York Herald*, 27 September 1845, 6 October 1845, 1 December 1845; *The Emancipator and Weekly Chronicle* (Boston), 24 September 1845; *Freeman's Journal and Daily Commercial Advertiser* (Dublin), 13 September 1845. See Frederick Douglass to Francis Jackson, 29 January 1846, reprinted in Foner, *The Life and Writings of Frederick Douglass*, 135; Douglass, *My Bondage and My Freedom*, 370–372; Douglass, *Life and Times*, 677–679; Blassingame, *The Frederick Douglass Papers*, 61–67, 71, 82–85, 89–93, 129–130, 139–143, 214–215; Alexander, *L'Acadie*, 261–262; Warburton, *Hochelaga*, 354–361; Cockrell, *Excelsior*, 315–324; Hutchinson, *The Story of the Hutchinsons*, 142–148.

72. *The Liberator*, 15 October 1841.

73. Douglass, "American Prejudice against Color," reprinted in Blassingame, *The Frederick Douglass Papers*, 63.

74. Douglass, *Life and Times*, 678.

75. Nathaniel Peabody (N. P.) Rogers to Charles Ray published in *The Colored American*, 3 October 1840; Charles Remond to William Lloyd Garrison, 25 April 1843, published in *The Liberator*, 28 April 1843.

76. Regarding Remond's upcoming abolitionist tour in England, see "From a Letter by Sarah Parker Remond to Unnamed Recipient," 18 September 1858, published in *The Liberator*, 19 November 1858.

77. Douglass, "An Account of American Slavery," reprinted in Blassingame, *The Frederick Douglass Papers*, 139–140.

78. Pettinger, "At Sea—Coloured Passenger," 153–154.

79. Ibid., 161.

80. Ibid.

81. Hutchinson, *The Story of the Hutchinsons*, 145. Douglass told an Irish audience "he had a great number of copies of his narrative; and, through these, the greater number of passengers soon became well acquainted with him." See Douglass, "The Cambria Riot, My Slave Experience, and My Irish Mission," reprinted in Blassingame, *The Frederick Douglass Papers*, 90.

82. *Albion: A Journal of News, Politics and Literature*, 21 December 1844.

83. Douglass, "An Account of American Slavery," reprinted in Blassingame, *The Frederick Douglass Papers*, 140.

84. Douglass, *Life and Times*, 678. Other observers remembered the extent of Douglass's mobility differently, however. John Hutchinson remembered that Douglass could only visit other sections of the ship if he was accompanied by his white comrades. See Hutchinson, *The Story of the Hutchinsons*, 145.

85. *The Liberator*, 26 September 1845.

86. *The Liberator*, 3 October 1845.

87. Douglass, *Life and Times*, 678.

88. *The Liberator*, 26 September 1845.

89. Cockrell, *Excelsior*, 320.

90. "Pro-slavery Row on the Atlantic," published in *The Liberator*, 10 October 1845.

91. Hutchinson, *The Story of the Hutchinsons*, 142. Judkins established the individualist demeanor among passenger-ship captains and was destined to become one of the most admired of Cunard's commodores. Historian Stephen Fox tells a story that, in a gale, Judkins refused to indulge a passenger's worry. The passenger asked the captain how far they were from land, and Judkins dismissively replied, "two miles," while he pointed his finger toward the ocean below. In another instance, a raucous argument occurred between circus promoter P. T. Barnum and Judkins during an 1847 crossing when Barnum wanted an American minister to give a Methodist sermon as opposed to the Cunard policy of allowing only Episcopal services to be conducted on board. Captain Judkins held his ground by threatening to put Barnum in irons and telling him to "shut up." Judkins did not easily kowtow to his passengers' whims and was unafraid to take charge of his own ship. See Fox, *Transatlantic*, 218; Barnum, *Struggles and Triumphs*, 243.

92. *The Liberator*, 26 September 1845.

93. Warburton, *Hochelaga*, 358–359; Hutchinson, *The Story of the Hutchinsons*, 146. Sir James Alexander remarked that "the planters had withstood emancipation songs such as: There is a country far away/ Friend Hopper says 'tis Canaday/ And if we reach Victoria's shores/ He tells us we are slaves no more./ Then haste all bondsmen let us go,/ And leave this Christian country, oh!/ Haste to the land of the British Queen,/ Where whips for negroes ne'er are seen." Certainly a song that positioned the British as morally superior to the Americans and their slave system would have caused friction during the voyage. See Alexander, *L'Acadie*, 262. The song is titled "A Song for Freedom" and is collected in Brown, *The Anti-Slavery Harp*, 57.

94. Frederick Douglass to Thurlow Weed, published in *The Liberator*, 16 January 1846.

95. Frederick Douglass to William Lloyd Garrison, published in *The Liberator*, 15 September 1845. Although Douglass originally identified the man as being from Connecticut in a letter to Garrison, he did not identify the man as being from the North in either of his memoirs—both published years later—but rather placed the blame for the riot on men from Georgia and New Orleans. This was most likely an abolitionist stratagem. See Douglass, *My Bondage and My Freedom*, 371; Douglass, *Life and Times*, 678. Others also identified the man as being from Connecticut: Judson Hutchinson said the "disturbance was commenced by a Connecticut Yankee, A Member of the Baptist Church." Judson's observation was an obvious indictment of the Baptists, who were generally proslavery. See *The Liberator*, 10 October 1845. A Douglass detractor concurred, writing "[Douglass] had proceeded but a few moments when a gentleman, a citizen of Connecticut, interrupted him." See *The New York Herald*, 1 December 1845.

96. Richards, *"Gentlemen of Property and Standing,"* 114–115. See also Kerber, "Abolitionists and Amalgamators," 30–31.

97. Hutchinson, *The Story of the Hutchinsons*, 146.

98. "Letter from Judson Hutchinson," reprinted in *The Liberator*, 10 October 1845. See also the letter from "Anonymous Traveler," reprinted in *The Liberator*, 3 October 1845. The Anonymous Traveler did not remember that Captain Judkins was the slaveholder referred to but thought another man made the same confession. But Judson's brother John also remembered that Captain Judkins claimed he was formerly a slaveholder. See Hutchinson, *The Story of the Hutchinsons*, 146. At twenty-three, Judkins would have been too young to have owned 200 slaves himself in 1834, at the end of West Indian enslavement. Instead, the captain must have been referring to losing the promise of owning his family's estate.

99. Douglass, *Life and Times*, 678–679; Warburton, *Hochelaga*, 359.

100. The story of the small man was one of Douglass's favorites to tell because it emphasized his own masculinity and the lack of that quality in his detractors. He told an Irish audience that the captain pushed down the smaller American, but when the American landed on the ground, he reached into his pocket. Douglass's heart sank because he believed the man was pulling out his Bowie knife, but instead the man pulled out his calling card and handed it to Captain Judkins, apparently an invitation to duel. The man told Judkins, "I'll see you in Liverpool." Judkins was nonplussed. This same diminutive dueler got into a spat with a Mr. Gough, a very tall, broad Irishman, whom Douglass described as "a man of gigantic size" and who sided with Douglass. Later, when the conversation continued in the *Cambria*'s grand saloon, several observers got a chuckle when the smaller man said that had he not been deterred, he would have thrown Mr. Gough into the ocean himself. Apparently, Mr. Gough looked on "with the most unfeigned delight." See Blassingame, *The Frederick Douglass Papers*, 91, 141; Warburton, *Hochelaga*, 361. See also *The Liberator*, 26 September 1845.

101. *The Liberator*, 10 October 1845; Hutchinson, *The Story of the Hutchinsons*, 147.

102. *The New York Herald*, 1 December 1845.

103. *The Boston Transcript*, published in *The Liberator*, 3 October 1845.

104. *The New York Herald*, 27 September 1845.

105. *The Liberator*, 26 September 1845.

106. Charles McIver to the editors of *The Liverpool Mercury*, reprinted in *The Liberator*, 14 May 1847.

107. Frederick Douglass to William Lloyd Garrison, published in *The Liberator*, 30 April 1847.

Epilogue

1. Craft and Craft, *Running a Thousand Miles*, 66–67.

2. "William P. Powell to Sydney Howard Gay [the editor of *The National Anti-Slavery Standard* (New York)], 12 December 1850," in Ripley, ed., *The Black Abolitionist Papers*, 234–238, quotation at 234.

3. Frederick Douglass, Victoria Hotel, Belfast [Ireland] to William Lloyd Garrison, Boston, Massachusetts, 1 January 1846, published in *The Liberator*, 30 January 1846.

4. Brown, *The American Fugitive in Europe*, 40.

5. Rice and Crawford, *Liberating Sojourn*; Blackett, *Building an Antislavery Wall* and *Beating against the Barriers*; Yellin, "Incidents Abroad," 158–172; Coleman, " 'Like Hot Lead to Pour on the Americans . . . ,' " 173–188; Peterson, "Literary Transnationalism," 189–208; Gerzina, ed., *Black Victorians, Black Victoriana*; Lorimer, *Colour, Class and the Victorians*.

6. Brown, *The American Fugitive in Europe*, 98; Greenspan, *William Wells Brown*.

7. Hadden, *Slave Patrols*, 10, 80, 124; Campbell, "The Seminoles, the 'Bloodhound War,' " 259–302.

8. Brown, *Narrative of William W. Brown*, 20–22; Greenspan, *William Wells Brown*, 56–57.

9. Douglass, "Farewell Speech to the British People, at London Tavern, London, England, 30 March 1847," and "The Right to Criticize American Institutions, a speech before the American Anti-Slavery Society, 11 May 1847," in Foner, *The Life and Writings of Frederick Douglass*, 231, 235.

10. Ward, *Autobiography of a Fugitive Negro*, 236.

11. McCaskill, "Ellen Craft," 96.

12. Ibid., 97.

13. "Ellen Craft to Editor, Anti-Slavery Advocate, 26 October 1852," in Ripley, ed., *The Black Abolitionist Papers*, 330–331, quotation at 330; *Frederick Douglass' Paper*, 4 February 1853.

14. Potter, *A Hairdresser's Experience*, 13.

15. "William Craft to Samuel May, Jr., 17 July 1860," in Ripley, *The Black Abolitionist Papers*, 478–480, quotation at 478.

16. *Birmingham Daily Post* (England), 2 November 1859; *Leeds Mercury*, 5 November 1859.

17. Frederick Douglass to William Lloyd Garrison, *The Liberator*, 30 January 1846.

18. "Letter from Williams Wells Brown," *The Liberator*, 2 November 1849. See also Brown, *The American Fugitive in Europe*, 110.

19. *The Liberator*, 2 November 1849.

20. Stowe, *Going Abroad*, 73.

21. Jacobs, *Incidents in the Life of a Slave Girl*, 184–185.

22. "Charles Lenox Remond to Thomas Cole, Edinburgh," *The Liberator,* 30 October 1840.

23. Jacobs, *Incidents in the Life of a Slave Girl*, 186.

24. "Charles Lenox Remond to Charles Ray, London," *The Colored American*, 3 October 1840.

25. "Speech by J. W. C. Pennington Delivered at Exeter Hall, London, England, 21 June 1843," in Ripley, *The Black Abolitionist Papers*, 129–133, quotation at 132.

26. "Alexander Crummell to John Jay, Liverpool, 9 August 1848," in Ripley, ed., *The Black Abolitionist Papers*, 142–148, quotation at 145.

27. "William P. Powell to Sydney Howard Gay, 12 December 1850," in Ripley, ed., *The Black Abolitionist Papers*, 234–238, quotation at 234.

28. "Speech by William Wells Brown Delivered at the Concert Rooms, Store Street, London, England, 27 September 1849," in Ripley, ed., *The Black Abolitionist Papers*, 176–181, quotation at 178.

29. Frederick Douglass, "Farewell Speech to the British People, at London Tavern, London, England, 30 March 1847," in Foner, *The Life and Writings of Frederick Douglass*, 209–210.

30. *The Switch*, published in *The Liberator*, 11 June 1847 (emphasis in original).

31. Frederick Douglass to William Lloyd Garrison, *The Liberator*, 11 June 1847.

Bibliography

Note on Sources

The research for this project began at a fortuitous moment in historical scholarship: the dawn of the age of digital humanities. As a result, many of the questions I address in this piece are answered, in part, because I had access to fully searchable, digital newspaper archives. For example, the conclusions I draw about how white northerners, up until the 1830s, used the word nigger to quote (and therefore mock) African American speakers, would not have been possible without searching across an enormous swath of newspapers and periodicals. Moreover, had I only relied on conventional research methods, uncovering the evidence, particularly that which highlights African American voices, would have been futile. Therefore, I have relied on several digital archives, mostly collections of newspapers, but also genealogical resources, to make my case. I am incredibly grateful to Smith College for investing in these databases, ones that benefit scholarship and teaching across the college in multiple ways. The databases most often used here include Accessible Archives: African American Newspapers, Readex's America's Historical Newspaper, Ancestry.com, Gale: News Vault: 17th–18th Century Burney Collection Newspapers, 19th Century British Library Newspapers, British Newspapers, and ProQuest Historical Newspapers.

Periodicals and Newspapers

Albion: A Journal of News, Politics and Literature (New York)

The American Anti-Slavery Reporter (New York)

The American Sentinel and Witness (Middletown, CT)

The Antheneum; or Spirit of the English Magazines (Boston)

The Anti-Slavery Record (New York)

The Birmingham Daily Post (England)

The Bookman, An Illustrated Magazine of Literature and Life (New York)

The Boston Commercial Gazette

The Boston News-Letter

The Christian Advocate and Journal (New York)
The Christian Citizen (Worcester)
The Christian Recorder (Philadelphia)
The Christian Register and Boston Observer
The Christian Watchman (Boston)
The City Gazette (Charleston)
The Colored American (New York)
The Columbian Centinel (Boston)
The Commercial Advertiser (New York)
The Constitution (Middletown, Connecticut)
The Daily Herald and Gazette (Ohio)
The Daily Ohio Statesman
The Derby Mercury (England)
The Emancipator (New York)
The Emancipator and Republican (Boston)
The Emancipator and Weekly Chronicle (Boston)
The Episcopal Recorder (Philadelphia)
The Evening Post (New York)
The Farmer's Cabinet (New Hampshire)
The Federal Gazette and Baltimore Daily Advertiser

Frederick Douglass' Paper (Rochester, New York)
Freedom's Journal (New York)
Freeman's Journal and Daily Commercial Advertiser (Dublin)
Friend, a Religious and Literary Journal (Philadelphia)
Harper's Monthly Magazine (New York)
The Herald of Freedom (New Hampshire)
The Illustrated London News
The Independent Gazetteer (Philadelphia)
Indiana Democrat
The Leeds Mercury
The Liberator (Boston)
The Liverpool Mercury
Lloyd's Weekly Newspaper (London)
The Maryland Gazette
The Massachusetts Ploughman and New England Journal of Agriculture
The Massachusetts Spy (Worcester)
The Milwaukee Sentinel and Gazette
The Mississippi Herald and Natchez Gazette
The Morning Chronicle (London)
The Morning Herald (New York)
The Nantucket Inquirer
The National Advocate (New York)

The National Aegis (Worcester)
The National Anti-Slavery Standard (New York and Philadelphia)
The National Banner and Nashville Whig
The National Era (Washington, D.C.)
The Newark Daily Advertiser
The New-Bedford Mercury
The New Bedford Register
The New Hampshire Patriot and State Gazette
New York Daily Times
The New York Evangelist
The New York Gazette
The New York Herald
The New York Mirror
New York Observer and Chronicle
The New York Spectator
The New York Times
The New York Tribune
The New Yorker
Niles' National Register (Baltimore)
Niles' Weekly Register (Baltimore)
The Norfolk Democrat
The North Star (Rochester)
The Norwich Packet (Connecticut)
The Ohio State Journal
The Oshkosh True Democrat
The Pennsylvania Freeman

The Pennsylvania Gazette
and Democratic Press
The Philadelphia National
Enquirer
The Providence
Courier
The Provincial Freeman
(Ontario)
The Public Ledger
(Philadelphia)

The Raleigh Register and
North Carolina Gazette
The Salem Gazette
Saturday Morning
Transcript (Boston)
The Scottish Press
The Switch (Albany,
NY)
The U.S. Democratic
Review (New York)

Vanity Fair (New York)
The Watchman (Mont-
pelier)
The Weekly Advocate
(New York)
The Wesleyan-Methodist
Magazine (London)
The Wisconsin Democrat
The Workingman's
Advocate (New York)

Other Primary Sources

Alexander, Sir James E. *L'Acadie; or Seven Years' Explorations in British America in Two Volumes*, vol. 2. London: Henry Colburn, 1849.

American Anti-Slavery Society. *The Anti-Slavery History of the John-Brown Year; Being the Twenty-Seventh Annual Report of the American Anti-Slavery Society.* New York: American Anti-Slavery Society, 1861.

The Annual Report of the Massachusetts Anti-Slavery Society. Eighteenth Annual Report, 23 January 1850, compiled in Annual Report, Massachusetts Anti-Slavery Society, vol. 18–24: *1850–1858*. Westport, CT: Negro Universities Press, 1970.

Annual Reports of the Railroad Corporations in the State of Massachusetts for 1840. Boston: Dutton and Wentworth, 1841.

Annual Reports of the Railroads in the State of Massachusetts. Boston: Dutton and Wentworth, 1838.

Anonymous. *The Laws of Etiquette; or, Short Rules and Reflections for Conduct in Society: By a Gentleman*. Philadelphia: Carey, Lea, and Blanchard, 1836.

———. *The Laws of Etiquette; or, Short Rules and Reflections for Conduct in Society: By a Gentleman*. Philadelphia: Lea & Blanchard, 1841.

Barnum, Phineas Taylor. *Struggles and Triumphs, or Forty Years' Recollections.* Buffalo, NY: Warren, Johnson, 1873.

Bibb, Henry. *The Narratives of the Life and Adventures of Henry Bibb, an American Slave: Written by Himself*. New York: Author, 1849.

Bird, Isabella Lucy. *The Englishwoman in America*. 1856. Madison: University of Wisconsin Press, 1996.

Blassingame, John W., ed. *The Frederick Douglass Papers: Series One, Speeches, Debates, and Interviews*, vol. 1: *1841–1846*. New Haven, CT: Yale University Press, 1979.

Boston and Providence Railroad Corporation. "Sixth Annual Report, 1838." In *Annual Reports of the Railroad Corporations in the State of Massachusetts for 1833–1840*. Boston: Dutton and Wentworth, 1841.

Branagan, Thomas. *Serious Remonstrances, Addressed to the Citizens of the Northern States, and Their Representatives . . . Consisting of Speculations and Animadversions, on the Recent Revival of the Slave Trade, Etc.* Philadelphia: Thomas T. Stiles, 1805.

Brown, James Scott, ed. *The Declaration of Independence; The Articles of Confederation; The Constitution of the United States*. New York: Oxford University Press, 1917.

———. *The Anti-Slavery Harp: A Collection of Songs for Anti-Slavery Meetings, Compiled by William W. Brown, A Fugitive Slave*. Boston: Bela Marsh, 1848.

———. *Clotel, or, the President's Daughter: A Narrative about Slave Life in the United States*. 1853. New York: Citadel Press, 1969.

Brown, William Wells. *The American Fugitive in Europe: Sketches of Places and People Abroad in the Travels of William Wells Brown*, edited by Paul Jefferson. 1855. New York: Markus Wiener, 1991.

———. *William W. Brown, an American Slave*. London: C. Gilpin, 1849.

A Century of Lawmaking for a New Nation: U.S. Congressional Documents and Debates, 1774–1875. Annals of Congress, 2nd Congress, 2nd Session. http://lcweb2.loc.gov/ammem/amlaw/lawhome.html.

Child, Lydia Maria. *An Appeal in Favor of That Class of Americans Called African*. New York: John S. Taylor, 1836.

Clay, Henry. "An Address: Delivered to the Colonization Society of Kentucky, at Frankfort, December 17, 1829, by the Hon. Henry Clay, at the Request of the Board of Managers of the American Colonization Society." Lexington, KY: Thomas Smith, 1829.

Craft, William, and Ellen Craft. *Running a Thousand Miles for Freedom*. 1860. Athens: University of Georgia Press, 1999.

Delany, Martin. *The Condition, Elevation, Emigration and Destiny of the Colored People of the United States*. Philadelphia: Author, 1852.

Dickens, Charles. *American Notes for General Circulation in Two Volumes*, vol. 1. London: Chapman and Hall, 1842.

Directors of the Boston and Providence Railroad Corporation. "Fourth Annual Report, 1836." In *Annual Reports of the Railroad Corporations in the State of Massachusetts for 1833–1840*. Boston: Dutton and Wentworth, 1841.

Directors of the Taunton Branch Railroad Corporation. "First Annual Report, 1836." In *Annual Reports of the Railroad Corporations in the State of Massachusetts for 1833–1840*. Boston: Dutton and Wentworth, 1841.

———. "Second Annual Report, 1837." In *Annual Reports of the Railroad Corporations in the State of Massachusetts for 1833–1840*. Boston: Dutton and Wentworth, 1841.

Dorr, David. *A Colored Man round the World, by a Quadroon*. Published by author. 1858.

———. *My Bondage and My Freedom*. 1855. In *Frederick Douglass Autobiographies*. New York: Library of America, 1994.

Douglass, Frederick. *Life and Times of Frederick Douglass*. 1881. In *Frederick Douglass Autobiographies*. New York: Library of America, 1994.

———. *Narrative of the Life of Frederick Douglass, an American Slave*. 1845. In *Frederick Douglass, Autobiographies*. New York: The Library of America, 1994.

Easton, Hosea. *A Treatise on the Intellectual Character and Civil and Political Condition of the Colored People of the U. States: And the Prejudice Exercised towards Them*. Boston: I. Knapp, 1837.

Elaw, Zilpha. *Memoirs of the Life, Religious Experience, Ministerial Travels, and Labours of Mrs. Zilpha Elaw, an American Female of Colour*. London: Author, 1846. In *Sisters of Spirit: Three Black Women's Autobiographies of the Nineteenth Century*, edited by William Andrews. Bloomington: Indiana University Press, 1986.

Foner, Philip S. *The Life and Writings of Frederick Douglass, Early Years, 1817–1849*. New York: International Publishers, 1950.

Goodell, William. *The American Slave Code in Theory and Practice: Its Distinctive Features Shown by Its Statutes, Judicial Decisions, and Illustrative Facts*. New York: American and Foreign Anti-Slavery Society, 1853.

Haliburton, Thomas Chandler. *Letter Bag of the Great Western or Life on a Steamer*. 1839. London: Richard Bentley, 1853.

Howard, Benjamin C. *Report of the Decision of the Supreme Court of the United States and the Opinions of the Judges Thereof in the Case of Dred Scott versus John F. A. Sandford*. December term, 1856. Washington, DC: Cornelius Wendell, 1857.

Hutchinson, John Wallace. *The Story of the Hutchinsons (Tribe of Jesse)*. Boston: Lee and Shephard, 1896.

Jacobs, Harriet A. *Incidents in the Life of a Slave Girl: Written by Herself*, edited by Jean Fagan Yellin. 1861. Cambridge, MA: Harvard University Press, 1987.

Janson, Charles William. *The Stranger in America: Containing Observations Made during a Long Residence in That Country*. London: J. Cundee, 1807.

"The Joint Special Committee to Whom Was Committed the Petition of Francis Jackson and Others, and Sundry Other Petitioners, for a Law Securing to Colored Persons Equal Rights in Rail-Road Accommodations." February 22, 1842, Senate Document No. 63. Massachusetts General Court, Boston.

Kemble, Frances Ann. *Journal of a Residence on a Georgian Plantation in 1838–1839*, edited by John A. Scott. Athens: University of Georgia Press, 1984.

Kollner, Augustus. *Common Sights on Land and Water: Delineated and Described for Young Children*. Philadelphia: American Sunday-School Union, 1852.

Lee, Jarena. *The Life and Religious Experience of Jarena Lee, a Coloured Lady*. Philadelphia: Author, 1846. In *Sisters of Spirit: Three Black Women's Autobiographies of the Nineteenth Century*, edited by William Andrews. Bloomington: Indiana University Press, 1986.

Lhamon Jr., W. T. *Jump Jim Crow: Lost Plays, Lyrics, and Street Prose of the First Atlantic Popular Culture*. Cambridge, MA: Harvard University Press, 2003.

Lieber, Francis. *The Stranger in America, or, Letters to a Gentleman in Germany*. Philadelphia: Carey, Lea & Blanchard, 1835.

Mars, James. *Life of James Mars, a Slave Born in Connecticut, Written by Himself*. 1864. Hartford, CT: Case, Lockwood, 1868.

Martin, Francois-Xavier. *The Office and Authority of a Justice of the Peace and of Sheriffs, Coroners, &c: According to the Laws of the State of North-Carolina*. New Bern, NC: Author, 1791.

Massachusetts House of Representatives. "Free Negroes and Mulattoes," January 16, 1822.

Massachusetts State Senate Unpassed Legislation. 1841 session, Docket 10903. SC1/series 231. Massachusetts Archives.

Massachusetts State Senate Unpassed Legislation. 1842 session, Docket 11057. SC1/series 231. Massachusetts Archives.

Moran, Benjamin. *The Journal of Benjamin Moran, 1857–1865*, vol. 1, edited by Sarah Agnes Wallace and Frances Elma Gillespie. Chicago: University of Chicago Press, 1948.

Murray, John. *Murray's Handbook for Belgium and the Rhine*. London: John Murray, 1852.

Nell, William Cooper. *Colored Patriots of the American Revolution with Sketches of Several Distinguished Colored Persons to Which Is Added a Brief Survey of the Condition and Prospects of Colored Americans*. Boston: R. F. Wallcut, 1855.

Northup, Solomon. *Twelve Years a Slave*, edited by Sue Eakin. 1853. Lafayette: University of Louisiana Press, 2007.

Potter, Eliza. *A Hairdresser's Experience in High Life*, edited by Xiomara Santamarina. 1859. Chapel Hill: University of North Carolina Press, 2009.

Quincy Jr., Josiah. *Figures of the Past from the Leaves of Old Journals by Josiah Quincy*. Boston: Roberts Brothers, 1883.

Rawick, George, ed. *The American Slave: A Composite Autobiography, Alabama and Indiana Narratives*, vol. 6. Westport, CT: Greenwood, 1972.

———. *The American Slave: A Composite Autobiography, Georgia Narratives*, vol. 12, parts 1 and 2. Westport, CT: Greenwood, 1972.

Ripley, Peter, ed. *The Black Abolitionist Papers*, vol. 1: *The British Isles, 1830–1865*. Chapel Hill: University of North Carolina Press, 1985.

Sancho, Ignatius. *Letters of the Late Ignatius Sancho, an African, with Memoirs of His Life by Joseph Jekyll*. 1802. Freeport, NY: Books for Libraries, 1971.

Smith, John. *The Generall Historie of Virginia by Captain John Smith, 1624; The Fourth Booke*, edited by John Gardiner Tyler. New York: Barnes and Noble, 1907.

Still, William. *The Underground Railroad: A Record of Facts, Authentic Narratives and Letters, &c.* 1872. Medford, NJ: Plexus, 2005.

Stowe, Harriet Beecher. *Sunny Memories of Foreign Lands*. London: T. Nelson and Sons, 1854.

United States Supreme Court. *The Case of Dred Scott in the United States Supreme Court; the Full Opinions of Justice Taney and Justice Curtis, and Abstracts of the Opinions of the Other Judges, with Analysis of the Points Ruled, and Some Concluding Observations*. New York: Greely and McElrath, 1857.

U.S. Department of Commerce, Bureau of the Census. *Negro Population, 1790–1915*. Washington, DC: U.S. Government Printing Office, 1918.

U.S. Department of State. *The United States Consular System: A Manual for Consuls, and Also for Merchants, Shipowners and Masters in Their Consular Transactions; Comprising the Instructions of the Department of State in Regard to Consular Emoluments, Duties, Privileges, and Liabilities*. Washington, DC: Taylor and Maury, 1856.

U.S. Passport Applications, 1795–1925. Ancestry.com.

U.S. Seamen's Protection Certificate, 29 October 1807, M1880 Roll 08. Ancestry
.com.

Walker, David. *Walker's Appeal, in Four Articles; Together with a Preamble, to the
Colored Citizens of the World, but in Particular, and Very Expressly, to Those
of the United States of America* (1829; repr. Boston, 1830), Sabin Americana,
1500–1926. http://galenet.galegroup.com/servlet/Sabin?dd=0&locID=
mlin_w_smithcol&dl=SABCPA1C36200&srchtp=b&c=1&d2=3&docNum
=CY3810684305&bo=walker%27s+appeal&h2=1&vrsn=1.0&b1=0X&d6=
3&ste=10&dc=tiPG&stp=DateAscend&d4=0.33&n=10&d5=d6. Accessed
21 December 2015.

Warburton, Esq., Eliot. *Hochelaga: Or, England in the New World*, vol. 2. London:
Henry Colburn, 1846.

Ward, Samuel Ringgold. *Autobiography of a Fugitive Negro: His Anti-Slavery
Labours in the United States, Canada, and England*. London: John Snow, 1855.

Weed, Thurlow. *A Chapter from the Autobiography of Mr. Thurlow Weed:
Stagecoach Traveling Forty-Six Years Ago*. Albany, NY: House of Charles Van
Benthuysen and Sons, 1870.

Wiggins, Rosalind Cobb, ed. *Captain Paul Cuffe's Logs and Letters, 1808–1817:
A Black Quaker's "Voice from within the Veil."* Washington, DC: Howard
University Press, 1996.

Wiley, Bell I., ed. *Slaves No More: Letters from Liberia, 1833–1869*. Lexington:
University Press of Kentucky, 1980.

Wilson, Harriet. *Our Nig or, Sketches from the Life of a Free Black, in a Two-Story
White House, North, Showing that Slavery's Shadows Fall Even There*. 1859. New
York: Vintage, 2002.

Secondary Sources

Alexander, Leslie M. *African or American?: Black Identity and Political Activism in
New York City, 1794–1861*. Champaign: University of Illinois Press, 2008.

Asim, Jabari. *The N Word: Who Can Say It, Who Shouldn't, and Why*. Boston:
Houghton Mifflin, 2007.

Bacon, Margaret Hope. *But One Race: The Life of Robert Purvis*. New York: State
University of New York, 2007.

Baptist, Edward. *The Half Has Never Been Told: Slavery and the Making of
American Capitalism*. New York: Basic Books, 2014.

———. "'Stol' and Fetched Here': Enslaved Migration, Ex-slave Narratives, and
Vernacular History." In *New Studies in the History of American Slavery*, edited
by Edward Baptist and Stephanie M. H. Camp, 243–274. Athens: University
of Georgia Press, 2006.

Bederman, Gail. *Manliness and Civilization: A Cultural History of Gender and
Race in the United States, 1880–1917*. Chicago: University of Chicago Press,
1995.

Beers, Henry Augustin. *Nathaniel Parker Willis*. Boston: Houghton, Mifflin, 1885.

Berlin, Ira. *Many Thousands Gone: The First Two Centuries of Slavery in North America*. Cambridge, MA: Harvard University Press, 1998.

Bernard, Emily. "Teaching the N-Word: A Black Professor, an All White Class, and the Thing Nobody Will Say." *American Scholar* 74 (2005): 46–59.

Biddle, Daniel R., and Murray Dubin. *Tasting Freedom: Octavius Catto and the Battle for Equality in Civil War America*. Philadelphia: Temple University Press, 2010.

Blackett, R. J. M. *Beating against the Barriers: The Lives of Six Nineteenth-Century Afro-Americans*. Ithaca, NY: Cornell University Press, 1986.

———. *Building an Antislavery Wall: Black Americans in the Atlantic Abolitionist Movement, 1830–1860*. Baton Rouge: Louisiana State University Press, 1983.

———. *The Underground Railroad and the Politics of Slavery*. Chapel Hill: University of North Carolina Press, 2013.

Blackwood, Sarah. "Fugitive Obscura: Runaway Slave Portraiture and Early Photographic Technology." *American Literature* 81 (March 2009): 93–125.

Blumin, Stuart M. *The Emergence of the Middle Class: Social Experience in the American City, 1760–1900*. New York: Cambridge University Press, 1989.

Bolster, W. Jeffrey. *Black Jacks: African American Seamen in the Age of Sail*. Cambridge, MA: Harvard University Press, 1997.

———. "'Every Inch a Man': Gender in the Lives of African American Seamen, 1800–1860." In *Iron Men, Wooden Women: Gender and Seafaring in the Atlantic World, 1700–1920*, edited by Margaret S. Creighton and Lisa Norling, 138–168. Baltimore: Johns Hopkins University Press, 1996.

Borome, Joseph A. "Robert Purvis and His Early Challenge to American Racism." *Negro History Bulletin* 30, no. 5 (May 1967): 8–10.

Bradlee, Francis B. C. *The Eastern Railroad: An Historical Account of Early Railroading in Eastern New England*. Salem, MA: Essex Institute, 1922.

Brinnin, John Malcolm. *The Sway of the Grand Saloon: A Social History of the North Atlantic*. New York: Delacort, 1971.

Brown, Sterling. "Negro Folk Expression: Spirituals, Seculars, Ballads and Work Songs." *Phylon* 14, no. 1 (1st Qtr., 1953), 45–61.

Bullard, Mary R. "Deconstructing a Manumission Document: Mary Stafford's Free Paper." *Georgia Historical Quarterly* 89, no. 3 (Autumn 2005): 285–317.

Camp, Stephanie. *Closer to Freedom: Enslaved Women and Everyday Resistance in the Plantation South*. Chapel Hill: University of North Carolina Press, 2004.

Campbell, John. "The Seminoles, the 'Bloodhound War,' and Abolitionism, 1796–1865." *The Journal of Southern History* 72, no. 2 (May 2006): 259–302.

Carter, Charles Frederick. *When Railroads Were New*. New York: Henry Holt, 1910.

Chiang, Connie Y. "The Nose Knows: The Sense of Smell in American History." *The Journal of American History* 95, no 2 (September 2008): 405–416.

Chideya, Farai. *The Color of Our Future: Race in the 21st Century*. New York: William Morrow, 1999.

Classen, Constance. "The Odor of the Other: Olfactory Symbolism and Cultural Categories." *Ethos* 20 (June 1992): 133–166.

Cockrell, Dale. *Demons of Disorder: Early Blackface Minstrels and Their World.* Cambridge: Cambridge University Press, 1997.

———, ed. *Excelsior: Journals of the Hutchinson Family Singers, 1842–1846.* Sociology of Music Series 5. Stuyvesant, NY: Pendragon, 1989.

Cohen, David S. "In Search of Carolus Africanus Rex: Afro-Dutch Folklore and Folklife in New York and New Jersey." *Journal of the African-American Historical and Genealogical Society* 5 (1984): 149–163.

Cohen, Patricia Cline. "Women at Large: Travel in Antebellum America." *History Today* 44 (December 1994): 44–50.

Cole, Simon A. *Suspect Identities: A History of Fingerprinting and Criminal Identification.* Cambridge, MA: Harvard University Press, 2001.

Coleman, Willi. "'Like Hot Lead to Pour on the Americans . . .': Sarah Parker Remond—From Salem, Mass., to the British Isles." In *Women's Rights and Transatlantic Antislavery in the Era of Emancipation*, edited by Kathryn Kish Sklar and James Brewer Stewart, 173–188. New Haven, CT: Yale University Press, 2007.

Cox, John D. *Traveling South: Travel Narratives and the Construction of American Identity.* Athens: University of Georgia Press, 2005.

Crockett, Hasan. "The Incendiary Pamphlet: David Walker's Appeal in Georgia." *Journal of Negro History* 86, no. 3 (Summer 2001): 305–318.

Crouthamel, James L., and Andrew Jackson. "James Gordon Bennett, the *New York Herald*, and the Development of Newspaper Sensationalism." *New York History* 54 (July 1973): 294–316.

Davis, David Brion. *The Problem of Slavery in the Age of Emancipation.* New York: Vintage, 2014.

Dollard, John. *Caste and Class in a Southern Town.* New York: Doubleday, 1957.

Dugaw, Dianne. "Female Sailors Bold: Transvestite Heroines and the Markers of Gender and Class." In *Iron Men, Wooden Women: Gender and Seafaring in the Atlantic World, 1700–1920*, edited by Margaret S. Creighton and Lisa Norling, 34–54. Baltimore: Johns Hopkins University Press, 1996.

Dunbar, Erica Armstrong. *A Fragile Freedom: African American Women and Emancipation in the Antebellum City.* New Haven, CT: Yale University Press, 2008.

Egerton, Douglas R. *He Shall Go Out Free: The Lives of Denmark Vesey.* New York: Rowman and Littlefield, 2005.

Epstein, Steven. *Speaking of Slavery: Color, Ethnicity, and Human Bondage in Italy.* Ithaca, NY: Cornell University Press, 2001.

Ewen, Elizabeth, and Stuart Ewen. *Typecasting: On the Arts and Sciences of Human Inequality.* New York: Seven Stories, 2006.

Ferranti, Michelle. "An Odor of Racism: Vaginal Deodorants in African-American Beauty Culture and Advertising." *Advertising Society Review* 11, no. 4 (2011). https://muse.jhu.edu/article/407304. Accessed April 2016.

Finkelman, Paul. "Chief Justice Hornblower of New Jersey and the Fugitive Slave Law of 1793." In *Slavery and the Law*, edited by Paul Finkelman, 113–141. Madison, WI: Madison House, 1997.

Fisch, Audrey A. *American Slaves in Victorian England: Abolitionist Politics in Popular Literature and Culture*. Cambridge: Cambridge University Press, 2000.

Fleetwood, Nicole R. "'Busing It' in the City: Black Youth, Performance and Public Transit." *The Drama Review* 48, no. 2 (T 182) (Summer 2004): 33–48.

Fox, Stephen. *Transatlantic: Samuel Cunard, Isambard Brunel, and the Great Atlantic Steamships*. New York: HarperCollins, 2003.

Frazier, Harriet C. *Runaway and Freed Missouri Slaves and Those Who Helped Them, 1763–1865*. Jefferson, NC: McFarland, 2004.

Freeman, Rhoda Golden. *The Free Negro in New York City in the Era before the Civil War*. New York: Garland Publishing, 1994.

Fryer, Peter. *Staying Power: The History of Black People in Britain*. London: Pluto, 1984.

Gassan, Richard H. *The Birth of American Tourism: New York, the Hudson Valley, and American Culture, 1790–1835*. Amherst: University of Massachusetts Press, 2008.

Gerzina, Gretchen Holbrook, ed. *Black Victorians, Black Victoriana*. New Brunswick, NJ: Rutgers University Press, 2003.

Giddings, Paula. *When and Where I Enter: The Impact of Black Women on Race, and Sex in America*. New York: Bantam, 1984.

Giesberg, Judith. *Army at Home: Women and the Civil War on the Northern Homefront*. Chapel Hill: University of North Carolina Press, 2009.

Gilman, Sander. *Difference and Pathology: Stereotypes of Sexuality, Race, and Madness*. Ithaca, NY: Cornell University Press, 1985.

Gilmore, Paul. "'De Genewine Artekil': William Wells Brown, Blackface Minstrelsy, and Abolition." *American Literature,* no. 69 (December 1997): 743–780.

Glenn, Evelyn Nakano. *Unequal Freedom: How Race and Gender Shaped American Citizenship and Labor*. Cambridge, MA: Harvard University Press, 2002.

Gomez, Michael A. *Exchanging Our Country Marks: The Transformation of African Identities in the Colonial and Antebellum South*. Chapel Hill: University of North Carolina Press, 1998.

Gough, Allison J. "Raising the Moral Conscience: The Atlantic Movement for African American Civil Rights, 1833–1919." PhD dissertation, Ohio State University, 2000.

Grant, H. Roger. *The Railroad: The Life Story of Technology*. Westport, CT: Greenwood, 2005.

Greenspan, Ezra. *William Wells Brown: An African American Life*. New York: W. W. Norton, 2014.

Gridley, J. N. "A Case under an Illinois Black Law." *Journal of the Illinois State Historical Society* 4 (January 1912): 400–425.

Gross, Ariela. *What Blood Won't Tell: A History of Race on Trial in America*. Cambridge, MA: Harvard University Press, 2008.

Grover, Kathryn. *The Fugitive's Gibraltar: Escaping Slaves and Abolitionism in New Bedford, Massachusetts*. Amherst: University of Massachusetts Press, 2001.

Gutman, Herbert. *The Black Family in Slavery and Freedom, 1750–1925*. New York: Pantheon, 1976.

Hadden, Sally E. *Slave Patrols: Law and Violence in Virginia and the Carolinas*. Cambridge, MA: Harvard University Press, 2001.

Hague, Euan. "'The Right to Enter Every Other State': The Supreme Court and African American Mobility in the United States." *Mobilities* 5, no. 3 (2010): 331–347.

Hamer, Phillip M. "Great Britain, the United States, and the Negro Seamen Acts, 1822–1848." *Journal of Southern History* 1 (February 1935): 3–28.

Harris, Leslie M. "From Abolitionist Amalgamators to 'Rulers of the Five Points': The Discourse of Interracial Sex and Reform in Antebellum New York City." In *Sex, Love, Race: Crossing Boundaries in North American History*, edited by Martha Hodes, 191–212. New York: New York University Press, 1999.

———. *In the Shadow of Slavery: African Americans in New York City, 1626–1863*. Chicago: University of Chicago Press, 2003.

Hartman, Saidiya. *Scenes of Subjection: Terror, Slavery, and Self-Making in Nineteenth-Century America*. New York: Oxford University Press, 1997.

Herndon, Ruth Wallis, and John E. Murray. "'A Proper and Instructive Education': Raising Children in Pauper Apprenticeship." In *Children Bound to Labor: The Pauper Apprentice System in Early America*, edited by Ruth Wallis Herndon and John E. Murray, 3–18. Ithaca, NY: Cornell University Press, 2009.

Hewitt, John H. "Mr. Downing and His Oyster House: The Life and Good Works of an African American Entrepreneur." *New York History* 74 (July 1993): 229–252.

———. "The Search for Elizabeth Jennings, Heroine of a Sunday Afternoon in New York City." *New York History* 71 (October 1990): 386–415.

Hietala, Thomas R. *Manifest Design: American Exceptionalism and Empire*, revised edition. Ithaca, NY: Cornell University Press, 2003.

Higginbotham, Evelyn Brooks. "African-American Women's History and the Metalanguage of Race." *Signs* 17, no. 2 (Winter 1992): 251–274.

Hine, Darlene Clark. *Hine Sight: Black Women and the Re-construction of American History*. Bloomington: Indiana University Press, 1994.

Hodges, Graham Russell. *David Ruggles: A Radical Black Abolitionist and the Underground Railroad in New York City*. Chapel Hill: University of North Carolina Press, 2010.

Hodges, Graham Russell, and Alan Edward Brown. *"Pretends to Be Free": Runaway Slave Advertisements from Colonial and Revolutionary New York and New Jersey*. New York: Garland, 1994.

Horton, James Oliver, and Lois Horton. "A Federal Assault: African Americans and the Impact of the Fugitive Slave Law of 1850." *Chicago-Kent Law Review* 68, no. 3 (June 1993): 1179–1197.

Hunt, Gaillard. *The American Passport: Its History and a Digest of Laws, Rulings, and Regulations Governing Its Issuance by the Department of State*. Washington, DC: U.S. Government Printing Office, 1898.

Jacobson, Matthew Frye. *Whiteness of a Different Color: European Immigrants and the Alchemy of Race*. Cambridge, MA: Harvard University Press, 1998.

Johnson, Howard. *The Cunard Story*. London: Whittet, 1988.

Johnson, Walter. "On Agency." *Journal of Social History* 37 (2003): 113–124.

———. *River of Dark Dreams: Slavery and Empire in the Cotton Kingdom*. Cambridge, MA: Harvard University Press, 2013.

———. "The Slave Trader, the White Slave, and the Politics of Racial Determination in the 1850s." *The Journal of American History* 87 (June 2000): 13–38.

———. *Soul by Soul: Life Inside the Antebellum Slave Market*. Cambridge, MA: Harvard University Press, 2001.

Jones, Martha S. *All Bound Up Together: The Woman Question in African American Public Culture, 1830–1900*. Chapel Hill: University of North Carolina Press, 2007.

Jones-Rogers, Stephanie. "If Only Trayvon Had Freedom Papers." In *History News Network*. http://historynewsnetwork.org/article/152622, 16 July 2013. Accessed 15 April 2016.

Jung, Moon-Ho. *Coolies and Cane: Race, Labor, and Sugar in the Age of Emancipation*. Baltimore: Johns Hopkins University Press, 2006.

Kahan, Michael Bruce. "Pedestrian Matters: The Contested Meanings and Uses of Philadelphia's Streets, 1850s–1920s." PhD dissertation, University of Pennsylvania, 2002.

Kantrowitz, Stephen. *More Than Freedom: Fighting for Black Citizenship in a White Republic, 1829–1889*. New York: Penguin, 2012.

Karsten, Peter. *Heart versus Head: Judge Made Law in Nineteenth-Century America*. Chapel Hill: University of North Carolina Press, 1997.

Kaye, Anthony. *Joining Places: Slave Neighborhoods in the Old South*. Chapel Hill: University of North Carolina Press, 2007.

Kelley, Blair Murphy. *Right to Ride: Streetcar Boycotts and African American Citizenship in the Era of* Plessy v. Ferguson. Chapel Hill: University of North Carolina Press, 2010.

Kelley, Robin D. G. *Race Rebels: Culture, Politics, and the Black Working Class*. New York: Free Press, 1994.

Kennedy, Randall L. *Nigger: The Strange Career of a Troublesome Word*. New York: First Vintage, 2003.

———. "Who Can Say 'Nigger'? and Other Considerations." *Journal of Blacks in Higher Education* 26 (Winter 1999–Winter 2000): 86–96.

Kerber, Linda K. "Abolitionists and Amalgamators: The New York City Race Riots of 1834." *New York History* 48 (January 1967): 28–39.

———. "Toward a History of Statelessness in America." *American Quarterly* 57, no. 3 (September 2005): 727–749.

Kerr-Ritchie, Jeffrey R. *Rites of August First: Emancipation Day in the Black Atlantic World*. Baton Rouge: Louisiana State University Press, 2007.

Lacey, Barbara E. "Visual Images of Blacks in Early America." *William and Mary Quarterly* 53 (January 1996): 137–180.

Laurie, Bruce. *Beyond Garrison: Antislavery and Social Reform*. Cambridge: Cambridge University Press, 2005.

Levine, Lawrence W. *Black Culture and Black Consciousness: Afro-American Folk Thought from Slavery to Freedom*. New York: Oxford University Press, 1977.

Litwack, Leon. "The Federal Government and the Free Negro, 1790–1860." *Journal of Negro History* 43 (October 1958): 261–278.

———. *North of Slavery: The Negro in the Free States, 1790–1860*. Chicago: University of Chicago Press, 1961.

———. *Trouble in Mind: Black Southerners in the Age of Jim Crow*. New York: Alfred A. Knopf, 1998.

Lockwood, Allison. *Passionate Pilgrims: The American Traveler in Great Britain, 1800–1914*. Rutherford, NJ: Fairleigh Dickinson University Press, 1982.

Lorimer, Douglas A. *Colour, Class and the Victorians: English Attitudes to the Negro in the Mid-Nineteenth Century*. Teaneck, NJ: Holmes and Meier, 1978.

Lott, Eric. *Love and Theft: Blackface Minstrelsy and the American Working Class*. New York: Oxford University Press, 1993.

Machar, Agnes Maule, and T. G. Marquis. *Builders of Canada from Cartier to Laurier*. London: Bradley-Garretson, 1903.

Mackintosh, Will. "'Ticketed Through': The Commodification of Travel in the Nineteenth Century." *Journal of the Early Republic* 32, no. 1 (Spring 2012): 61–89.

Mahar, William J. "Black English in Early Blackface Minstrelsy: A New Interpretation of the Sources of Minstrel Show Dialect." *American Quarterly* 37 (Summer 1985): 260–285.

Majewski, John. *A House Dividing: Economic Development in Pennsylvania and Virginia before the Civil War*. Cambridge: Cambridge University Press, 2006.

Masur, Kate. *An Example for All the Land: Emancipation and the Struggle over Equality in Washington, DC*. Chapel Hill: University of North Carolina Press, 2010.

McAllister, Marvin. *Whiting Up: Whiteface Minstrels and Stage Europeans in African American Performance*. Chapel Hill: University of North Carolina Press, 2011.

McCaskill, Barbara. "Ellen Craft: The Fugitive Who Fled as a Planter." In *Georgia Women: Their Lives and Times*, vol. 1, edited by Ann Short Chirhart and Betty Wood, 82–108. Athens: University of Georgia Press, 2009.

McDaniel, W. Caleb. *The Problem of Democracy in the Age of Slavery: Garrisonian Abolitionists and Transatlantic Reform*. Baton Rouge: Louisiana State University Press, 2013.

McFeely, William S. *Frederick Douglass*. New York: W. W. Norton, 1995.

McKittrick, Katherine. *Demonic Grounds: Black Women and the Cartographies of Struggle*. Minneapolis: University of Minnesota Press, 2006.

Melish, Joanne Pope. *Disowning Slavery: Gradual Emancipation and "Race" in New England, 1780–1860*. Ithaca, NY: Cornell University Press, 1998.

Menschel, David. "Abolition without Deliverance: The Law of Connecticut Slavery, 1784–1848." *The Yale Law Journal* 111 (October 2001): 183–222.

Miles, Tiya. *Ties That Bind: The Story of an Afro-Cherokee Family in Slavery and Freedom*. Berkeley: University of California Press, 2005.

Miller, Floyd J. *The Search for a Black Nationality: Black Emigration and Colonization, 1787–1863*. Urbana: University of Illinois Press, 1975.

Minardi, Margot. *Making Slavery History: Abolitionism and the Politics of Memory in Massachusetts*. New York: Oxford University Press, 2010.

Minicucci, Stephen. "Internal Improvements and the Union, 1790–1860." *Studies in American Political Development* 18 (Autumn 2004): 160–185.

Mitchell, Michele. *Righteous Propagation: African Americans and the Politics of Racial Destiny after Reconstruction*. Chapel Hill: University of North Carolina Press, 2004.

Moulton, Amber D. "Closing the 'Floodgate to Impurity': Moral Reform, Antislavery, and Interracial Marriage in Antebellum Massachusetts." *Journal of the Civil War Era* 3 (March 2013): 2–34.

Mulvey, Christopher. *Transatlantic Manners: Social Patterns in Nineteenth-Century Anglo-American Travel Literature*. Cambridge: Cambridge University Press, 1990.

Nash, Gary B. *Forging Freedom: The Formation of Philadelphia's Black Community, 1720–1840*. Cambridge, MA: Harvard University Press, 1988.

Nash, Gary B., and Jean R. Soderlund. *Freedom by Degrees: Emancipation in Pennsylvania and Its Aftermath*. New York: Oxford University Press, 1991.

Needler, Geoffrey D. "An Antedating of 'Nigger.'" *American Speech* 42 (May 1967): 159–160.

Neuman, Gerald. "The Lost Century of American Immigration Law (1776–1875)." *The Columbia Law Review* 93, no. 8 (December 1993): 1833–1901.

Nightingale, Carl H. *Segregation: A Global History of Divided Cities*. Chicago: University of Chicago Press, 2012.

Norton, Mary Beth. *Liberty's Daughters: The Revolutionary Experience of American Women, 1750–1800*. 1980. Ithaca, NY: Cornell University Press, 1996.

Parker, Kunal. "Citizenship and Immigration Law, 1800–1924: Resolutions of Membership and Territory." In *The Cambridge History of Law in America*, vol. 2, edited by Michael Grossberg and Christopher Tomlins, 168–203. New York: Cambridge University Press, 2008.

——. "Making Blacks Foreigners: The Legal Construction of Former Slaves in Post-Revolutionary Massachusetts." *Utah Law Review* 75 (2001): 75–124.

Perkins, Howard C. "A Neglected Phase of the Movement for Southern Unity, 1847–1852." *Journal of Southern History* 12, no. 2 (May 1846): 153–203.

Peterson, Carla. "Literary Transnationalism and Diasporic History: Frances Watkins Harper's 'Fancy Sketches,' 1859–1860." In *Women's Rights and Transatlantic Antislavery in the Era of Emancipation*, edited by Kathryn Kish Sklar and James Brewer Stewart, 189–208. New Haven, CT: Yale University Press, 2007.

Pettinger, Alasdair. "At Sea—Coloured Passenger." In *Sea Changes: Historicizing the Ocean*, edited by Bernard Klein and Gesa McKenthum, 149–166. New York: Routledge, 2004.

Power-Greene, Ousmane. *Against Wind and Tide: The African American Struggle against the Colonization Movement*. New York: New York University Press, 2014.

Pryor, Elizabeth. "'Jim Crow' Cars, Passport Denials and Atlantic Crossings: African-American Travel, Protest and Citizenship at Home and Abroad, 1827–1865." PhD dissertation, University of California, Santa Barbara, 2008.

Rael, Patrick. *Black Identity and Black Protest in the Antebellum North*. Chapel Hill: University of North Carolina Press, 2002.

Rediker, Marcus. "Liberty beneath the Jolly Roger: The Lives of Anne Bonny and Mary Read, Pirates." In *Iron Men, Wooden Women: Gender and Seafaring in the Atlantic World, 1700–1920*, edited by Margaret S. Creighton and Lisa Norling, 1–33. Baltimore: Johns Hopkins University Press, 1996.

Rice, Alan J., and Martin Crawford, eds. *Liberating Sojourn: Frederick Douglass and Transatlantic Reform*. Athens: University of Georgia Press, 1999.

Richards, Leonard. *"Gentlemen of Property and Standing": Anti-Abolitionist Mobs in Jacksonian America*. Oxford: Oxford University Press, 1970.

Riddell, William Renwick. "The Fugitive Slave in Upper Canada." *Journal of Negro History* 5 (July 1920): 340–358.

Robertson, Craig. *The Passport in America: The History of a Document*. New York: Oxford University Press, 2010.

——. "'Passport Please': The US Passport and the Documentation of Individual Identity, 1845–1930." PhD dissertation, University of Illinois at Urbana-Champaign, 2004.

Rockman, Seth. *Scraping By: Wage Labor, Slavery, and Survival in Early Baltimore*. Baltimore: Johns Hopkins University Press, 2009.

Roediger, David. *The Wages of Whiteness: Race and the Making of the American Working Class*. 1991. London: Verso, 1999.

Ruchames, Louis. "Jim Crow Railroads in Massachusetts." *American Quarterly* 8 (Spring 1956): 61–75.

Salter, Mark B. *The Passport in International Relations*. Boulder, CO: Lynne Rienner, 2003.

Schor, Joel. *Henry Highland Garnet: A Voice of Black Radicalism in the Nineteenth Century*. Westport, CT: Greenwood, 1977.

Scott, James C. *Domination and the Arts of Resistance: Hidden Transcripts*. New Haven, CT: Yale University Press, 1990.

Sheriff, Carol. *The Artificial River: The Erie Canal and the Paradox of Progress, 1817–1862*. New York: Hill and Wang, 1996.

Siebert, Wilbur H. *The Underground Railroad from Slavery to Freedom*. New York: Macmillan Company, 1898.

Smallwood, Stephanie E. *Saltwater Slavery: A Middle Passage from Africa to American Diaspora*. Cambridge, MA: Harvard University Press, 2008.

Smith, Mark. *How Race Is Made: Slavery, Segregation, and the Senses*. Chapel Hill: University of North Carolina Press, 2006.

——. *Sensing the Past: Seeing, Hearing, Smelling, Tasting, and Touching*. Berkeley: University of California Press, 2007.

Smith, Rogers M. *Civic Ideals: Conflicting Visions of Citizenship in U.S. History.* New Haven, CT: Yale University Press, 1997.

Springer, Haskell. "The Captain's Wife at Sea." In *Iron Men, Wooden Women: Gender and Seafaring in the Atlantic World, 1700–1920,* edited by Margaret S. Creighton and Lisa Norling, 92–117. Baltimore: Johns Hopkins University Press, 1996.

Stansell, Christine. *City of Women: Sex and Class in New York, 1789–1869.* Urbana: University of Illinois Press, 1987.

Stewart, Catherine A. *Long Past Slavery: Representing Race in the Federal Writers' Project.* Chapel Hill: University of North Carolina Press, 2016.

Stovall, Tyler. *Paris Noir: African Americans in the City of Light.* Boston: Houghton Mifflin, 1996.

Stowe, William W. *Going Abroad: European Travel in Nineteenth-Century American Culture.* Princeton, NJ: Princeton University Press, 1994.

Stuckey, Sterling. *Slave Culture: Nationalist Theory and the Foundations of Black America.* New York: Oxford University Press, 1987.

———. "Through the Prism of Folklore: The Black Ethos in Slavery." *Massachusetts Review* 9, no. 3 (Summer 1968): 417–437.

Sweet, John Wood. *Bodies Politic: Negotiating Race in the American North, 1730–1830.* Philadelphia: University of Pennsylvania Press, 2007.

Swift, David E. *Black Prophets of Justice: Activist Clergy before the Civil War.* Baton Rouge: Louisiana State University Press, 1989.

Taylor, George Rogers. *The Transportation Revolution, 1815–1860.* New York: M. E. Sharpe, 1951.

Thornton, John. *Africa and Africans in the Making of the Atlantic World, 1400–1680.* Cambridge: Cambridge University Press, 1992.

Torpey, John. *The Invention of the Passport: Surveillance, Citizenship and the State.* Cambridge: Cambridge University Press, 2000.

Turner, Edward Raymond. *The Negro in Pennsylvania: 1639–1861.* Washington, DC: American Historical Association, 1910.

Usrey, Miriam L. "Charles Lenox Remond, Garrison's Ebony Echo: World Anti-Slavery Convention, 1840." *Essex Institute Historical Collections* 106, no. 2 (April 1970): 112–125.

Waldstreicher, David. *Slavery's Constitution: From Revolution to Ratification.* New York: Hill and Wang, 2009.

Walker, George. *The Afro-American in New York City, 1827–1860.* New York: Garland, 1993.

Walvin, James. *Black and White: The Negro and English Society, 1555–1945.* London: Penguin Press, 1973.

Washington, Margaret. *Sojourner Truth's America.* Urbana: University of Illinois Press, 2009.

Welke, Barbara Y. *Recasting American Liberty: Gender, Race, Law, and the Railroad Revolution, 1865–1920.* Cambridge, MA: Harvard University Press, 2001.

———. "Rights of Passage: Gendered-Rights Consciousness and the Quest for Freedom, California, 1850–1870." In *African American Women Confront the*

West, 1600–2000, edited by Qunitard Tayler and Shirley Ann Wilson Moore, 73–93. Norman: University of Oklahoma Press, 2003.

Wesley, Charles H. "The Concept of Negro Inferiority in American Thought." *Journal of Negro History* 25 (October 1940): 540–560.

White, Barbara A. "Afterword: New Information on Harriet Wilson and the Bellmont Family." In Harriet E. Wilson, *Our Nig; or, Sketches from the Life of a Free Black, in a Two-Story White House, North, Showing that Slavery's Shadows Fall Even There*, iii–liv. New York: Vintage, 2002.

White, Shane. *Somewhat More Independent: The End of Slavery in New York City, 1770–1810*. Athens: University of Georgia Press, 1991.

Wilentz, Sean. *Chants Democratic: New York City and the Rise of the American Working Class, 1788–1850*. 1984. New York: Oxford University Press, 2004.

Williams, George W. *History of the Negro Race in America from 1619 to 1880*, vol. 2. New York: G. P. Putnam's Sons, 1882.

Williams, Raymond. *Keywords: A Vocabulary of Culture and Society*. New York: Oxford University Press, 1983.

Windley, Lathan A., ed. *Runaway Slave Advertisements: A Documentary History from the 1730s to 1790*, vols. 1–4. Westport, CT: Greenwood, 1983.

Wise, Steven M. *Though the Heavens May Fall: The Landmark Trial That Led to the End of Human Slavery*. Cambridge: Da Capo, 2005.

Wolf, Eva Sheppard. *Almost Free: A Story about Family and Race in Antebellum Virginia*. Athens: University of Georgia Press, 2012.

Wong, Edlie L. *Neither Fugitive nor Free: Atlantic Slavery, Freedom Suits, and the Legal Culture of Travel*. New York: New York University Press, 2009.

Wood, Marcus. *Blind Memory: Visual Representations of Slavery in England and America, 1780–1865*. New York: Routledge, 2000.

Woodson, Carter G., ed. "Eighteenth Century Slaves as Advertised by Their Masters." *Journal of Negro History* 1 (April 1916): 163–216.

Woodward, C. Vann. *The Strange Career of Jim Crow*. New York: Oxford University Press, 2002.

Yee, Shirley J. *Black Women Abolitionists: A Study in Activism, 1828–1860*. Knoxville: University of Tennessee Press, 1992.

Yellin, Jean Fagan. "Incidents Abroad: Harriet Jacobs and the Transatlantic Movement." In *Women's Rights and Transatlantic Antislavery in the Era of Emancipation*, edited by Kathryn Kish Sklar and James Brewer Stewart, 158–172. New Haven, CT: Yale University Press, 2007.

Zilversmit, Arthur. *The First Emancipation: The Abolition of Slavery in the North*. Chicago: University of Chicago Press, 1967.

Zylstra, Geoffrey. "Whiteness, Freedom, and Technology: The Racial Struggle over Philadelphia's Streetcars, 1859–1867." *Technology and Culture* 52, no. 4 (October 2011): 678–702.

Index

black activists (*continued*)
39–40, 41, 43, 167n88; transatlantic travel of, 2, 4, 7–9, 38, 41, 44, 101, 103–104, 118–119, 126, 129, 130–136, 140–148, 149, 150; use of term "colored," 1–2, 161n4. *See also* abolitionists and abolitionist movement; activist respectability; colored travelers

Blackett, R. J. M., 129

blackface cultural production: and antiabolitionist sentiment, 31; antiblack rhymes, 39, 167n86; Jim Brown as character of, 32; Jim Crow as stage character of, 31–33, 39, 76–77, 86, 91–92; and Jim Crow song, 32–33, 92; in letters to the editor, 19–21, 91, 164–165n33; "Life in Philadelphia" series, 27–30; literary blackface, 19–23, 36–37, 91; minstrelsy, 31–33, 86, 92, 122–123; proto-blackface productions, 19; and use of term nigger, 5, 26–27, 29–33, 38, 39, 41; used to feminize black men, 21, 24; white abolitionists' distaste for, 94

black laborers: conflict with black middle class, 13–14, 37–38, 167n83; and indentured servitude, 16; perceived as part of an immutable social class, 11, 16; and respectability, 37–38, 167n83; slavery associated with, 16, 46; on strategies for liberation, 14; use of term nigger, 5, 11, 13, 14, 15, 17, 19, 24, 25–26, 35, 38, 39, 41

black lexicon: and Atlantic World, 17–18; nigger as part of, 5, 15, 16, 17, 18–20, 22–25, 26–27, 30–31, 163n6, 164–165n33; whites ventriloquizing, 25, 31, 33

black men: and direct confrontation, 88–89, 99; masculinity, 7, 21, 24, 29, 70–71, 94–95, 150–152; in portraits of runaway slaves, 52, 53–54, 55;

self-liberation on public conveyances, 57

black middle class: and direct confrontation as strategy, 89; rejection of roles as laborers, 11, 14, 17, 30, 37–38; and respectability, 37, 70–71, 87. *See also* black activists; colored travelers

black mobility: and black sailors, 110–111, 114, 138, 178n44; and confinement of enslaved people, 46–47; contests over freedom of, 3–4, 158–159; of enslaved and free servants, 57, 58, 63–64, 68, 69, 116–117, 171n79; and free papers, 109, 111–114; Jim Crow stage character and, 31, 33, 92; and passports, 4, 7, 110–111, 114, 116–118, 122, 123, 125; and politics of exclusion, 64–69, 72, 74; popular culture's attack on, 1, 2, 9, 46, 50–55, 63, 157; and portraits of runaway slaves, 50–54, 169n33, 169n34; stakes of, 62–64, 88; surveillance documents impeding, 108–114; surveillance of, 47, 48, 49, 95, 150; the term nigger as obstacle to, 5, 10–11, 14, 26, 29–30, 31, 39, 40, 67; and transatlantic travel, 127. *See also* colored travelers; criminalization of black mobility; railroads; segregation; stagecoaches

black women: access to streetcars, 60; attacks against black femininity, 29, 95; black (male) activists' protection of, 70–71; and constraints on open protest, 82; covert travel on public conveyances, 72–74, 137; and direct confrontation as protest strategy, 88, 89, 96, 98–99; and gendered freedom, 150, 152–153; and legal claims against railroad segregation, 98–99; in portraits of runaway slaves, 52–53; and railroad segregation, 82, 95; as runaway slaves, 53; and segregation on public conveyances, 62, 70–71, 72; self-liberation on public conveyances, 57–59, 170n45; transatlantic travel of, 139–140, 141, 149, 152–153, 183–184n70; vulnerability when traveling, 70–71, 74, 95

bloodhounds, 150–151

Body, Rias, 110

Bolster, W. Jeffrey, 138

Boston and Providence Railroad (B&P), 76, 78–80, 81, 89, 95, 97, 100, 101

Boston Vigilance Committee, 100

Brown, Liza, 23

Brown, William Wells: *Clotel,* 36–37; as delegate to Peace Congress in Paris, 103, 118, 154–156; on freedom, 150–152; in Great Britain, 149; passport request of, 103, 104, 106, 116, 118–119, 121, 122, 180n82; on return to U.S., 159; on use of term nigger, 36

Browne, John, 116

Buchanan, James, 118

Buffum, James, 89, 140, 142

Calhoun, John C., 119

Cambria (steamship), 126, 131, 133, 134, 139, 140–148, 154, 184n71, 186n100

Camp, Stephanie, 19, 46

Carney, Cornelia, 23, 24

Carter, Bernard M., 136–137

Cass, Lewis, 106–107

Child, Lydia Maria, 72–74

citizenship: and antislavery politics, 119–120; as birthright, 103, 105–106, 115–116, 124; and black activism, 35, 36, 45, 78, 85–88, 95, 97, 103–104, 114–115, 121–125; and Colored Convention movement, 2; and equal access to public space, 2, 7, 85–87, 88, 91, 95, 97, 102; of former slaves, 105–106; passports denoting, 7,

103–104, 105, 106, 107, 109, 114–115, 117, 118, 119, 121, 122–124, 125, 158, 176–177n7; and poor relief, 105–106; precarity of for free people of color, 113–114, 156; public conveyances as sites to assert, 2, 4, 6, 45, 61–62, 64, 67, 68, 69, 70, 71, 74, 102, 158–159; and racialized nature of, 49, 95, 103; and republicanism, 26; and respectability, 38, 87, 167n83; travel as component of, 2, 3, 4, 6, 7, 45, 47–48, 59, 61–62, 64, 67, 68, 69–75, 102, 149–150, 157, 158, 170n49

civil rights movement, 3. *See also* equal rights movement

Classen, Constance, 171n76

Clay, Edward, 27–30

Clay, Henry, 49

Clayton, John M., 103, 115, 116–120, 122, 179n73

Cobden, Richard, 154–155

Cohen, Patricia Cline, 60, 82

Collins, John Anderson "J. A.," 84

The Colored American, 36, 49, 76, 87, 88, 167n3, 182n9

Colored Convention movement, 2

colored travelers: black activists adopting term, 1–2, 161n4; depots and stations as sites of conflict for, 63; direct confrontation used by, 78, 84, 85, 87–88, 90; freedom defined by, 3, 4, 8–9, 69, 127, 129, 150–153, 155–156, 159; protest letters of, 69–70, 72; and railroad segregation, 81–82, 83, 90–95, 101, 158; segregation and protest on public conveyances, 60, 61–64, 72–74, 76–77, 80, 90, 102; and transatlantic travel, 129, 136–137, 150–156; travel as component of citizenship for, 2, 4, 6, 45, 61–62, 64, 67, 68, 69, 70, 71, 149–150. *See also* black mobility; criminalization of black mobility; passports

Connecticut, 11, 16, 47, 168n12

Cornish, Samuel, 3, 36, 70–71, 77, 87–88, 95, 159

Cox, John, 108, 177n25

Craft, Ellen, 53, 57–58, 112, 140, 149, 152–153, 170n45, 183–184n70

Craft, William, 57–58, 112, 149, 153, 183–184n70

Crandall, Prudence, 122

Crawley, Charles, 24

criminalization of black mobility: and access to public conveyances, 45–47; and the age of segregation, 44, 63, 78; and antiblack vigilantism, 6, 75, 82, 109; as conceptual framework, 6, 46–55; to delimit black international travel, 117–119; and deputization of U.S. whites, 6, 9, 46–48, 77, 83; and "Jim Crow car," 81, 82, 83; and legislation, 46, 47, 48, 49–51, 74, 157, 168n7; and passports, 105; and racialized surveillance documents, 7, 108, 110–114, 123; and runaway slave advertisements, 50–54, 55; in twenty-first century, 9, 168n7.

Crummell, Alexander, 156

Cuffe, Paul, 3, 61–62, 65–66, 90, 97

Cunard, Edward, 132, 133

Cunard, Samuel, 130, 132–133, 138, 177n26

Cunard Steamship Company: crews of steamships, 135; Frederick Douglass's transatlantic voyage of 1845 on, 8, 40, 126, 127–128, 131, 132–133, 134, 136, 139, 140–148, 154, 184n71, 185n84; multinational clientele of, 133; and segregation, 133, 141–142, 144–145, 148; and transatlantic travel, 130, 141–142, 177n26, 183–184n70

Dallas, George Mifflin, 107

dandyism, 37, 38

Davis, Carrie, 110

Davis, Clarissa, 170n45

Delany, Martin, 38, 113

Democratic Party, 119, 120

Dickens, Charles, 133–134

direct confrontation, as protest strategy, 78, 84–85, 87–90, 95, 98–100, 102, 136–137, 142, 148

Dollard, John, 171n76

domestic labor, 37–38, 90

Douglass, Frederick: antislavery lecture attempt on *Cambria,* 126, 131, 143–147, 186n95, 100; as colored traveler, 11; effect of slavery on ability to travel, 1; on free papers, 112; in Great Britain, 149, 151–152; Hutchinson Family Singers' "The Fugitive's Song" dedicated to, 53–54; *Narrative of the Life of Frederick Douglass* and, 142; and protests on public conveyances, 67–68, 70, 77, 84–85, 96, 102, 126–128, 140–148; radicalism of, 126–127, 142, 146, 148; on railroad segregation, 77, 84, 85, 96, 102, 127, 140, 141; on steamship segregation, 70, 132–133, 141; transatlantic voyage in 1845, 8, 40, 126, 127–128, 131, 132–133, 134, 136, 139, 140–148, 154, 184n71, 185n84; use of term nigger in the writings of, 40

Downing, Thomas, 97–98, 166n56

Dred Scott v. Sandford (1857), 7, 103, 115, 122, 123

Eastern Rail Road (ERR), 69, 80, 81, 83, 84, 96, 99, 100, 101

Easton, Hosea, 10, 11, 17, 31, 151, 161n4

Elaw, Zilpha, 165n40

Emancipation Proclamation, 124

enslaved people: abroad marriages of, 53; agency of, 163–164n19; and "black geographies," 46–47; citizenship status of former slaves, 105–106; and fungibility of captive body, 52, 169n35; legacy of, 13, 26; "rival geographies" of, 19; runaway slave advertisements, 50–54, 55, 169nn33, 34; and self-liberation on public conveyances, 55–59; slave economy, 53, 56–57, 132; and slave songs, 19, 23–25, 165nn48, 51; use of term nigger, 23–25, 165n48; and verbal isolation of, 17; and whites' fears of insurrection, 21, 26, 110, 111, 178n44

enslavement: and antislavery politics, 119–120; black activists on effect on freedom, 85–86; and gradual abolition in North, 11, 14, 16, 48, 162n3, 164n21, 174n46; and passports for colored travelers, 104, 107, 120; and racialized surveillance documents, 109–114; and "statutory slavery," 16; and U.S. Constitution, 156; David Walker's indictment of, 12, 13

Epstein, Steven, 169n33

equal rights movement: access to public conveyances as symbol of, 45, 69–72, 158; black activists linking abolition to, 85–86; and criminalization of black mobility, 75; and protest strategies of black activists, 6, 69–72, 95; and respectability, 87–88

etiquette, 60, 69, 170n55

Europe: black belief of egalitarianism in, 4, 8, 147; passport system in, 108; and transatlantic travel of black abolitionists, 127, 149

Fisch, Audrey, 129

foreignness, as concept to exclude African Americans, 21, 105, 106–107, 109, 113, 114

Fourteenth Amendment, 106, 124

Fox, Stephen, 185n91

freedom: access to public conveyances as symbol of, 45, 69–72; and

black activists' legal claims, 97; black activists on enslavement's effect on, 85–86; colored travelers defining, 3, 4, 8–9, 69, 127, 129, 150–153, 155–156, 159; gendered freedom, 142, 149–153; and passports, 108–109; precarity of, 113, 158; and railroad segregation, 82; and transatlantic travel, 142, 149–153; whites' fears of black freedom, 20, 21, 26, 27, 29–31, 40, 45, 148

Freedom's Journal, 38, 40, 70–71, 87, 129, 167n88

free papers, 109, 111–114, 158

Free Soilers, 119, 120

Fugitive Slave Act (1793), 48, 85, 129

Fugitive Slave Law (1850), 50, 112–113, 121

Garnet, Henry Highland, 62

Garrison, William Lloyd: on black mobility, 171n79; Frederick Douglass's correspondence with, 40, 143, 145, 186n95; and Robert Purvis, 136; Charles Remond's relationship with, 100; on stagecoach travel, 64; transatlantic travel of, 133; "Traveller's Directory" published by, 101, 176n96

gender: and black activists' protests of segregation, 70–71; and black mobility, 52–53; constraints on open protest, 82; and direct confrontation as protest strategy, 88, 89; of Jim Crow character, 94–95; and moral improvement, 36; and protection of ladies' cabins, 60, 62, 89, 134; and self-liberation on public conveyances, 57; use of term nigger associated with, 163n6. *See also* black men; black women; gendered freedom

gendered freedom, 142, 149–153

Georgia, 112

Kennedy, Randall, 14
Kerber, Linda, 104

Lee, Jarena, 165n40
legislation: black migration limited by,
    48–49; and criminalization of black
    mobility, 46, 47, 48, 49–51, 74, 157,
    168n7; curfew laws of the North,
    47; *Dred Scott v. Sandford* (1857), 7,
    103, 115, 122, 123; fugitive slave laws
    (1793) and (1850), 48, 50, 85,
    112–113, 121, 129; gradual abolition
    laws, 11, 16; laws limiting black
    mobility in southern states, 1, 7, 47,
    109, 110, 111–114; laws targeting free
    black people in Massachusetts, 48;
    Negro Seamen Acts, 110–111; *Plessy
    v. Ferguson* (1896), 3; and racial sepa-
    ratism, 49; and segregation, 1, 3;
    "separate but equal," 1; Separate
    Car Act of Louisiana, 158; and slave
    pass system, 109, 110, 111; *Tennessee
    v. Claiborne,* 122
letters to the editor: black activists'
    protest letters on exclusionary
    episodes, 69–70, 72, 74, 76–77,
    117–118; blackface cultural
    production in, 19–21, 91,
    164–165n33
The Liberator, 40, 101, 124, 167n86,
    176n96, 181n104
Liberia, emigration to, 8, 116, 162n15
Lincoln, Abraham, 124
Litwack, Leon, 176n7
Lorimer, Douglas, 129
Lott, Eric, 92
Louisiana, 111, 113, 158
lynching, 39, 90, 95, 174n46
Lynn Anti-Slavery Society, 96

McKittrick, Katherine, 46
McLane, John, 115
Madison, Betsey, 70–71
Mann, Daniel, 99–100
manumission papers, 49

Marcy, William L., 122
Mars, James, 16
Martin, John Sella, 124
Martin, Trayvon, 168n7
Maryland, 110
Massachusetts: antiabolitionist ferment
    in, 80; blacks' lack of legal recourse
    in, 20; and debates on black migra-
    tion, 48; and debates on passports,
    120; as free state, 11, 16, 164n21; laws
    targeting free black people in, 48;
    railroad segregation in, 78, 94, 95, 99,
    100–102, 127, 130, 159; status of free
    people of color in, 105–106
Massachusetts General Court, 78, 100
Melish, Joanne Pope, 16, 19, 164n21,
    168n12
Mexican-American War, 119
Middle Passage, 127
Minardi, Margot, 164n21
minstrelsy. *See* blackface cultural
    production
Mississippi, 112
Missouri, 112
Monroe, James, 115
Montgomery Bus Boycotts, 3,
    158–159
moral improvement, 37, 69, 70, 74, 85,
    86–87, 90
Murray's *Handbook for Travel,* 109

Native Americans, 47, 49, 60
Needler, Geoffrey D., 164n20
Negro Seamen Acts, 110–111
Nell, William Cooper, 121, 122
New Bedford and Taunton Line
    (NB&T), 80, 81, 84, 98, 100
New Hampshire, 11, 16, 164n21
New Jersey, 11, 16, 49
New York, 11, 16, 49, 86
New York City, 85, 91
New York Committee on
    Vigilance, 85
New York State Anti-Slavery Society,
    71

nigger: author's note on term, 5–6, 163n6; black activists on term, 12, 38–41; black activists' rejection of term, 35–38, 40; black activists' use of term, 5, 12, 19, 35, 37, 38, 39–40, 41, 43, 167n88; in blackface cultural production, 19–21, 26–27, 29–33, 38–39, 41, 164–165n33, 167n86; complicated usages of, 12–15; etymology of term, 5–6, 11, 12, 164n27; as labor category, 11, 14, 16–17, 24–25; and politics of respectability, 37, 38; as racial epithet, 5, 10–11, 12, 14, 25–27, 29–35, 39, 41, 43, 45, 86; as social identity, 18, 19, 21–23, 25, 27, 36, 37, 41; term used as verbal assault of colored travelers, 10–11; violence and, 26–27, 39, 40, 41

Noah, Mordecai, 166n57

North Carolina, 110, 113, 178n44

The North Star, 118

Northup, Solomon, 113

Norton, Mary Beth, 21

Ohio, 48

"Our Nig or, Sketches from the Life of a Free Black...", 22–23, 41–43

Parker, Kunal, 105

Parks, Rosa, 3, 158–159

passports: and black mobility, 4, 7, 110–111, 114, 116–118, 122, 123, 125; of black sailors, 7, 109, 110–111, 114, 158, 178n44; William Wells Brown's request of, 103, 104, 106, 116, 118–119, 121, 122, 180n82; citizenship articulated by, 7, 103–104, 105, 106, 107, 109, 114–115, 117, 118, 119, 121, 122–124, 125, 158, 176–177n7; of colored travelers, 4, 7, 103, 108, 114, 115–116, 120, 121, 123, 176–177n7; loyalty pledge for, 180–181n100; and surveillance, 105, 108–109

Paul, Nathaniel, 129, 159

Paul, Susan, 3, 72

Pennington, J. W. C., 3, 11, 38–39, 99, 132, 156, 159

Pennsylvania, 11, 16, 48

people of color, use of term, 161n5

Pettinger, Alasdair, 141–142

Philadelphia, 29

Phillips, Wendell, 100, 118

Plessy, Homer, 158

Plessy v. Ferguson (1896), 3

policing. *See* criminalization of black mobility; surveillance

poor relief, and citizenship status, 105–106

poor whites, 24, 40, 81, 82, 91

popular culture. *See* blackface cultural production; Jim Crow; runaway slave advertisements

Potter, Eliza, 153

Powell, William, 149–150, 156

prejudice: and nigger as epithet, 39, 41; and passport denials, 107; and railroad segregation, 86–87; Charles Remond on, 44; slavery as the cause of, 86–87; and stagecoach segregation, 72; and steamship segregation, 141; and transatlantic travel, 155–156

The Provincial Freeman, 70

public conveyances: black activists on equal access to, 3–4, 6, 7, 45, 69–72, 77, 78, 158; black women disguised as men on, 57–59, 170n45; black women's covert travel on, 72–74, 137; colored travelers' fight for citizenship on, 2, 4, 6, 45, 61–62, 64, 67, 68, 69, 70, 71, 74, 102, 158–159; cost of, 59, 60, 63; dangers for colored travelers, 44, 61, 62, 63; enslaved people's self-liberation on, 55–59; etiquette on, 60, 170n55; expanding infrastructure of, 44, 59; and modernization, 45, 81, 130; physical intimacy of accommodations, 64–65, 67, 72, 133, 134–135, 138–139, 142, 147; and segregation, 2, 6, 44, 46, 60,

and imperialism, 170n49; as public conveyances, 45, 59; segregation on, 60, 62, 64, 67, 70–71, 76, 83, 89, 126–127, 130, 131, 132–133, 140–141, 159; and transatlantic travel, 108, 126, 127, 128, 130–136, 140–148; travel time on, 170n48

Still, William, 56, 58, 59, 73, 170n45

Stonington Line, 76, 83, 85, 89

Stowe, Harriet Beecher, 108, 135–136

streetcars: black activists' fight for equal access to, 4, 78, 97, 99; as public conveyances, 45; segregation of, 70, 78, 97, 102; as symbols of progress, 80; women's access to, 60

Stuckey, Sterling, 15

surveillance, 6, 7, 46–55, 91, 95, 105, 108–114, 150–151, 157–158

Sweet, John, 50

Taney, Roger, 122, 124, 181n104

Taylor, Zachary, 119–120, 122

technology: role in segregation, 6, 78, 80–81, 86; and transatlantic travel, 108, 130

Tennessee, 102, 122, 158

Texas, 49

Thomas, J. A., 122–123

Thornton, John, 17–18

transatlantic travel: of black activists, 2, 4, 7–9, 38, 41, 44, 101, 103–104, 118–119, 126, 129, 130–136, 139–148, 149, 150, 152–153, 183–184n70; and gendered freedom, 142, 149–153; multicultural nature of, 138; racial liminality of, 139–140, 143, 147, 148; segregation in, 126–127, 128, 130–136; stakes of, 127–128; and white supremacy, 133

Transcontinental Railroad, 78

travel (equal access to): of black middle class, 60–61, 74; as component of citizenship, 2, 3, 4, 6, 7, 45, 47–48, 59, 61–62, 64, 67, 68, 69–75, 102, 149–150, 157, 158, 170n49; and

oppressive nature of white supremacy, 3; as type of currency, 2, 59–62; and white middle class, 60, 81, 108, 109, 130; whiteness as basis for, 48, 60, 168n18; of white women, 60, 62, 66. *See also* black mobility; criminalization of black mobility; railroads; stagecoaches

Tubman, Harriet, 53

Turner, Nat, 111, 178n44

Underground Railroad, 58–59

U.S. Congress: and antislavery politics, 119–120; and black citizenship, 122; and criminalization of black mobility, 49–50

U.S. Constitution (1787), 46, 47–48, 106, 156

U.S. Department of State: passport procedures of, 104, 107, 116, 117–118, 120, 121–122, 123, 124, 127, 180–181n100; passports (or certificates of protection) approved for enslaved and free black servants, 115–117, 118, 120; passports approved for colored travelers, 4, 7, 103, 108, 114, 115–116, 121, 123; passports refused to colored travelers, 7, 103, 104–105, 107, 114, 115, 116, 117–118, 119, 121, 122–123, 125, 158, 176–177n7, 179n73

U.S. Supreme Court: on black citizenship, 103; right to domestic travel based on whiteness, 168n18; "separate but equal" accommodations ruling, 3

Van Buren, Martin, 93

Van Renselaer, Thomas, 63–64

Vaux, Robert, 115

Vermont, 11, 16, 164n21

Vesey, Denmark, 111

vigilantism: antiblack vigilantism in public space, 6, 7, 9, 46, 47, 50–51, 157; and antinativist sentiment, 57; and lynching, 174n46; and public

vigilantism (*continued*)
conveyances, 6; and racialized surveillance documents, 109; and railroad segregation, 82–83; of transatlantic travel, 8; white supremacy fostering, 67

Virginia, 110, 112, 113, 128, 181n7

Walker, David: *Appeal*, 2, 12–14, 40, 111; on black laborers' use of term nigger, 38; use of black sailors to disseminate writings, 111; use of term colored, 2; use of term nigger, 11, 13, 14, 15, 16–17, 18, 40

Ward, Samuel Ringgold, 132, 133, 141, 152

Webb, Frank, 184n70

Webb, Mary, 140, 184n70

Weems, Ann Maria, 58–59, 170n45

Welke, Barbara, 170n49

Wells, Ida B., 158

West Indian Emancipation, 114, 129, 136, 146, 186n98

Wheatley, Phillis, 128

Whig Party, 120

White, Essex, 115–116

White, Shane, 18, 19

white laborers, 25–26, 60

white middle class: reformers protesting railroad segregation, 85; and respectability, 69, 88; travel (equal access to), 60, 81, 108, 109, 130; and use of term nigger, 14, 40

whites: anxieties about black freedom and social mobility, 20, 21, 26, 27, 29–31, 40, 45, 148; attitudes toward passports, 108–109; black mobility attacked by, 1, 2, 63; as deputies policing black mobility, 47, 48, 49; fears over black international travelers, 120; and meaning of term nigger, 17, 25; as patrollers in slave pass system, 46–47, 110; and

political aims of segregation, 68; racism of, 2–3, 5; use of term nigger, 5, 8, 10–12, 14, 16, 22, 23, 25, 26–27, 29–34, 36, 40, 67, 167n88; David Walker's indictment of, 12

white supremacy: and characteristics of U.S. racism, 8; emancipation destabilizing, 174n46; racial boundaries of, 44, 63–64, 91, 115, 125, 159; and segregation, 69, 70, 89, 90, 99, 102; state laws supporting, 49; and transatlantic travel, 133; travel (equal access to) as illustrative of oppressive nature of, 3, 69, 70; and use of term nigger, 15, 24, 26, 38; vigilantism fostered by, 67

white working class: and abolitionists, 94; and blackface cultural production, 91, 92; citizenship of, 95; and colored travelers, 70, 94; and racial divide with people of color, 81; and railroad segregation, 94–95; as servants, 90; treatment of women, 60, 170n55. *See also* white laborers

Williams, Peter, 116, 121, 122

Williams, Raymond, 163n6

Wilmot Proviso, 119

Wilson, Harriet, 22–23, 36, 41, 43, 165n40

Wirt, William, 122

Wong, Edlie, 97, 111, 177n7, 179n73

Wood, Peter, 17

Works Progress Administration (WPA) ex-slave narratives, 19, 23, 24, 110, 163n6

World's Anti-Slavery Convention, London, 38, 44

Wright, Theodore, 71

Zylstra, Geoff, 70